When Only One Converts

When Only One Converts

Lynn Nordhagen

Our Sunday Visitor Publishing Division
Our Sunday Visitor, Inc.
Huntington, Indiana 46750

*We dedicate this book to St. Joseph, who in his marriage
definitely got more than he bargained for.*

O Joseph,
  with the white of your years refracted
  into a rainbow of promises
  that the Lord is about to keep,
    you cover your family as a coat
    angelically patched together in dreams.

O Woodworker,
  the young God apprenticing under you
  uses simple patterns
    — a manger, a yoke, a cross —
    in his arduous project of repair.

I, under repair, have returned
  to hometown Rome,
  to be counted, I suppose,
  and taxed in my human resources.
    Shut away from downtown's attentions,
    I lodge at the edge
    of this house of bread.
  I follow dreams far afield
  to give haven to my Lord and my Lady
  and to their servants, my family.

So foster me, faith-father,
  in labor driven by hope,
  in a gift for fairness,
  in a steady hearth-fire of devotion,
    till like you I finish this course
    and may then speed the heedless world's restoration
    from a more intimate and effective distance,
    there in the expansive bond of triune holiness.

Larry Dimock

Acknowledgments

I would like to thank everyone who has contributed to this work, particularly those who gave permission to reprint material that has appeared in other publications, among them Queenship Publishing Company, Santa Barbara, California, for "Love Compelled Me to Wait" by Paul Thigpen, which appeared in Marcus Grodi's book *Journey's Home*; and *The Catholic Faith* magazine, published in San Francisco, California, for "A Marriage Saved in Heaven: Elisabeth Leseur's Life of Love" by Robin Maas, which appeared in the January/ February 1997 edition. I would also like to thank all the authors for their generosity in sharing their stories. Their candid soul-searching was done in a spirit of love for those in similar circumstances. May their witness to God's grace be an inspiration to all of us to humbly strive for our perfect unity in Christ.

Readers who are interested in learning more about conversion stories are encouraged to visit the following websites:

http://members.aol.com/Rom4Five/coradcor.html
http://members.aol.com/Rom4Five/mixedmarriage.html

Contents

Introduction
ROBIN MAAS, PH.D.
11

Preface: A Family Tradition
LYNN NORDHAGEN
23

1 ✤ A Pilgrim's Progress
WILLIAM J. CORK, D. MIN.
27

2 ✤ Into Harbor
LARRY DIMOCK
51

3 ✤ An Ongoing Journey
CHARLES DEWOLF
59

4 ✤ The Making of a Fool
JUSTIN CASE
81

5 ✤ Different Timetables
BRUCE SULLIVAN
93

6 ✤ Love Compelled Me to Wait
PAUL THIGPEN
101

7 ✤ Converting One at a Time
DAVID K. DEWOLF
109

8 ✤ A Protestant's Prayers
KAREN PETERSON
125

9 ❧ A House Divided

Michael J. Bolesta, M.D.

137

10 ❧ As Christ Loved the Church

Barbara G. Brown

153

11 ❧ Joy and Sorrow

Maxine Smith

165

12 ❧ The Two Shall Become One

Tim and Mary Drake

181

13 ❧ Burdens as Blessings

Michele L. Fitzpatrick

197

14 ❧ Your Pride, My Prejudice, and 'Festina Lente'

Lynn Nordhagen

207

15 ❧ Biblical Submission: An Interview with Kenneth Howell

Lynn Nordhagen

213

16 ❧ The Courage to Love

Gregory K. Popcak, MSW, LCSW

233

17 ❧ A Marriage Saved in Heaven: Elisabeth Leseur's Life of Love

Robin Maas, Ph.D.

251

Recommended Reading

265

Introduction

By now I consider myself something of a connoisseur of conversion accounts. I began reading them — on the sly — in my early twenties, much, I suppose, like someone in pursuit of forbidden fruit. Like so many other Protestants raised in pre-Vatican II times, I had been imbued with a fervent anti-Catholicism. The insidious power of Rome, I was taught, was something to be feared and despised; and I could give no rational account of my interest in reading the narratives of those who had finally succumbed to that spiritually insidious influence. I would read in spurts and then back off, frightened of my own fascination.

This schizophrenic attraction-repulsion dynamic continued for over twenty years until I, too, finally succumbed and became, against every youthful prejudice, a *Catholic*. That was over eleven years ago; and since that time I have had ample opportunity to reflect not only on my own lengthy and convoluted odyssey but on the phenomenon of conversion to Catholicism in general. It is an endlessly fascinating subject, and in every conversion account I read, I inevitably find at least one echo of my own experience — often much more.

Without a doubt, the feature that seems most consistently a part of the majority of conversion accounts is a preoccupation with the issue of "truth." Some are drawn to Catholicism because of the beauty and richness of its tradition and, in particular, the almost palpable sense of mystery that inheres in Catholic worship still — despite the drastic architectural and liturgical prunings inflicted on the Church in the name of conciliar reform. Often a hunger for the Eucharist provides the final impulse that propels one to risk every other certainty for this one compelling good. But always, the question that haunts the process of conversion is the metaphysical one. Whether I like this Church or not is beside the point. What I need to know is this: Is what she teaches *true*? Is the Catholic Church what she claims to be? If she is, then, like Peter, I really have no choice: ". . . To whom shall we go? You have the words of eternal life" (John 6:68).

The second most predictable feature I find in conversion accounts is the requirement of sacrifice. Just as the course of true love never does run smooth, so also does a real conversion *cost*. Leaving aside conversions of convenience (usually for the sake of family harmony), those that are the consequence of genuine soul-searching almost always face some obstacle that, at least initially, appears almost insuperable. This may take the form of tremendous resistance from family members, the risk of social ostracization, even loss of a job. Often the greatest obstacle lies within and entails the surrender of a particular image we have of ourselves, our personal history, and, of course, our future. Whatever shape the challenge takes, something that always appears to have great value must be risked. So the convert finds himself facing significant loss for the sake of promised gain: ". . . Go, sell what you possess and give to the poor, and you will have treasure in heaven; and come, follow me" (Matthew 19:21).

Finally, what I have come to see with increasing clarity over time is that the search for truth and the requirement of sacrifice are yoked together. If the truth is the pearl of great price, then it is worth *everything else*, and there is a sense in which we will never have enough resources of our own to purchase it. We don't simply sell all that we own to buy it; we, in effect, go into debt. We mortgage our hopes and discover only slowly how much will be required of us.

The typical Protestant looking at Catholicism from the outside in looks for an intellectual solution to the question *Is it true?* The solution is sought in books, usually apologetical works that address the specific kinds of issues that spring from the "Protest" that gave birth to their denomination: for example, the authority of Scripture, the problem of believer's baptism, or the meaning of justification and the role of works in the salvation of the soul. The more serious a student of theology the potential convert is, the more important this quest for an intellectual solution becomes and the more easily distracted he or she tends to be from other issues that may ultimately be much more of a stumbling block on the road to Rome. *Satisfy my mind,* we say, and the rest will fall into place.

Alas, it seldom works this way. I would venture to say that the mind is the easiest thing to satisfy in this quest. Far more troublesome and duplicitous is the heart. If the mind seeks to *know* truth, the heart must itself *be true*; and the heart, much more than the mind, is defended against truth. Changing your mind can be a startling and sobering experience. Allowing your heart to be changed is painful. The heart, much more than the mind, wants to be left in peace, in the dark.

The problem lies in our truncated vision of truth. It's all a matter of doctrine, we think — of propositions, proven true or false, to which we say a simple yes or no. What I learned from my own conversion and continue to see replicated over and over again is that the truth we seek will, sooner or later, lay claim to *everything* about us: our minds, our hearts, our occupations, and, inevitably, every significant relationship we have — especially our marriages. Whatever in our lives — our self — is disordered, incomplete, wounded, or grounded in falsity must either be redeemed or dispensed with. Because, as our Lord said, God's reign does work like leaven. It permeates every molecule of the loaf, transforming it into something entirely new.

The emotional reordering in our lives that truth requires may need to occur before the conversion is technically completed or, as in my own case, it may occur in the wake of one's reception into the Catholic Church. It depends on the nature of the obstacle and all of the other particulars that determine our lives at any point in time.

"Do not think that I have come to bring peace on earth; I have not come to bring peace, but a sword. For I have come to set a man against his father, and a daughter against her mother, and a daughter-in-law against her mother-in-law;

and a man's foes will be those of his own household" (Matthew 10:34-36; cf. Luke 12:51-53).

These words of Jesus are among the most troubling in the Gospels. How could a God whom we claim is *Love Itself* be a cause of division among family members? Why, we ask, would the evangelist include such a disturbing passage if he wanted his account to draw people to Christ? There is only one reason for including such discouraging words: *Jesus actually said them*; and, further, the experience of the first Christians must have borne this prediction out. Indeed, historians tell us that this painful division within families is precisely what did occur as the Apostles began to preach that the long-awaited Messiah had finally come, that he had been put to death on a cross and had, against all reason, been raised from the dead.

The Gospel was — and still is — a scandalous proposition to pious Jews accustomed to interpreting their beloved Scriptures in ways that entirely exclude a crucified messiah, and utter foolishness to the Greeks, those worldly-wise and skeptical souls who condescendingly told St. Paul that sometime when they were not so busy, they would hear what he had to say (cf. 1 Corinthians 1:23; Acts 17:32). Today's converts to Catholicism are drawn mainly from contemporary equivalents to these same ancient subjects of Christian evangelization. They may, for example, be drawn from those among us who have given their allegiance to culturally acceptable and therefore "worldly" (*secular*) explanations of reality, or they may already be sincere, even zealous, followers of Christ. Every family, it seems, still contains "Greeks" and "Jews" (in this sense) — which is why conversion continues to cause painful separations in families.

A convert coming out of an unchurched, religiously liberal, or indifferent family is usually thought to have "flipped out." Generally labeled a "fanatic," he or she becomes an enigma to loved ones, an embarrassment. Such converts may meet with hostility, but more often it is ridicule and disdain. "Ex-Greeks," these newborn Christians must learn, little by little, what the Lord requires of them and as their conviction grows, so does their pain at seeing those they love deprived of the grace of Christ. They cannot fathom the monumental indifference of their loved ones to the issues of eternity, and therein lies their suffering.

Those whose conversion occurs in a context of preexisting religious zeal, usually of a conservative Protestant or sectarian type, face a different set of problems that are no less isolating and, if anything, more excruciatingly painful. Such converts are not considered lunatics by their loved ones but *traitors*. And beyond bewilderment or contempt, treachery evokes hatred and rage.

Because the stories in this collection are by "ex-Jews" rather than "ex-Greeks," they make for particularly painful, if engrossing, reading. They are representative of a whole new wave of conversions to Catholicism coming out of conservative, evangelical Protestant churches. These are the stories of the people who were already "believers" — persons zealous for the Lord and for the Bible as the sole "Rock" on which their Christian conviction rested. And because the Protestant ethos defines itself and feeds off of anti-Catholicism — we are *not that* — a defection to the Church of Rome within the ranks is experienced as nothing less than tragic. In the concrete details of the conversions included here we see how accurate our Lord's words about the effect of his coming and his call really are. The Truth that is Christ is a sword first, and only later bread, then balm.

Scripture attests that, virtually immediately in the life of the infant Church, thorny pastoral problems relating to the conversion of married people presented themselves. Paul's letters address, very strategically, the problem of the Christian married to an unbeliever:

> To the rest I say, not the Lord, that if any brother has a wife who is an unbeliever, and she consents to live with him, he should not divorce her. If any woman has a hus-

band who is an unbeliever, and he consents to live with her, she should not divorce him. For the unbelieving husband is consecrated through his wife, and the unbelieving wife is consecrated through her husband. Otherwise, your children would be unclean, but as it is they are holy. But if the unbelieving partner desires to separate, let it be so; in such a case the brother or sister is not bound. For God has called us to peace. Wife, how do you know whether you will save your husband? Husband, how do you know whether you will save your wife?

Only, let every one lead the life which the Lord has assigned to him and in which God has called him.

— 1 Corinthians 7:12-17

It is St. Paul who tells us that *in Christ* we become a "new creation," echoing the Lord's teaching that we must be "reborn" (cf. John 3:3). A true conversion changes us profoundly; and change, as we all know, can be frightening. Human nature does not want to consent to what it cannot control. So there are few things that can be more threatening than to watch the person you married and thought you "knew" slowly but surely begin to become *someone else*. Watching anyone you think you know well and on whom you are more or less emotionally dependent would be unsettling; but when it is someone with whom you are "one flesh," then the stakes are suddenly raised very high indeed. As marital counselors are quick to tell us, when one spouse changes, the other has to change, too — what else can "one flesh" mean? But there is no predicting precisely what this change will be.

What is clear from St. Paul's advice is that a decision for Christ in his Church has the effect of shining a laserlike light on the life of all those involved. The clarity of self-definition that conversion requires puts intense pressure on the unconverted mate. He or she may bolt — or not. But the believer is to remain in the union as long as the unbelieving or unconverted spouse is willing.

There is a reason for this: The union, *qua union*, is sanctifying — and no less so because the marriage may be a difficult one. In God's providential design for life *in Christ* lived under fallen conditions, the faith of one supplies for the other by virtue of the fact that they are "one flesh." And those converts who suffer the pains of spiritual loneliness because they attend Mass unaccompanied by their spouses need to remember that while God works reliably through the sacraments his grace is not limited to these channels alone.

What the convert to Catholicism doesn't immediately comprehend is that the spiritual loneliness he or she suffers may just as easily be shared by a cradle Catholic married to another such. To be "Catholic" is not necessarily to be on a quest for truth, for *God*. It is often the case that spouses raised as Catholic may suddenly find a chasm opening up in their relationship when one of them suddenly becomes very intentional in the practice of the faith and the other realizes, implicitly, that one's partner in life has suddenly been gripped by a Presence whose mysterious power is formidable and therefore threatening.

There is no guarantee that the person we fall in love with will remain as we initially experienced him or turn out to be what we want him to be. Indeed, this almost never happens. The inexorable reality of life is change. And the key to change is the mystery of human freedom — the inscrutable but sublime choice of the originating Source of all freedom to share the risk, so to speak.

"So have no fear of them; for nothing is covered that will not be revealed, or hidden that will not be known" (Matthew 10:26).

The kind of change conversion requires is like the tilling of soil. It is an "unearthing" designed to create the conditions necessary for sowing seed so that in the future there will be a harvest. It has to happen, but in the process much may get turned up that we would rather not have to face. Yet face it we must, for if the field remains studded with stones and infested with weeds, nothing will thrive in it. Moreover, the longer we have remained "untilled," the more disturbing will the process be when we finally consent to be "furrowed." What we see in conversion accounts is that a quest for truth, once it is undertaken, takes us places we would rather not go. We learn, perhaps to our chagrin, that much more than the mind must be saved from error.

The classic conversion story in Protestantism involves a sinner coming to his senses, finally facing his morally bankrupt condition and his own helplessness to "save himself." Pleading for mercy and forgiveness, the truly repentant sinner suddenly finds himself "justified," *counted worthy*, not because of his own merits but because of Christ's. The Love that is forgiveness frees and heals. The soul, newly born in this experience of grace, is now ready to live a very different kind of life. Christ has changed him by accepting him *as he is*.

Conversion accounts in the Catholic tradition are usually very different. They are generally not about the search for acceptance or forgiveness but are much more likely to be quests fueled not by a sense of helplessness and remorse but by *hunger*. Persons are drawn — or driven — to Catholicism by an awareness, conscious or otherwise, that they are lacking something. The hunger is often recognized first as a hunger of the mind for truth. Eventually, it is recognized as being a much more global lack. What satisfies the mind must, in the end, satisfy the soul as well. And the soul on the way into the Catholic Church finally recognizes that what he hungers for is *food* — the Bread of Life we call the Eucharist, Jesus Christ himself made present in the sacrifice of the Mass.

Every conversion account is necessarily unique, and the path truth takes must follow the interior twists and turns peculiar to the personal history and individual psyche of the convert. In some cases, what is troubled and false in the self and in our family relationships must be recognized and corrected before it is possible to enter the Church. In others, the "unearthing" cannot really occur until truth has already begun to be assimilated in and through access to the sacraments.

Such was the case in my own conversion. I converted in midlife — a time of upheaval for most people, a nature-made fork in the road when all the circumstances of life conspire to force us to face up to things that, in our youth, we were able to ignore or conceal. My hard-won interior consent to "becoming Catholic" was the conclusion of a struggle I had anticipated and, to a certain extent, welcomed; and the immediate consequence of my conversion was a kind of happiness and contentment I had never known before.

Happiness *heals*. As a consequence of my conversion I did begin to change in a whole host of ways, and, before too long, all hell broke loose. While my husband had offered no strong objections to my conversion at the time it occurred, he soon found much to complain about. In the first place, I believe my own very evident happiness and contentment only served to make my husband much more consciously discontented than he already was, and over a period of time he became utterly miserable, blaming his unhappiness on me and, especially, on my conversion. The newly received Catholic is very often a person "in love" — a condition impossible to disguise from the person we live with; and the obvious response to seeing one's spouse "in love" is jealousy. For a period of time it looked like things were spinning out of control in my marriage.

At the same time, the experience of receiving the Truth that is Christ daily in the consecrated Host was having its own relentless but entirely unanticipated effect on me. And then, one day, I woke up and said, "There *is* something wrong — and it's not just with the marriage but with *me*."

Sustained by the Bread that is Truth and a long-established practice of daily prayer, I sought professional help for a problem I hadn't even known existed and which was rooted in the losses and suffering of early childhood. What I learned was that many deep-rooted problems in my marriage were a consequence of this hidden sorrow, and with the help of a very skilled counselor I submitted my heart to the steel-sharp "plough" that is truth so that everything that might hinder the harvest might be thrown up and discarded. I had reached a point where I was sufficiently supported by what the Church was offering me to be able to deal with the pain, uncertainty, and confusion that inevitably accompany an extended process of self-examination; and I was determined to keep at it until I had plumbed the depths of what I didn't know. I wanted to leave no stone unturned.

My husband quickly followed suit, and he, too, began a course of therapy. We spent an extended period of time on this joint project. Slowly and imperceptibly, problems in the relationship began to resolve themselves, and my husband's hostility to my conversion dissolved. In the subsequent years he has moved increasingly closer to the positions of the Church on almost every issue of significance and frequently accompanies me to Mass. He knows — and has said — that when the moment of "truth" comes to him it will be to Catholicism that he will turn.

The stories in this particular collection of conversion accounts all witness to the strength and complexity of both the marital bond and the inexorably magnetic pull of Catholicism. Some of these accounts include happy resolutions to the initial rupture caused by the conversion of one spouse. Others remain unresolved but hopeful — even where further rupture has occurred.

I am especially pleased that the editor of this valuable collection of conversion narratives has chosen to include my account of the very difficult but utterly remarkable marriage between two cradle Catholics, Felix and Elisabeth Leseur. The witness of Elisabeth Leseur to her ex-Catholic, zealously atheistic husband has provided support and encouragement in the difficult moments of my own marriage as nothing else has by relativizing my personal suffering and, I believe, substantiates my earlier claim that simply having a spouse whose religious affiliation is or once was identical to your own is no guarantee of spiritual companionship.

The unresolved cases documented here represent in their very irresolution a vivid reminder that subsequent generations continue to pay the collective cost of the tragic rending of Christ's seamless garment, the horrendous wounding of the Body that occurred in the Protestant Reformation. The suffering of both spouses that comes when one says "Yes" to apostolic Christianity and the other says "No" — or *"Not yet"* — cannot be dismissed or minimized. In their "one flesh," that cosmic wound remains open and visible — a reminder of the Lord's own atrocious pain in the sacrifice offered on Calvary. Yet while it is appropriate for the converted spouse to pray and offer sacrifice for the unconverted beloved, those of us who watch and wait may find that the Lord is ready to use that wound to accomplish much more than the temporal happiness we long to see realized in our marriages.

ROBIN MAAS, PH.D.
PROFESSOR OF SPIRITUALITY,
JOHN PAUL II INSTITUTE FOR
STUDIES ON MARRIAGE AND
FAMILY
WASHINGTON, D.C.

Preface: A Family Tradition

If your family tree is anything like mine, fighting about religion is practically a tradition. In my family it goes back at least to my great-grandparents.

Great-grandpa was Catholic, and great-grandma was Protestant. My grandmother's only memory of religion in her home is that her parents fought about it. Grandma herself seemed to choose either no religion, or all religions, depending on how you look at it.

My mother was raised without benefit of any faith, but converted to the Catholic Church along with my father. On his side of the family, his grandmother was a devout Catholic, but his parents were silent about religion as he was growing up. His mother's anti-Catholicism overwhelmed whatever Catholic sentiments his father may have still harbored. But he converted as a young man, with my mother, and they set out to raise a large Catholic family in the 1950s and 1960s, keeping their Catholic faith through thick and thin.

I am the oldest daughter, one of three practicing Catholics among my siblings. Four are evangelical Protestants, and I have been a Protestant twice myself.

Both times that I returned to the Catholic Church,[1] I contemplated my family tree. I had plenty of doctrinal issues to resolve, but there were also marriage and family issues, which loomed like charged thunderheads over the horizon of my conversion journey, and which reminded me that this conflict is "in my blood."

This book comes from my experience of finding that many other converts and returning Catholics have had the same emotional family battles over religion, that many marriages have felt the threat of disunity coming against what they thought was the very basis of their marriage, their unity in Christ. How dare one of the spouses upset the applecart so thoroughly by becoming of all things — Catholic?

What This Book Is Not

Although I and most of the contributors to this book are of the Roman Catholic faith, we want to make it clear that it is not an attempt to persuade the non-Catholic partners in marriage to convert. We are not here to prove the truth of the Catholic faith, but to help both Catholic and non-Catholic spouses to understand the conversion experience and how it can affect a marriage. The Catholic faith is so all-encompassing that misunderstanding and fear are not surprising reactions. That is something we understand from our personal experience of first being horrified at the thought of becoming Catholic. Some of our spouses have converted, sooner or later, and some have not.

We are not marriage counselors. None of us claims to have solved all our problems. Our focus is on imparting what we have been through, and praying that our readers will be encouraged by our experience. Yes, we have had fights into the wee hours of the morning. We have been worried sick over what this will do to our children's faith. We have met with our own pastors and counselors, and agonized over the disunity we never expected. We are sinful human beings living with other sinful human beings, yet writing from our most idealistic selves, trying to both encourage others and admit our own failures.

In spite of dark days of doubt, through fear and anger and pain, we have not only survived, but have even grown spiritually, and for the most part come to some sense of resolution within our marriages. We know that the peace and joy can return, and the marriage can be stronger. Our children can know that Christ is still the basis for our unity, not the reason for our strife. The world can still know that we are Christians by our love. And at the heavenly wedding banquet, celebrating the marriage of Christ and his Church, we will feast together in perfect unity.

The recent increase in conversions[2] naturally brings more marriages into the rough waters raised by religious differences. While we have no easy solutions, we offer hope and compassion. Even mixed marriages of long duration can benefit from reawakening to the potential for dialog and deep understanding that comes from discussing such momentous things with a spouse. The potential for studied indifference or even habitual indifference is to be guarded against in all our relationships.

Both joy and sorrow come with conversion. There is the exhilaration of discovery, the sense of adventure, the peaceful rest of coming home, the eagerness to share. All these come with the process. Yet there is grieving for the past and for old friends who will not or cannot share your enthusiasm. Trying to communicate with those who don't understand brings loneliness and frustration. If even your own spouse does not understand, the sorrow is greatly intensified, and there is a tendency to build defensive walls. Yet the meaning of your relationship is challenged and all your spiritual resources are called upon to deepen and even redefine the relationship, to continue to grow in the oneness God intends for marriage. A sense of relief, new hope, and courage arise when we know that others have been there before us. Often, our healing begins in being understood at last.

To the non-Catholic spouse, too, we hope the insights and stories we offer will be helpful. Each of us has been a non-Catholic, and can identify with *not* understanding Catholic doctrine, customs, or culture. We have been on both sides of the fence, and so we extend to you this invitation to grow in understanding of your converting "other half."

Even in same-faith relationships, our marriages need healing, as do all our relationships this side of heaven. We can learn to ask each other's forgiveness. We can grow in patience and empathy with each other. We must strive to show love constantly, to emphasize the unity we do have, not only as married couples, but also as believers in Christ. We must keep trying to understand each other, and never give up. In this way, we hope to become one, as Jesus prayed for all who are his (cf. John 17:11). Without trying to "fix" each other, we must put our relationship in God's hands, and leave the fixing to him.

LYNN NORDHAGEN

Endnotes

1. See *Envoy Magazine*, March-April 1998, "Once, Twice, Three Times a Catholic."

2. See *New Oxford Review*, March 1996, "Why Are So Many Converting?" by Kenneth J. Howell.

Chapter 1

A Pilgrim's Progress

by William J. Cork, D. Min.

I dreamed, and behold, I saw a man clothed with rags, standing in a certain place, with his face from his own house, a book in his hand, and a great burden upon his back. I looked, and saw him open the book, and read therein; and as he read, he wept and trembled; and, not being able longer to contain, he brake out with a lamentable cry, saying, "What shall I do?"

In this plight, therefore, he went home, and restrained himself as long as he could, that his wife and children should not perceive his distress; but he could not be silent long, because that his trouble increased.

I saw in my dream that the man began to run. Now, he had not run far from his own door, when his wife and children perceiving it, began to cry after him to return; but the man put his fingers in his ears, and ran on, crying, "Life! life! eternal life!" So he looked not behind him, but fled towards the middle of the plain.

> — John Bunyan,
> *The Pilgrim's Progress*

Like Bunyan's hero, I set out one day on a journey of faith that separated me, spiritually, from those I loved most. They cried after me to return, but I kept going, oblivious to their pleadings. For sixteen years I traveled alone, without looking back.

In the summer of 1999, while my wife was away for a seven-week vacation, I paused to reflect on what this journey has meant. But that's getting ahead of myself.

Joy and I were married on May 23, 1982, at the end of my sophomore year. At the time, we were both Seventh-day Adventists. Joy's father, an SDA pastor, performed the ceremony at the Village Church of Seventh-day Adventists in South Lancaster, Massachusetts. I had just finished my sophomore year at Atlantic Union College, and intended to enter the Adventist ministry.

On that spring day, however, we thought only of one another. After the exchange of vows, Joy took my hands in hers, looked into my eyes, and sang:

> I bring to thee, the song my soul is singing;
> I give to thee, my love forever true.
> God knows my heart, he knows I love you only;
> Ah, life is sweet when all is lived for you.
>
> Day unto day with Christ enthroned, exalted,
> Our home with love shall ever hallowed be.
> Life's dearest joys will grow the deeper, sweeter:
> Love shall abide through all eternity.
>
> — Albert Simpson Reitz,
> "Love Shall Abide" (© 1938)

After the reception, we drove my boss's old Chevy Vega up to the mountains of Vermont for our honeymoon, which we spent at a friend's rustic camp. We celebrated our first Sabbath together with a communion service; as the sun went down, we lighted kerosene lamps, read John 13, and then knelt to wash one another's feet.

From time to time over the next week we would wander into the nearby towns for sightseeing and browsing in used-book stores. One treasure we found on that trip was a hundred-year-old richly illustrated edition of John Bunyan's classic, *The Pilgrim's Progress*. We could not have known that it would prove to be a prophetic choice.

Beginnings

My mother became a Seventh-day Adventist in high school. My father had little interest in religion at the time — though he did insist on having me baptized as an infant at the Methodist church near our home. My mother, however, assumed responsibility for our religious training, and faithfully took us to Sabbath school. About the time I was fourteen I began considering that I might be called to the ministry, and adult friends encouraged me. When it was time to go to college, I selected Atlantic Union College in South Lancaster, Massachusetts; in the summer of 1980, I asked my dad to drive me to the train station in Chicago.

My father had become a Christian while I was in high school. Not long after I went to college, he took an additional step in his journey, and joined the Adventist church. What should have been a time of celebration became an occasion for cynicism on my part. That's not an unusual attitude for a know-it-all college freshman, of course. And I was a young adult in a period brimming with cynicism. Watergate was still a recent memory, and the corruption of Nixon had been followed by the incompetence of Ford and Carter. Within Adventism, this was a period of theological ferment. Australians Desmond Ford and Robert Brinsmead questioned the Adventist views of salvation and the judgment. California pastor Walter Rea was shocked to discover evidence that Ellen G. White, an Adventist founder, did not give credit to sources whose phraseology she "borrowed." Ford's expulsion from the Adventist ministry after a "trial" at a church camp at Glacier View, Colorado, sparked what seemed to be an exodus (or a "shaking") of Adventist pastors and seminarians. Some became evangelicals; others started independent "Evangelical Adventist" churches.

I was in the right time at the right place to be affected by these debates. I was suspicious of authority, and in my senior year of high school I had experienced an "Evangelical awakening" due in part to Desmond Ford. I was a religion major, and I had an interest in church history — especially the history of Adventism. I started out looking objectively at the debates (or so I told myself), but I quickly became a passionate partisan. During my junior year at Atlantic Union, I used my "bully pulpit" as student newspaper editor to hurl verbal grenades at the Adventist leadership for its handling of the situation. For example, I drew an editorial cartoon, which featured the SDA General Conference president, Neal Wilson, at the wheel of a ship; behind him was a life preserver with the name *Titanic*. The caption read, "God himself couldn't sink this ship!"

By this time I was married. Joy had known of my interest in the church controversies before we married, but she could not understand why I was so taken with them, or why I would let them trouble my faith. So we didn't talk about it much.

When I published a letter in the student paper announcing my resignation — which I said was prompted by my disagreement with fundamental Adventist teachings — it took many people by surprise. Someone took a copy to Joy's parents, and after a few days, they wrote separate letters to me. I recently reread them. Their love and concern are evident on every page. They told me of having many sleepless nights because they thought I was making a terrible mistake.

In the next few days, I tried to step back and look carefully at the path I was on. I corresponded with respected Adventist pastor George Vandeman. I had a long intimate conversation in my living room with Elder John Loor, president of the Northern New England Conference (which ended with us on our knees in prayer). One of my teachers, Jim Valentine, tried to discuss the theological issues with me from a sympathetic perspective. But I had made up my mind, and the break was inevitable.

I had what I thought were very good reasons. As I would

articulate it in years to come, I would say that having been raised in a legalistic and sectarian environment, I had two critical issues: the Gospel and the church. I liked what Ford and Brinsmead were saying about the Gospel's message of unconditional forgiveness, but I didn't think forming a splinter movement of a splinter movement was the answer. My study of the church's history opened to me the continuity of the faith of the ages; experiences with other Christians led me to seek out new and wider forms of fellowship. The Gospel, I came to believe, must create a community of faith in continuity with the preaching of the Apostles. It must draw us toward other believers, not away from them.

There were other factors influencing me, not directly related to the Adventist debates. Some had to do with the nature of my education. My Scripture professors introduced me to form and redaction criticism; this led me to seek the authority of Scripture not in a process of verbal inspiration, but in Scripture's transmission in and through a community of faith. Theology professors took us to lectures in Boston to hear such theologians as Wolfhart Pannenberg, Charles Hartshorne, and Langdon Gilkey. And my history professors pushed me continually back to the sources of Christian thought.

But even before I published that inflammatory cartoon and the resignation letter, an event had occurred which had tipped the scales in favor of leaving. It was February 1983, and one of my professors took us to the annual Congress of the Evangelism Association of New England. Francis Schaeffer was the main speaker. As I gazed upon that diverse crowd of Adventists, evangelicals, Catholics (in habit and collar), and charismatics (waving their hands), I was overwhelmed by a sense of our unity in Christ, and the need to seek fellowship with these brothers and sisters. At that moment, the Adventist sitting next to me poked me in the ribs with his elbow and muttered, "It's too bad these people don't know the Truth." That was all I needed. My brother-in-law was also looking at other religious options, and visiting different churches. I called him when I got home and asked where he was going the next day — I wanted to join him. We visited a Presbyterian church in Clinton, Massachusetts; I started attending regularly, and in June 1983 I wrote a letter of resignation to the Adventist church where I was a member.

Joy found herself pulled between me and her parents; as I've already mentioned, my own father had joined the Adventist church not long before. In such emotionally charged surroundings, Joy was not about to even consider leaving; when her brother formally left, it was a second blow to her family. She has remained a dedicated Adventist to this day. Our marriage could have been shattered at that time had it not been for one of my professors, to whom I went for counseling. He helped me see that one who undergoes a conversion experience goes through the same sort of grief process as one who is watching a loved one die — and the convert's family and friends go through a parallel process. There will be anger, and denial, and depression, he warned. And so there was. This professor helped me to identify it — but it didn't disappear. It was hidden, and would smolder for many years.

Starting Over

Because of this emotional upset in my family, I chose to stay close to Adventism for a while. I finished my B.A., and accepted a teaching assistantship at Loma Linda University in Riverside, California, to begin graduate study in church history. My responsibilities there included giving occasional lectures in the undergraduate church history survey, and helping to edit *Adventist Heritage: A Journal of Adventist History.*

In our first months in Riverside I investigated a number of churches of different denominations, and Joy visited them with me. One Sunday in October 1984, I decided to visit a nearby Lutheran church (Luther had been a great influence, so I figured I owed it to him). It turned out to be "Reformation Day," and a skinny high school student stood in the pulpit clad in a brown robe to read one of Luther's sermons.

In the Lutheran confessions, I heard the New Testament Gospel — in forceful Germanic tones that went well with the tune of "A Mighty Fortress" playing in the back of my mind. In the Lutheran liturgy and especially the Eucharist, I recognized the body and blood of Christ, and felt connected to the church of all ages. Lutheranism united for me the Evangelical and Catholic dimensions of the Christian faith.

At the same time, I found that many of the things which attracted me to Lutheranism raised another question: Why not go "all the way"? Become a *Roman* Catholic? I had too many years of anti-Catholic propaganda ringing in my ears to consider that. And yet Rome was clearly becoming less of a threat. Later that school year, I took a course on the "History of the Papacy and Roman Catholicism" from my department chair, Professor Paul Landa. He had the entire class read the documents of Vatican II, and required that we visit a Catholic church and write a report on the Mass. On the side, Paul introduced me to John Henry Newman's *Essay on the Development of Christian Doctrine*, saying it was the best argument in favor of Catholicism and that no Protestant had yet given an adequate response.

Due to financial constraints, Loma Linda was not able to guarantee me scholarship funding for the next year. I began to think it was time to transfer to a seminary, and Joy agreed. Paul suggested I consider Gettysburg Lutheran Seminary; he said if I were going to continue in church history, Luther scholar Eric Gritsch would be a great mentor. He also introduced me to the book Gritsch wrote with Robert Jenson, *Lutheranism: The Theological Movement and Its Confessional Writings*.

In this work, which is the standard introduction to the Lutheran confessions used in ELCA seminaries, Gritsch and Jenson define Lutheranism as a movement of Evangelical reform within the Catholic Church. Their premise is that the

Lutheran confessions (the *Confessio Augustana* in particular) are not a constitution to begin a new church, but manifestos of reform which assume Catholic dogma and practice wherever the same is not criticized.

This resonated with my own growing understanding of Lutheranism as a *via media* between Rome and the excesses of the Reformed Protestantism of Calvin and Zwingli. But this raised other questions, questions inspired by Newman's *Essay.* Is such a *via media* really possible? If one accepts the Catholic principle of the faithfulness of Christ to his Church through time, will not one be pushed eventually to seek communion with Rome?

I transferred to Gettysburg Seminary in the fall of 1985, endorsed by the Pacific Southwest Synod of the Lutheran Church in America. Joy was regarded with great skepticism by some in the administration. In one of our first conversations, Dean Gerhard Krodel (a former Luftwaffe pilot with a thick Bavarian accent we all loved to imitate) leaned back in his chair and said, "Now, I don't say this myself, but you are going to find yourself in a parish one day and they are going to say to you, 'If you can't convert your own wife, what the hell business do you have preaching to us?' So, what you should do is go down to the bookstore and get a copy of Werner Elert's book, *The Structure of Lutheranism* — that will give you everything you need to convert your wife."

The next few years were busy. I finished my M.A. in church history the following spring, with a thesis on the abolitionist and transcendentalist Theodore Parker. I continued on for the Master of Divinity degree, taking some classes through the Washington Theological Consortium at Catholic seminaries. I joined the Army Reserve Chaplain Candidate program, and completed a unit of Clinical Pastoral Education at Walter Reed Army Medical Center. In 1987, Joy and I drove back to Riverside for my year-long internship at Trinity Lutheran; while there, we visited many old Franciscan missions. Returning to Gettysburg for my senior year, I became a member of the

Brothers and Sisters of Charity, Domestic, an ecumenical Franciscan community founded by John Michael Talbot. Each of these experiences put me into contact with Catholics, with whom I began to form very close friendships.

Despite Dean Krodel's insistence that I try to convert my wife, she was not intimidated. She was an active part of the seminary community; she sang in the Festival Choir and, in my senior year, she ran the Seminary Child Care Co-op. And she did all this while continuing to be active in her own church. She would continue this balancing act in the years to come in the parishes I would serve as pastor.

I graduated from Gettysburg in May 1989. I was called to be pastor of the Thompsontown Lutheran Parish in Juniata County, Pennsylvania, and was ordained on June 11. Ten days prior to this, Joy entered the hospital with severe hemorrhaging; our son Andrew was born late that night, two months premature, due to a placental abruption. He was in the hospital for two months as I began my ministry. The cumulative stress was more than I had ever imagined possible.

During my time at Gettysburg, I had many conversations with fellow students about the forthcoming merger that would result in the formation of the Evangelical Lutheran Church in America. We were troubled by the fact that the merger process had decided to put off discussion of theological issues until after the merger. We felt it was becoming just another mainline Protestant church, with no commitment to either Scripture or the Lutheran confessions.

The Lutheran identity crisis was clearly illustrated by my experiences at Thompsontown. This was a two-church parish. Emmanuel, in town, had kneelers in the pews, and a hand-carved Tyrolean crucifix over the altar; it used wine for communion, but thought that communion should be held only once a month. Centre, in the country, was indistinguishable from a Methodist or Reformed church; it used grape juice for communion, sang Evangelical Sunday school songs, but was a very close, supportive community of faith. On top of the personal stress I was experiencing with my family, I soon found myself reviving thirty-year-old jealousies between the two churches. Though I was liturgically more in synch with Emmanuel, I was personally attracted to the people at Centre — part of this was due to the fact that Joy's Adventist faith was an issue with some of the gossips at Emmanuel, but not at Centre, where she was well loved. I exacerbated these tensions by defending a more Catholic view of ordained ministry over against congregationalism (translate that as meaning that I insisted on my authority as pastor when frustrated by snowballing criticism!).

I resigned after a year. That summer, to gain some healing and some perspective, I attended a conference for priests, deacons, and seminarians at the Franciscan University of Steubenville. I was subscribing to the charismatic Catholic magazine *New Covenant*, and had seen in an advertisement that Father Francis Martin would be one of the speakers. I had taken a class from Francis on the "Letter to the Romans" at the Dominican House of Studies, and I had been very impressed with the way he dealt with the hermeneutical disagreements between Lutherans and Catholics. The worship services and the talks were all inspiring, but it was the private conversations that I remember best.

One day I was talking to some priests about differences between Catholics and Lutherans over the Eucharist. Lutherans believe that the Eucharist is the body of Christ — at least as long as the liturgy lasts. A question arises with what happens afterward. Lutheran theologians have either said it goes back to being mere bread (so that one Lutheran church I preached at had no problem throwing the leftover bread to the birds!), or they avoid the problem by consuming all the bread during the liturgy. And yet we had no problem taking communion to the sick without reconsecrating it!

One of the priests listened to all my objections and excuses and quietly said, "When God gives a gift, he doesn't take it back."

That night, when the evening meeting ended, I found myself in a stampede of priests rushing downhill from the red-and-white tent to the chapel. The assembly fell into hushed silence as the body of Christ was exposed in the monstrance. Priests fell on their faces. I was speechless. A feeling of awe overwhelmed me, and all my objections fell away as I found myself praying, "My Lord and my God!"

Another day that week I was walking with a priest and we came across another group of priests. After some casual conversation, one suggested praying the Rosary. I tried to back out gracefully. A priest (the same one from the other day!) pressed the point. I nervously remembered a quote from Lutheran theologian Gerhard Forde about "not talking to dead people." The priest looked me in the eye and replied, "Don't you believe in the communion of saints?" I had no response.

The climax of the week for me was a gut-wrenching experience of profound grief and alienation as I sat alone in the pew while the priests and deacons around me went forward to receive the body and blood of our Lord — we fell on each other's shoulders and cried.

The next few months passed in a blur. I finished Phase II of the Army Chaplain Officer Basic Course at Fort Monmouth, New Jersey. One morning the drill sergeant sang as we ran, "I wish somebody would start a war — Hey!" That evening he told us he was never singing that again — Saddam Hussein had invaded Kuwait. I spent that fall on active duty at Fort Bragg, North Carolina, helping out at the 82d Airborne Division Memorial Chapel as the soldiers of the division were being transported to Saudi Arabia to defend President Bush's "line in the sand."

I thought I might be called to active duty; instead, that Christmas I was called to be pastor of Shepherd of the Hills Lutheran Church in Montpelier, Vermont. If I could have been a "Catholic" sort of Lutheran anywhere, it would have been here: we reserved the Blessed Sacrament, had weekly Eucharist, "smells and bells" — even a touch of charismatic praise.

One of the church's traditions was to use Luther's *Formula Missae* as the order of service on Reformation Day. This was Luther's 1521 revision of the Mass. Luther had kept it in Latin, with German Scriptures and hymns and a German sermon, but this parish did it all in English. For Reformation Day 1991, I suggested doing it in Latin, as Luther had intended (contrary to myth, he never had a problem with the Latin Mass as such, but thought it should be retained as an option). We used sixteenth-century Lutheran hymns in English, and kept the Scriptures of the sermon in English, but the rest was in Latin, in a simple chant setting. This was one of the best received liturgies I ever did anywhere.

And yet, in spite of all this romantic Romanism, it seemed to me that the parish was congregationalist in the extreme. We had discussions at council meetings about whether we should spend the money to send delegates to the synod assembly, and whether we should pay for all members to receive the ELCA's magazine, *The Lutheran*. I interpreted this as a suspicion of the larger church — not that I blamed the members entirely. In 1990 the ELCA published a study on human sexuality that declared that Scripture and church tradition had no answers to contemporary questions on sexuality, and that the church must seek its message in an ahistorical "radical imperative." I wrote a review of the study that was published as the editorial in *Lutheran Forum*. I found myself giving up hope that a "Catholic" version of Lutheranism would ever amount to anything other than a sectarian option within a generic old-line Protestant denomination.

I continued dialogue with many Catholic priest friends, especially those I worked with now that I was a chaplain in the Vermont National Guard; I also began meeting regularly with the local Catholic pastor "for coffee." I made my permanent profession in the Brothers and Sisters of Charity. I attended other priests' conferences at Steubenville. But I put off making any kind of decision on "the Catholic question."

But then, in 1992, Shepherd of the Hills faced a financial

crisis. The members had bought a building right before the previous pastor left, and then had a long interim without a full-time pastor. This was the first time this small congregation had ever tried to pay for both a pastor and a building. They had counted on growth in membership, but it never came. In fact, our attendance and giving dropped as we grappled with revelations of some of the deeds of my predecessor. When the treasurer suggested that they might have to cut me to half time, I agreed that this was the best course of action. (Yet when they actually voted to do it at the annual meeting, I was in shock. It was a very bitter pill to swallow.)

This decision provided me with the opportunity to face the other issue I had been trying to avoid, Hamlet-like, for so long. I told Joy that I was going to write a letter to Cardinal Bernard Law of Boston; her only response was, "I always knew it would come to this." I visited Law in early April 1992, and then told my Lutheran bishop, Bob Isaksen. I began to apply for jobs in Catholic settings; Cardinal Law put me in touch with friends of his in the business world. I wanted to wait until my family was taken care of until I did anything drastic; but as time went by, it became clear that I would just need to "jump." Bob called me in early October and said that he had talked with Law, and they felt it best for me to resign the following week. My head began to spin; "Can I wait till the end of the month?" Bob agreed. Ironically, that meant that my final sermon as a Lutheran pastor was on Reformation Sunday.

I took the last few days of October as vacation, and the last four hours of my ordained ministry were spent watching my brothers in a community theater performance of *Camelot*. As "Arthur" mused on what had led him to war with Lancelot, his beloved Jenny deep within the besieged castle, I mused on the path that had brought me to this point. The next day, I got a phone call from the Pentagon; they were wondering if I would be interested in going on active duty as a chaplain. I told them to call back in a couple of days. "Can I delay this decision?" I wondered. Bob Isaksen called to clarify where I stood; I told him that it was over, and that I considered myself no longer an ELCA pastor. On November 11, 1992, in a private ceremony attended by some priests, deacons, and Franciscan friends, I was received into the Catholic Church.

'Further Up and Further In'

For the next eighteen months I was unemployed, with a wife and two children (Aimee was born in March 1992, also premature). I looked for any kind of work — I continued to work part time for the Vermont National Guard, I wrote regularly for the diocesan paper, and I got a position preaching Catholic parish missions — but it still wasn't enough. When the money in the bank slowly dribbled away, I swallowed my pride and signed up for food stamps. Two months later our income was so low that we were eligible for welfare. And I wondered whether I had done the right thing. On top of it all, Aimee was diagnosed with a congenital hip dislocation, and she would spend three-and-a-half years undergoing repeated hospitalizations in an attempt to correct it. A Methodist pastor friend got her admitted to the Shriners Hospital in Springfield, Massachusetts — and during each of her hospitalizations, Joy stayed by her side day and night.

That was a trying time. It gave me a lasting love for St. John of the Cross, especially his book *The Dark Night of the Soul*.

The worst experience, perhaps, was the difficulty of finding a job in a Catholic church. I sent out hundreds of inquiries, got handfuls of responses and three or four interviews, at which I kept coming in second. I grew angry with the patronizing excuses that people gave for not wanting to hire me: "We don't think it would be just to pay you only $20,000 a year"; "We don't think it would be fair to your family to move so far"; "Would you accept a janitorial position at $6 an hour, an hour's drive from your house?"

Yet God was faithful. Whenever it seemed as if the darkness would envelop us completely, a ray of light would shine. My pastor would pay bills that I was unable to pay. Another priest friend would send me checks of $200 or $500. At Easter, I received a card from Cardinal Law. He told me he wished he could be doing more for us. He added, in a footnote, that there was a gift in the card, a token of his care; "Consider it a little Easter egg." It was a check for $900. He also arranged for me to receive a $600-a-month stipend from a special fund that the Archdiocese of New York had set up for clergy converts.

In July 1994, thanks to a chance conversation between my daughter's godfather and a priest in another diocese, I finally got a full-time position as a parish director of religious education. I was responsible for religion classes for kids of all ages, for sacramental preparation, and for classes for adults. Over the next few months, I found myself in the middle of a parish conflict that was unlike anything we had experienced in any other setting. I began to think that I had made a stupid mistake by putting my family in a situation where this could happen. I decided to investigate the possibility of a return to Lutheranism.

I contacted Bishop Isaksen and began a discernment process toward reinstatement. I took tests and psychological evaluations, and had several interviews with a committee. During one of these sessions, someone asked a question that threw me for a loop: "What can you say positive about Adventism?" She explained, "Obviously this is an issue affecting your marriage; if you can only see the negative aspects of your Adventist upbringing, how can that not negatively impact your relationship with Joy?" I thought of a couple of points (the Adventist concern for the whole person, its realization that the kingdom of God will never be established by man, and another point or two), but I was troubled by the question, and would mull it over from time to time in the years to come.

The committee eventually decided to place me in a kind

of second internship to feel me out a little further. Now was the time that I would have to make a decision: would I stay in the Catholic Church, or, now that the door was open, would I return to my previous life? Would going back be easier for my family, or would it be merely running from some troubles in my present situation? With these questions in mind, I met with the pastor they wanted to put me with and discovered that he was exactly the kind of pastor I had been, with the same questions and concerns that had sent me to Rome in the first place.

I needed time to pray, and the next weekend I went on a retreat. I had written to some Catholic friends, and some had sent letters of counsel. On the long drive to the retreat center, I reviewed all of this advice, and the history of the previous couple of years. About halfway there, it struck me that I was on the verge of making a very stupid decision. I had stayed faithful to Christ and his Church through eighteen months of unemployment, and now, after a bad experience in one parish I was ready to throw the towel in and go back. I thought of several Scriptures that touch on the theme of looking back; I realized that whatever God was calling me to, it was not a return to the Lutheran ministry. I thought to myself, "There is no going back. Christ never calls us backward; he only calls us forward." After the retreat, I returned home determined to stick with the situation. I went to my pastor in the Sacrament of Reconciliation, and was able to talk freely about the difficulties, and my struggles—and to receive the grace of Christ. Things improved, and the next six months brought a healing in many fractured relationships.

But at that point I began to see that I needed to be in another position — one better suited to my interests and talents, and to the needs of my family. I had long thought about the possibility of campus ministry, and in November 1996 I was hired as a campus minister at St. Mark's University Parish, the Newman Center at the University of California at Santa Barbara. UCSB was a vibrant campus, and I was able to be involved in many ecumenical and interfaith projects (the focus of the Doctor of Ministry studies I had begun a year earlier). Because of the high cost of living, Joy returned to work as a preschool teacher for the first time since our son was born.

When it came time for me to select a doctoral project, I decided to develop an ecumenical version of the parish mission I preached for Isaiah Ministries. This project gave me the opportunity to reflect on the most pressing ecumenical question in my life: my relationship with my wife. I returned to the question posed by that Lutheran committee member: "What can you say about Adventism that is positive?" My answer to this question turned into a book manuscript, *That All May Be One: Reflections on Christian Unity.* I intended it to be a tool for Christians of different backgrounds to use in exploring their own faith journey, and the journeys of other Christians. It would be one component of the "Isaiah 43: Regathering" ecumenical parish mission.

I did a trial run of the mission in November 1997 at St. Mark's, which involved Lutherans, Episcopalians, Presbyterians, Orthodox, evangelicals, and charismatics. In February 1998 I was part of another exciting ecumenical event, as members of those same faiths (and more) came together to sponsor a ten-day "Veritas Forum" at UCSB, the goal of which was to confront the secular campus with the Christian claim that there is such a thing as Truth, and that this Truth is found in Jesus Christ.

At the height of these personal successes, I saw that the stress of having to work was wearing down Joy. I knew that I wouldn't be able to negotiate much of an increase in salary next time around, and once more began the task of looking at other possibilities. That summer I was hired as Director of Young Adult and Campus Ministry for the Diocese of Galveston-Houston, a newly created position in a large diocese — a position that would allow for lots of creativity and imagination. And a significant salary raise and a drop in the cost of living meant that Joy could stay home with the kids.

A Look Back

As I sit down to write this, it has been a year since we came to Houston. This is one of the longest summers of my life, since Joy and the kids are in the middle of a seven-week visit to her parents in Vermont. Before they left, Joy and I had been experiencing some increased tensions over our differences in faith. This year the kids have become much more involved in activities at the Adventist church, and to my annoyance they have no interest in coming to Mass with me. It's been almost seven years since I became a Catholic, and I have begun to speak with my bishop about the possibility of ordination to the priesthood. It would be an answer to prayer for me — but I must ask what effect it would have on Joy and the kids.

For a long time the spiritual side of our marriage has been in an uneasy détente; rather than discussing our differences (which often leads to an argument), we have too often found it easier just to avoid talking about it. I have to admit that the arguments are always my fault — that anger at Adventism which has smoldered for sixteen years flaring up once more.

Some months ago, Lynn Nordhagen told me about this book, and asked me to write a chapter. I had dashed something off, but she wanted a revision. As I stared at what I had written, and compared it with the questions I was asking about the state of my marriage, I began to wonder if I had anything at all to say on the subject that would benefit anyone.

I recently read a book by the Jewish campus minister at Oxford University, Rabbi Shmuley Boteach, entitled *Kosher Sex*. The teachings of Jewish mysticism on marriage assume that we are married to the person God has chosen for us. We should not be annoyed by our differences with that person, or (if we are still searching) try to find someone who thinks like us in all things — rather, we need someone who is *unlike* us. We are essentially incomplete, fragmented, and need to find our "soul mate" to be a whole person. I had tried to cut off my Adventist past, and everything associated with it; yet here I am, not only married to an Adventist, but to a gentle, loving woman for whom the Adventist faith has been a consistent source of strength through all the trials I have inflicted upon her (Cardinal Law once said, "Joy must be a saint to put up with you!"). I cannot be a whole person, and we cannot have the kind of marriage God intends for us, unless I can look anew at Adventism, and release that anger that has been a third party in our relationship.

And so, during this seven-week retreat, I've been taking a new look at where I have come from. This chapter began as a triumphalistic apologetic entitled "From Sectarianism to the Communion of Saints," which was published in a book about clergy converts. I wanted to turn it into just a story of a pilgrim's journey — and the effect of that journey on his family.

I concluded the original essay by saying that if I were to summarize the primary reason I became a Catholic and why I remain one, I think the best answer comes from Cardinal John Henry Newman's *Essay on the Development of Christian Doctrine*:

> Whatever history teaches, whatever it omits, whatever it exaggerates or extenuates, whatever it says and unsays, at least the Christianity of history is not Protestantism. If ever there were a safe truth, it is this.
>
> And Protestantism has ever felt it so. . . . This is shown in the determination already referred to of dispensing with historical Christianity altogether and of forming a Christianity from the Bible alone. . . . Our popular religion scarcely recognizes the fact of the twelve long ages which lie between the Councils of Nicaea and Trent, except as affording one or two passages to illustrate its wild interpretations of certain prophecies of St. Paul and St. John. . . . To be deep in history is to cease to be a Protestant.

I was a novice church historian when I first read those words, and yet even then I felt their truth. I had already experienced the pull of the faith of the Fathers of the Church; I had experienced the sense of mystical union through the Eucharist and baptism; I had learned to say "Amen" to the truth in Augustine, the Cappadocians, Francis and Dominic, Aquinas and Bonaventure, Vatican II and John Paul II. When that priest asked if I believed in the communion of saints, I had to say, "Yes! Of course I do!"

But now I need to add something to that. I need to ask myself if I can also recognize as my brothers and sisters the heroes of the Reformation: Martin Luther, Ulrich Zwingli, Menno Simons, Jean Calvin. And then comes the next step — can I in any degree embrace Ellen White and William Miller?

During one of my parish missions, my priest partner chastised me in private for quoting from Protestants. He saw this as a sign that I had not fully embraced Catholicism. In a recent Internet discussion, I found other Catholics expressing surprise that I would try to understand the anti-Catholic attitudes of many Protestants. In another discussion, a celebrated Catholic apologist viciously attacked me for speaking gently of Martin Luther. All struck me as arrogant: "We alone have the truth. We alone have experienced the Spirit of God. You knew nothing of the Gospel before you became Catholic."

But as I look at the Adventists close to me, who have stood by me all these years, I cannot accept that triumphalism. I compare the cockiness of those comments (and stronger things I have said!) with the love and humility shown to me. If it is true that "by their fruits you will know them," which of us has borne the sweeter fruits?

As I said above, the other day I reread the letters my in-laws wrote at the time I left Adventism. These letters do not defend the teachings of Adventism. They do not claim Adventism as the "true church." Rather, they are humble expressions of their love and support for one they saw to be wrestling in faith — even if they could not understand the questions that troubled me.

My father-in-law said: "Oh yes, I should note why our hearts have been sad, and sleep has evaded us. We received a phone call from someone about a letter that appeared in the 'Lancastrian.' It left us shocked — especially because we had no advance warning — except some perceptive intuition. Yet, we realize that God has a purpose for your life. Humanly we have wondered if the method you used was the most appropriate and if it was not a bit hasty. Yet, we are all growing — and if we grow with Christ and let him lead — the final outcome is what is important. . . . God isn't finished with any of us yet. We must all stay close to him so that we can be led to (not run ahead of) him and thus accept the victory over the adversary that Jesus has made possible for us."

He added as a postscript: "For out of much affliction and anguish of heart I wrote unto you with many tears; not that ye should be grieved, but that ye might know the love which I have more abundantly unto you" (2 Corinthians 2:4).

My mother-in-law wrote: "Perhaps this whole experience can help us to understand God better. Moses had to learn humility in the wilderness before God could use him. He had the best education that the times could provide but was too sure of himself, and God put him in a quiet spot herding sheep to learn lessons of humility and patience. Perhaps you, too, Bill, have lessons God wants you to learn before you can be a successful soul winner for him. Don't be discouraged — be willing to let God lead you — when the time is *right* and our hearts are right he *will* lead us to just the spot on earth where we can work for him. . . . Every day we pray for you and lately with saddened hearts our thoughts are often lifting heavenward in your behalf. . . . 'The fruit of the Spirit is love, joy, peace, longsuffering, gentleness, goodness, faith, meekness, temperance, against such there is no law' (Galatians 5:22-23). . . . 'Be strong and of a good courage; be not afraid, neither be thou dismayed: for the Lord thy God is with thee whithersoever thou goest' (Joshua 1:9). . . . Our tomorrows are in God's hands. Ours is today to enjoy, have confidence, and trust in our heavenly Father. God bless you both as you daily seek to become more and more like Jesus so that we will all be ready to receive him with joy and gladness at his coming — his *soon* coming."

That's the spirit that both Joy and her parents have continued to display these past sixteen years or so.

I still believe that God does not call us backward, only forward. But whatever is in front of us, we will only get there because of God's leading throughout our lives — even in circumstances where we only caught a glimpse of light in the midst of darkness. For many years Joy and I have lived parallel lives — from this point on we need to journey together.

Postscript

Another year has gone by. Some seeds were planted in my reflections of last summer that are starting to blossom. For the first time in seventeen years, we are praying together as a family. We've each given a little. Joy and I have begun to close each day with some quiet time together, followed by Night Prayer. After the first couple of days of Night Prayer, in which I tried to do it "by the book," with each of us alternating parts, I could see that Joy wasn't entirely comfortable. We talked about it. She couldn't see how reading something out of a book was prayer—especially some of the night-time psalms that are rather gloomy: "my only friend is darkness." I shared how each of these psalms has come to trigger memories for me; that particular psalm reminds me of dark days when we could not pray together, and we were suffering in isolation during family crises. We changed the way of praying after that. We lie close together, and I pray the psalms softly. We pray the responsory together. We take time for voicing our petitions or concerns, joining Joy's accustomed way of praying with this ancient prayer of the Catholic Church.

Joy also suggested that she and the kids would begin joining me for Mass (at least two or three times a month). She was not comfortable sending the kids off to religious education at my parish, but suggested that I do some home-schooling, so we could study together as a family. I could not ask for more.

On my part, I suggested that instead of watching TV on Friday night while Joy and the kids tried to find quiet time to observe the Sabbath in another part of the house, we make this a family day. We have begun the practice of praying a modified version of Evening Prayer as a family on Friday and Saturday evenings at sundown, marking the beginning and end of the Sabbath (and the beginning of the Lord's Day) with the Service of Light. Our kids love rituals—and they love to see us praying together, instead of arguing. Andrew is still not sure about Mass some days, but then I remind him that among his favorite videos are a cartoon series on famous saints: St. Francis of Assisi, St. Patrick, St. Francis Xavier.

I've made some other changes, too. I'm washing the dishes. And taking out the garbage. Without complaining. That was the hardest change of all.

> God knows my heart, he knows I love you only;
> Ah, life is sweet when all is lived for you.

Chapter 2

Into

Harbor

by Larry Dimock

When a couple marries, the partners bring many dreams with them. They want to live up to each other's expectations. They even hope to change for the sake of the other. When Gail and I got married during college, we prided ourselves on knowing each other well and on communicating and compromising for the sake of the relationship. When I proposed to study for the Congregational ministry, like my father and my mother's father, Gail was very supportive. She worked to put me through Harvard Divinity School. I was able to spend time after classes tending our new baby while she worked. Then, ordained to be pastor of a rural church outside Seattle, I immersed myself in its life, especially in leading a number of Bible study groups. Gail dived right in too, serving in several capacities and enjoying the instant social network afforded to a minister's wife.

Neither of us anticipated the drastic change that occurred four years into my ministry. It was 1976. In search of truth for myself and my congregation, I stumbled upon the apostolic nature of the Church, as sharply portrayed by G. K. Chesterton in *The Everlasting Man*. He showed through history the supernatural tenacity of the Church in holding to her founder's legacy and also her resilience against decay, as if Christ's promised presence to her were actually happening. I had never considered how necessary this divine support was. Regardless of anything I did not yet know about the Roman Catholic Church, I noticed that her unique self-recognition as the true Church resonated with Jesus' own confession of Messiahship and divinity. The Church now seemed to be echoing to me a question parallel to his: Who do you say that I am? Somehow I knew. This key slid perfectly into the slot of years of questions. It only remained for me to turn the key.

I resigned my position the very next Sunday, explaining my intention to go over to the Roman Catholic Church. I was matching in action the sudden sureness of my new conviction that the Catholic Church is this apostolic church. I believe that this decisiveness in me was a grace from God. I had great joy and little pain. It seemed less a choice of mine than a crucial response to an event that had come upon me — crucial in the sense described by the Second Vatican Council that "they could not be saved who, knowing that the Catholic Church was founded as necessary by God through Christ, would refuse either to enter it, or to remain in it" (*Lumen Gentium*, 14).

My parishioners were dumbfounded. This was not the kind of thing even gossips would know what to do with. Most of the congregation recognized the sincerity of my conviction, but no one understood it and, to my chagrin, no one was much interested to learn what was so wonderful in what I had found. My parents and relatives were also confused but didn't bother me about the decision. Maybe they knew how stubborn I could be. Hardest hit was Gail. Pregnant with our third child, she was naturally hurt by my unilateral destabilizing of our future. She did not share in what the Catholic Church meant to me, not having wrestled with theological issues in the way I had. She had a more right-brained way of relating to God and church than I. Gail had been breezing along in the role of minister's wife, and here I was, pulling that magic carpet out from under her. She said I was crazy to be doing this so quickly, without planning a way into the future. I couldn't explain to her satisfaction my compelling sense that I couldn't hold this kind of thing in, that I had to act on it.

I was happy to be received into the Catholic Church. But eventually months of odd jobs, liquidating savings, and getting a cold shoulder from Catholic schools where I thought I might teach left me needing a sign from God of what to do. Only St. Paul's advice kept occurring to me: "Work with your hands." Almost arbitrarily, I made my way into the electrical trade. I was glad to have concrete things to achieve, calluses to develop, and sore muscles to tend, in place of the anxieties and uncertainties I had been under. The economic breech was starting to mend, but the marriage was still hurting.

Disunity in religion puts a special strain on a marriage when it occurs after the knot has been tied. Gail and I wrestled over where our girls would attend religious education classes and where our new baby, Carl, should be baptized. I won out. And when it came to birth control, I pressed my Church's position on Gail's conscience (or on her sexual needs, I suppose) till she accepted natural family planning — in practice if not fully from the heart. To Gail it wasn't fair: I was getting my way in one thing after another, and she was the one having to adjust. I could use my arsenal of arguments to make her look unreasonable, while her strongest feelings about a matter were ineffective with me. The one-sidedness I had shown when I tossed away three years of professional education and four of practice was continuing.

I did feel for Gail in her predicament, though. I just didn't know how to mesh my new identity with my fidelity and love for her. I may have gone back on whatever promises I made at ordination, but those were not on a par with my marriage vows to love, honor, and cherish her, for better and for worse. I assumed God was involved in our marrying and that he meant for these two to somehow be one flesh till death. Where in all this were our vaunted skills at communication? Wouldn't they be able to help us through these difficulties? On invitation, we revived them for a while by making a Marriage Encounter weekend. But communication wasn't what it used to be. Before, it had often been a sweet exchange by flower and bee. Now, often enough, it was an exchange of venom by wasp and spider. Differences, perhaps irreconcilable, were threatening to slay our legacy of care for each other. Ultimately, this deliberate communication seemed to reopen wounds that were possibly trying to heal far below the surface of what we could do. The proof of our "for better or worse" pledge was not going to come from words of complaint or persuasion. Rather, it would come from a forbearing silence and from daily gestures of courtesy and practical compromise, made as a sacrifice and as a prayer to God that our stony hearts might be softened again somehow.

One gesture we did make — I don't remember which of us suggested it — was to attend both of our churches together once a month. This was important to us. Even though we only kept it up for about a year, we were showing each other that we hoped to regain some closeness, while not knowing how it could come about.

About five years into our new world order, Gail began coming to Mass every Sunday, leaving her friends at the Congregational church behind. I didn't know quite what this meant. Only later did she tell me. She had always scorned the way spouses of Catholics would become Catholic for no apparent motive of their own. She was not going to be another such case. However, on a meditative retreat one weekend with a friend, Gail was willing to listen to see if God had anything particular to tell her. A simple statement came to her: "Go to the Catholic Church." Not what she wanted to hear! She knew what was being said, but she took a year before feeling able to make this move.

It was another two years before Gail presented herself for the sacrament of confirmation. By then she had already joined the choir and the women's group and endeared herself to many in the parish. If I didn't throw a party at her full entry into the Church, it wasn't just to keep from the appearance of "I told you so." It was also from something stingier in me. Though I was glad our outward disunity was ending, I was distrustful of her motives. Like the Prodigal Son's older brother, the only decent motive I seemed to recognize was the type that had moved me. According to the tapes playing in my constricted heart, full intellectual conviction was the only solid foundation. As if the organic gestation that had fashioned her obedience were not from God, perhaps even more solidly than my mental conception! For such a conception will miscarry if it does not grow into the full-term person. Gail's development as a Catholic did not lack belief-content, however. She came in with a much greater awareness of doctrine than most. She was perhaps more humble than I under the mysteries these propositions describe, and so she was less strident. Talking should not exceed walking.

In fact, my walk had a stumbling way about it. Once the faith crisis I had imposed on Gail found some resolution, dormant difficulties of mine reasserted themselves. How could I, who had trained to be a professional, find life satisfying as a layperson? How could I resist having a critical eye and ear about the liturgy and the preaching? I couldn't easily keep from saying internally, "I would not have treated this Scripture the way this priest is doing." And what sort of piety was really my own, now that my "public piety" was gone? I had to struggle with these sorts of things. In addition, I was concerned that my "rock-solid" Church was being destabilized following the reforms of the Second Vatican Council. (Was this Gail's revenge? Now I got to see how it felt to lose security and have no control over events around me!)

Sorting out which changes are real and which are local personal agenda, which upheavals must be supported or endured and which resisted — this has been exhausting. In this desert of mine, the Spirit has given me some refreshment in Marian spirituality, in reflection on her apparitions, and by further study of Scripture and of St. Thomas Aquinas. Once again, these were not to Gail's taste, but we were getting more used to differences that this "universal" faith magnified between us. Maybe some appreciation and even adoption of each other's ways was starting to creep in.

Gail's growth has proceeded in an interesting direction. Her social sense and her energy for serving found an outlet in volunteer secretarial work in our parish. Her success with newsletters, bookkeeping, organization, and the RCIA (Rite of Christian Initiation of Adults) has brought her now to a full-time salaried position administering a mission-church in another part of the parish. In effect, she is a minister's wife glorified, or at least professionalized. She has grown to love the life that developed in her. The conception of God's grace in us may itself actually be as tender as Christ's coming to the Virgin Mary, but in this life we do not receive such tenderness without some pain, since we carry the sorrow of Eve in us as well.

What can be distilled so far, from twenty-two years of waves? What can we learn from this wake that still grinds and laps at Gail and me since the Catholic ship came in — into the little harbor of our marriage? The lessons gained are nothing very new. I may have heard them stated at some time in my past or preached them myself, but when they come about in the flesh, they seem less like truth, more just plain experience, opaque and raw.

I see that what I am in our marriage can be a cross for my spouse. This is either because I really am "a pain" or else because she is not ready to understand something good that I bring. More likely there will be a mixture of these two reasons. So when I am a cause of pain to her, I should stay humble enough to change where I should, but patient enough for her to grasp whatever good she can. Just as the sign of the cross is the gesture used for a blessing, I should not shrink from being an occasion of suffering to my spouse in respect to something I am certain is good. Knowing her difficulty with it, I should not insist on its reception, should even lighten her cross by extra sympathy; but knowing its goodness, I should not expect its ultimate full rejection. If for a time there is rejection, I can either accept this as Christ did, or else I will suffer because of a pride that takes it too personally. (Or again, a mixture.) In either case, the difficulty enables further conversion in both of us.

Some imperfection in need of conversion clings to the Church herself. Her union with Christ is incomplete, as she, the Bride, is added to, adorned, and cleansed, in preparation for their day of consummation in heaven. Though not yet ready for that, she is led on by the perfect husband. In love he is patient and persistent. He takes initiative in many ways, and she is surprised, but by his good heart, dying of love, he draws consent and wonder from hers.

And with marriage being patterned after the relation of Christ and the Church, we should not be surprised to see stresses that the Church bears reflected directly in marriages. If the Church has experienced separations among the baptized, we can pray and work for their reunion by the very way we treat one another when we find divisions (and not just religious ones) in our marriages.

The effect of recent conversions to Catholicism by so many of us who officially represented Protestantism is not clear. These conversions might actually be prophetic, rather than having "effect." Something is happening or about to happen toward the healing of divisions in the Body of Christ, I believe. My wife's entering into Rome may give some ex-pastors hope for their wives, but the fulfillment, if it comes, may await a more general reconciliation and unification of the Church. That would be part of what the pope refers to as a second Pentecost, and it could be closer at hand than we dare imagine, thanks to God's merciful power.

A final biblical footnote. As I recall the sheer length of time involved for both Gail and me, I am amazed. Many marriages have battled or suffered as long for the sake of worldly goods. How much better if the perseverance is for eternal goods! The

Scripture is about Jacob and Rachel and her father, Laban. Just to gain her as his wife, Jacob had to labor under Laban and his conniving for twenty years. Still he labored gladly, knowing that God was blessing him at every step. May God keep us in his grace, so as to assure us of his knowledge of our needs, and to give us good hope of his blessed provision.

Chapter 3

An Ongoing Journey

by Charles DeWolf

Until at least my mid-adolescence, Catholicism was the last religion to which I might have imagined myself converting. Psychologists or students of the conversion experience may find nothing startling in this, but the thought still fills me with a mixture of wonder and mirth.

My four brothers and I grew up in what I would characterize as a "staunchly moderate" Protestant family. Our father was a pastor, first Presbyterian, then Methodist. I was still a small boy at the time of our denominational shift, though I do recall being instructed one night, as we were preparing for bedtime prayers, that henceforth we would ask forgiveness of "trespasses" instead of "debts."

At least by the standards of today, my siblings and I were biblically literate. During my early adolescence, we undertook the reading of the Scriptures every morning at breakfast, beginning with Genesis and ending with the final "amen" of the Book of Revelation.

This is not to imply that we grew up in sheltered piety or that we lived in a constant state of tension with the secular world. In fact, it was not in encountering "the ungodly" that I experienced early culture shock but rather in discovering classmates so benighted as to be scandalized by the theory of evolution.

My hostility toward those we came to know as Fundamentalists easily extended to Roman Catholics, though this was then magnified by the social and cultural prejudices that American Protestants of that era typically bore. Most objectionable, in my mind, was their exclusivity.

Catholic classmates dared to speak of the only true church. Like the Fundamentalists, Catholics believed in a literal hell and then made matters even worse by inventing such absurdities as purgatory and limbo. We learned that they prayed to statues, worshiped Mary, and were slavishly obedient to a supposedly infallible pope in faraway Rome. When a friend went to a nun for tutoring in mathematics, only to fall into her clutches and convert, I thought this was vivid proof of Catholic deviousness. Anti-Romanism, I should say, did nothing to make me a more devout Protestant. In fact, many of my objections to Catholicism overlapped with doubts about our own faith. Particularly objectionable was the Trinitarian doctrine that turned gentle Jesus into a god.

In such views, I was encouraged by a long-time family friend: a Unitarian minister of Jewish origin. Being more sympathetic to the Christian element in Unitarianism than many or most of his co-believers, he had an amiable relationship with my father. They were happy to find common ground, while cheerfully accepting their theological differences. From his half-Irish mother, with a Catholic father and a proud and domineering Anglo-Protestant mother, my father had inherited a dislike for religious contentiousness of all kinds. Ironically enough, this must have been reinforced by the attitude of my paternal grandfather, who erupted in anger over his son's decision to become a minister. I should say that my father hardly fit the stereotype of the pompous "marshmallow Christians" my grandfather, a Mason, seems to have despised. In fact, as he related to me in later years, he had begun his training for the ministry at a time when the pendulum had clearly swung away from the optimistic progressivism and theological minimalism that characterized, for example, the Social Gospel movement.

Still, even as I was growing up, the Methodist church was

latitudinarian enough to include both semi-Fundamentalists and quasi-Unitarians. Besides, of far more immediate relevance to my contemporaries than the fine points of Trinitarianism was the social code that distinguished the righteous from the fallen. The mark of a good Methodist boy or girl was not a notarized affirmation of the creeds; it was good, clean living: no smoking, drinking, or misbehavior in the backseat of automobiles. (Catholics, as we well knew, were shockingly tolerant of the first two vices; as for the third, there was always "confession," which, we again understood, was nothing but the most cynical of ruses.)

Lacking both the will and the means to commit social heresy, I chose, as my avenue of teenage rebellion, matters of faith instead of morals. In this, I was no doubt also taking the less hazardous course. My mother, proud of being ever "open to new ideas," was quite willing to undertake safaris into the intellectual wilds, as long as they offered mental exercises that did not undermine the common decency. She had no apparent qualms, for example, about taking on Samuel Beckett's *Waiting for Godot*, despite the author's avowed atheism. On the other hand, I distinctly remember that her response to Boris Pasternak's *Dr. Zhivago* was decidedly cool: the story, it seemed to her, appeared to condone adultery.

One Sunday morning, as we were reciting the Apostles' Creed, I decided on an impulse that I would not pretend to affirm what, in fact, I did not believe. Quietly but firmly, I closed the hymnal.

A lady in the pew behind me observed this. More amused than shocked — she herself having been of vaguely Unitarian sympathies — she reported the incident to my father, who then raised the issue over the Sunday dinner table. Freedom of conscience, my father declared in exasperation, does not include the right to scandalize the faithful — or embarrass one's parents.

As if unsatisfied with limiting my unorthodox views to religion, I soon began looking into the realm of politics as well.

Even during the supposedly repressive 1950s and the early 1960s, there was ample access to trendy, excitingly dangerous ideas. On trips to my native Berkeley, where my father had grown up and attended the university, I had my first intimations of an exotic but strangely appealing counter-culture, where sandals and beards were — or so I imagined — the mark of the intellectual. In San Francisco, I eagerly bought the left-wing weeklies sold at street-corner newspaper stands. My parents looked on my growing interest in socialism with a mixture of amusement and annoyance. Their generation, they insisted, had been through it all and seen quite clearly that it was another one of those fine ideas that, in practice, turn out to be disastrous.

Such was not, of course, the line of argument most likely to dissuade the would-be utopian. Having no personal responsibility for the means of production I thought belonged in the hands of the proletariat, I was free to concentrate on the fantasy vision, not the grubby reality. It was less the scientific socialism of Karl Marx that moved me than what might be called the science-fiction socialism of H. G. Wells. I was, at the same time, enthralled by the early novels of Arthur C. Clarke, once described as an "atheist mystic." I was particularly haunted by *Childhood's End*, which depicts the earth ruled by a race of wise and benevolent aliens who happen to have the appearance of huge winged devils. Vastly more intelligent than humans and virtually immortal, they act as the midwives for the final stage in terrestrial evolution: the collectivization of all intelligence and its absorption into a vast galactic Overmind. This is not to say that I was quite prepared to surrender belief in a personal God. Forty years later, it is hard to remember the fluctuating state of my adolescent mind, but I can easily imagine that what I wistfully sought was an accommodation between the God of Scripture and "that grand totality of which we are all a tiny part." This was Emerson's Oversoul — or what I have come to call "the Big Blob."

There were starker options: a science teacher of mine, married to a Catholic but himself an agnostic, spoke approvingly in off-the-record bull sessions of Deism, which he described as the belief that "God created the world in six days and hasn't done a damn thing since." With its touch of profanity, I felt a certain thrill in repeating the statement, but I did so neither happily nor with true conviction: I still wanted the God of Abraham, Isaac, Jacob, Moses, David, Isaiah, and, yes, even Jesus. So, faithfully but unwittingly following in the steps of many a hedger, I attempted to make my peace with revealed religion by turning the concept of revelation on its head. The religious history of humankind, I reasoned, was a developmental process, with Judaic monotheism as its greatest triumph. To say that God speaks to his people was simply a figurative way of describing the constant refining of humanity's spiritual and moral "insights." (Idealistic young people have a way of rediscovering bad ideas.) My rejection of Christian orthodoxy stemmed primarily from my uneasiness with the idea of God's unambiguous intrusion into human history: it seemed so parochial, so primitive. Such notions as the Incarnation and the Atonement — Methodists admittedly played them down a bit — suggested very serious intrusion indeed.

While I found Jesus so compelling a figure that I had no wish to abandon him, I was repelled by the idea that he was divine, except in the sense that all humans share the "divine spark" — and Jesus clearly to the greatest degree of any human who had ever lived. (The question of what precisely gave him even that status did not occur to me.) Simply put, what I wanted out of "religion" was an intellectually palatable worldview that also managed to provide emotional warmth and personal reassurance: the more inclusive (that is, the vaguer) in its actual claims, the better. Christianity, I felt, would be a nifty faith if it were not encumbered by irrational dogma. Methodism was fortunately not as mired in it as was Catholicism, but there were still too many vestiges of narrow-mindedness and backwardness, obscuring the sublime vision of the Big Blob.

Of the quasi-pantheism that I found then so progressive, C. S. Lewis has written:

> Pantheism is congenial to our minds not because it is the final stage in a slow process of enlightenment, but because it is almost as old as we are. So far from being the final religious refinement, Pantheism is in fact the natural bent of the human mind. . . . Platonism and Judaism, and Christianity (which has incorporated both) have proved the only things capable of resisting it. It is the attitude into which the human mind automatically falls when left to itself.
>
> — *Miracles*

I do not know how I might have responded if I had read these words then instead of later: as Lewis himself reminds us, through the words of Aslan the Lion in *The Chronicles of Narnia*, we are not given to know what might have happened. I do remember, however, that when my maternal grandmother lent me *The Great Divorce*, I was very much taken with the author's hauntingly vivid imagination. Still, I was quite unwilling to accept his basic premises: that hell did indeed exist and that human beings might freely choose it.

Disillusionment in Germany

In the summer of 1962, my life was altered forever by the beginning of a much longed-for adventure in Germany as an exchange student. My paternal grandmother had generously provided the financial means, but the immediate sponsoring agency was the International Christian Youth Exchange (ICYE), an interdenominational organization with links to the World Council of Churches.

The beginnings of my new life in Germany did not bring me any closer to orthodox Christianity. My host-mother, a nominal Lutheran, faithfully paid her church taxes and nearly as faithfully stayed home on Sunday morning so that we might enjoy coffee, toast, and classical music. Somewhat to my relief, she explained that while she and her son, a boy then fifteen, were entirely supportive of the Church's overall purpose, they did not believe in miracles, fairy tales intended strictly for the lesser orders. Her husband's family, old Prussian aristocrats, had been split by a conversion of some of their members to Catholicism, and the bitterness had remained. To the extent I understood their antipathy, I was only too happy to reinforce it.

"Exulting to the heavens, downcast to death," says young Egmont in a play written by Goethe as an equally young man. I heard the words more than once from my host-mother as a reminder that the movements of youthful emotions are those of a roller coaster. Certainly my experience in Germany included moments of what seemed to be both great happiness and great misery.

This went beyond the usual emotional throes of adolescence and even sporadic homesickness, of which I suffered few pangs. There was, after all, the excitement of living in Europe, whose languages and culture I still cherish.

The temptation to despair came from the terrible suspicion that, in the end, neither the religion in which I did not believe nor the ersatz-religion that I had tried to construct was anything more than self-delusion. Camus's antihero might speak of the "benign indifference of the universe," but I still desperately wanted something a bit more user-friendly. After all, even Friedrich von Schiller, hardly an orthodox Christian, had written an egregiously sentimental poem, made world-famous by Beethoven's Chorale Symphony, in which we are assured: "O'er the starry vault of heaven must surely dwell a loving father."

"Blessed is the man who walks not in the counsel of the wicked," begins the Psalms, "nor stands in the way of sinners, nor sits in the seat of scoffers; but his delight is in the law of the Lord, and on his law he meditates day and night." While I shall not malign old, long-lost companions of various nationalities by describing them as "wicked," I will say that I had freely chosen the company of scoffers. As for the subject upon which I obsessively "meditated," it took as its unhappy premise the notion that "truth," if there was any to be had, could lie virtually anywhere — except in the biblical faith. I was the opposite of the latchkey-seeking drunkard in the oft-cited joke: I was quite deliberately scrounging about in the dark, convinced that the key to the Father's house could not possibly have been left under the light of the designated lamp-post.

Physically exhausted and emotionally drained, I came home one late November afternoon from a retreat in Radevormwald. My host-mother took one look at me, exclaimed "Du, Junge!" and promptly ordered me to get a long sleep. Waking up in the middle of the night, I began reading a book lent to me by one of the girls in the group: Kahlil Gibran's *The Prophet*. To confess that even now I can recite passages from that work fills me with even greater embarrassment than to admit that I also know all of the words of Schiller's "Ode to Joy." As for Gibran, all I shall say in sheepish self-defense is that his language, imagery, and "mystical drawings" — the latter quite rightly said to be reminiscent of William Blake — seem to have drugged many more hard-headed minds than my own: "And you, vast sea, sleepless mother, who alone are peace to the river and the stream, only another winding will this stream make, only another murmur in this glade, and I shall come to you, a boundless drop in a boundless ocean."

Again, as C. S. Lewis suggests, there appears to be a powerful impulse in the human spirit, both intellectual and emotional, to believe in absolute monism, that is, to regard all differences, all distinctions, as ultimately illusory. The great appeal of all Romantic artists of pantheistic inclination is that even as they celebrate the merely phenomenal, in its poignant, transient beauty, they constantly hint at the same underlying truth: the boundless ocean.

When I mentioned *The Prophet* to a British teacher, he nodded, and said that if I liked Gibran, I should also read Hermann Hesse. It was only later, however, that I happened to pick up Hesse's *Siddhartha* in a used-book store. This time the language was German, but the message and — perhaps more importantly — the hypnotic effect of what can only be called the Jungian imagery and style were remarkably the same. Yet it was also while I was still in Germany that I read yet a work that had a far greater, long-range impact on my thinking. It was a two-volume book I spotted one day while wandering about a university library. It was in English: *The Nature and Destiny of Man*. The author had a German name, but apparently he was an American theologian: Reinhold Niebuhr. His profession made me suspicious. (I had no idea at the time that he had been one of my father's professors.)

Opening the book to the first page, I was immediately drawn to Niebuhr's discussion of self-awareness. How is it, I had asked myself, self-absorbed teenager that I was, that consciousness can contemplate itself: Where, I wondered, in all the mirrors of the mind was the "ultimate me"? Niebuhr takes this peculiar capacity as his point of departure and suggests that it is precisely this partial self-transcendence that makes sin possible, specifically the sin of pride and rebellion against God. Of course, I had learned in Sunday school about free will and the choice between good and evil, but I had also always assumed that bad behavior was simply the result of a poor social environment and inadequate information. Furthermore, the words of our Lord seemed to support this view: "Judge not lest ye be judged"; "Let him who is without sin among you cast the first stone"; "Father, forgive them, for they know not what they do." Yet between Voltaire's rationalistic and relativistic "To understand is to forgive all" and the mystery of divine grace fell a shadow I utterly failed to see. If human beings at their worst were, I reasoned, merely confused and ill-informed, then they were essentially innocent, which meant that they were also essentially good. Thus, the message of the Gospels seemed to blend perfectly with the words of Gibran: ". . . Only then shall you know that the erect and the fallen are but one man, standing in twilight between the night of his pigmy-self and the day of his god-self."

I cannot explain how it is that I was at all receptive to Niebuhr. My strong inclination was, after all, to feel, as the yuppie generation would put it, "uncomfortable" with the very idea of "sin." All I can say is that what he said made logical and psychological sense. My own experience told me that when I did something of which I was ashamed, it was not a distant and exotic pigmy-self that was to blame; it was my own willful me. At the tender age of seventeen or eighteen, I clearly did not understand all of Niebuhr's treatise. Yet the overall thrust of the argument, with its devastating critique of human pretentiousness and its wonderfully plausible defense of the biblical faith, held me firmly in its grasp. Suddenly it seemed that we human beings could sin after all, and it was not against the Big Blob that we sinned; it was against God our Creator.

A journey had begun, and though it took many long twists and turns, I vaguely sensed even then that the Hound of Heaven was on my trail.

Returning to Europe

In the autumn of 1965, I was, to my great delight, in Europe again, this time for study in southern France. I had become an almost stereotypical wanna-be Berkeley radical. I qualify the description with "almost" not because I was any less self-righteous, opinionated, or quarrelsome than most — in fact, I was usually spoiling for a fight — but rather for two seemingly paradoxical reasons.

On the one hand, I had been drawn not to the (grossly overrated) "idealism" of the New Left but rather by what I took to be the tough-minded realism of the Old Left. Not to put too fine a point upon it, I had become convinced that the only way to defeat "capitalist imperialism" — and end the escalating war in Vietnam — was not to shun the Communist cause but rather to embrace it. I had no use for goody-goody Norman Thomas socialists, with their fastidious attachment to the niceties of bourgeois democracy; I admired the "hard lads," those who had no fear of being called Bolsheviks. (Later, when opposition to the American war effort went from the radical fringes to become a mass movement, I was both bemused and annoyed by the "give-peace-a-chance" types. Both logically and empirically, I knew, "peace" was just a euphemistic way of referring to a Communist victory.) Marxism appealed to me in somewhat the same way that Niebuhr had — and not coincidentally. Niebuhr was critical of Marx but readily conceded that the old revolutionary often had a shrewder insight into the dark side of human nature, with all its greed, selfishness, and ulterior motives, than did idealistic reformism.

On the other hand, there was one important characteristic of leftist radicalism that troubled me: general indifference to religious faith and specific hostility to Christianity. For all the thrill I felt in spouting bloodthirsty Marxist-Leninist slogans, I had no use for the "scientific atheism" taught in Communist countries or the crude reductionism that treated all religion as simply an instrument of the ruling classes. In my wistful hope for accommodation, I readily drifted into a kind of doublethink. It even made "social" sense: then as now, left-leaning secularism was the intellectual fashion, and the desire to be "with it" was terribly seductive.

France offered a particularly striking example of the two powerful forces in both conflict and coexistence: the Communist Party and the Catholic Church. My French friends tended to be disgruntled members — or at least on the fringes — of either one or the other.

However reluctantly, I had to admit that the more accommodating of the two were the Catholics. It was they who said, for example, that Albert Camus was really at heart a religious person and that if he had lived, he would surely have turned to the Church. A Communist friend of mine, on the other hand, on noticing that I was reading one of Camus' philosophical works, gave me a disapproving look and remarked that I should wean myself of bourgeois idealism. During the Christmas holidays, I found myself accompanying a fellow student on a retreat to a Benedictine monastery in Hautes-Pyrenees. He was himself a nonpracticing Catholic and a political radical-to-be, but he had a genuine interest in monasticism and a lingering, if ambivalent, attachment to the faith. Though we were not particularly close friends, I was grateful to know someone with similar sympathies.

What struck me about the monks was that they hardly resembled the ethereally cerebral, emaciated ascetics of my imagination. Many were strong young men, their ruddy cheeks proof of years spent working in the open air. They spoke little, relying more often on gestures than words.

We would rise in the wee hours of the morning to join them in chanting the Glory Be in Latin; *"Gloria Patris, et Filio, et Spirtui Sancto"* was the constant refrain. The knowledge that these words had been sung for countless generations of monks and would be sung by countless generations more filled me with awe and wonder: *"Sicut erat in principio et nunc et semper et in saecula saeculorum. Amen."* There was, I am sure, more than a bit of "medieval romanticism" in my emotions. Yet in the serenity and beauty of the chant, I had an intimation of timelessness, filling me with an intense yearning that went far beyond my meager understanding of either the day-to-day life of the monastery or the intensity of faith that clearly lay behind it.

I returned to the flatlands transfixed — and equally confused. It was clear enough to me that if ever I were to make a genuine religious commitment, it would be to Catholicism. Alas, however, that was still a dauntingly big "if."

Journeying to Japan

I have often said half-seriously that I first came to Japan in order to learn enough Japanese to read *Snow Country* by Yasunari Kawabata in the original. Kawabata had just been awarded the Nobel Prize for literature in 1968. In January 1969, I had come to Japan from Korea on holiday, where I read Edward Seidensticker's translation of the novel with great interest. My more practical reasons, however, had more to do with friendship and career aims: half a dozen American friends from Peace Corps days were there, and I thought that knowledge of a second East Asian language would be useful for graduate school. I had no intention of staying longer than a year or two. How little we know! That was thirty years ago. I have sometimes wondered what my parents would have said if someone had told them at the time of my birth that their son would spend most of his life involved with and speaking the languages of two nations that were once America's bitterest enemies. Born at the end of April 1945, just before Hitler's suicide and the end of Nazi Germany, I have, of course, no memory of the war, but I still have special reasons for being haunted by it. At the time, far across the Pacific, Japan was still holding out, despite the firebombing of its urban centers. In mid-July of that year, the city of Hitachi, an industrial center northeast of Tokyo, was bombarded from the sea. Tome Suda, my future mother-in-law, had seen her children evacuated, but she had remained behind. She says she remembers cartloads of the dead being borne away. A month later, her husband, a soldier in Manchuria, was captured by Soviet troops and taken to Siberia.

Yoshizo Suda, one of the few survivors of that ordeal, returned to Japan in 1947. In the early autumn of the next year, he became the father of his fourth child and second daughter, Keiko, a name that literally means "blessed child." Born into the postwar generation, she was indeed fortunate. Her only childhood memory of soldiers would be of American GIs passing through her neighborhood in jeeps. During her early years, as Japan was rising from the ashes, her hometown grew into a prosperous company town.

Keiko was working at Hitachi Research Laboratory when I first met her. It was a cold Saturday morning in November. She had brought over mandarin oranges to an American friend of mine, whom I was visiting. The three of us sat on the tatami mats of the house that would later be mine, next to the frosted windows, and talked.

At the time, having been in Japan for barely a month, I spoke little Japanese, unlike my friend, a former Peace Corps comrade. Keiko had learned English in school and was, in fact, one of the students at the language school where my friend was teaching and I was soon to teach. Still, she much preferred to speak Japanese. In an attempt to communicate — or at least to compete — I wrote Chinese characters on the windows.

We were married two years later. Her father had initially threatened to disown her if she married "the enemy," dismissing as nit-picking the argument that I was, after all, American, not Russian. In the end, however, he graciously relented and even paid for the Shinto ceremony. Keiko had suggested a church wedding, but as I was no longer a practicing Protestant and not yet a Catholic, I discouraged the idea.

On to Hawaii

After eight months in Tokyo, Keiko and I moved to Honolulu, where I entered graduate studies in linguistics at the University of Hawaii. For the next five years, interrupted only by a stay in the Palauan islands of Micronesia, where I studied the Western Austronesian language spoken there, we enjoyed the balmy weather and multicultural life of Oahu. In May 1977, our first son, Michael Robert Yukio, was born.

Before our marriage and even long thereafter, Keiko and I hardly spoke of religion. This was not because I thought it unimportant or regarded it as "too personal" to discuss, even between husband and wife. I still enjoyed a good debate, perhaps especially when it involved the herds of "freethinking individualists" and their all-too-predictable prejudices against the biblical faith. Keiko was, however, a special case, though to explain it I must first put what I take to be her perspective on the issues in a broad cross-cultural context.

In Europe, nonbelievers or former believers in theistic religion, particularly among the intellectual classes, may readily describe themselves, logically enough, as atheists. In America, perhaps for cultural at least as much for philosophical reasons, one may prefer to hedge by describing oneself as agnostic. Yet even so, there is an either-or to be confronted, making genuine neutrality at best problematic. This is not necessarily because nonbelievers are surrounded by believers; in fact, they may not be, as anyone who has lived among American academics can attest. Rather, it is, I would suggest, because we products of Western culture, for all of our secularization, still care about the answer. In Europe, atheism was, at least until relatively recently, a viable career option for succeeding generations of intellectuals. Bertrand Russell and Jean-Paul Sartre are just two outstanding examples of philosophers who spent their lifetimes tirelessly contending that the very idea of God is logically impossible and mischievous to boot.

The vast majority of Japanese, having never been theists, are not inclined to be zealous atheists either. Even the Sino-Japanese equivalent of the term, *mushinron-sha*, literally "no-god-theorist," is seldom heard, except perhaps among Western-oriented academicians. The far more common phrase used by Japanese to explain their lack of personal or institutional disposition to any faith is *mushukyo*, literally "without religion."

Western visitors to Japan, enthralled with the mystique of "Oriental spirituality" and led on well-trodden tours of Buddhist temples and Shinto shrines, may be misled into thinking that most Japanese are steeped in religious beliefs that differ from those in the West in content but not intensity.

The assumption that most Japanese are nontheistic, pantheistic, or animistic may inspire a sense of exoticism; the realization that most Japanese cannot be bothered with any of the above, on the other hand, is likely to be simply mind-boggling.

Like the great majority of Japanese, Keiko's parents were "nuptial Shintoists, funereal Buddhists." More than most urbanites today, they knew and observed the customs. Yet perhaps even more than their highly secularized compatriots, they were strictly nominal adherents. Once, not long after meeting Keiko, I accompanied her to a Shinto shrine, where she showed me the simple purification ritual one undertakes before clapping one's hands and beseeching the deities for favors. Having long associated Shinto with militarism and emperor-worship, I still found the mere presence of shrines somewhat ominous. Keiko, more in her carefree behavior than in her words, helped me to grasp the simple, happy-go-lucky character of the religion. I vaguely remember asking her in those early days whether she believed in the gods. Her response was to the effect: "Not really, but there's no harm in it."

Much later, while walking down a street in Tokyo, our minds on the possibility of marriage, Keiko spied the office of a fortune-teller. On an impulse, she went upstairs for a consultation, only to return a few moments later. When I asked what had happened, she said that the fee was a third more than she was willing to pay. "Yes, but, after all, you do believe in it, don't you?" I protested. "Yes," she replied, "but not to the tune of three thousand yen!"

After graduating from high school, Keiko attended a conservative Protestant mission college, where religion classes and chapel attendance were mandatory. She seems to have cheerfully accepted the requirements as part of education, grateful for the interesting and useful information they offered. She says, however, that while a very small number of her classmates agreed to be baptized, the thought of joining them never occurred to her. My sense that Keiko's family as a whole may be even less "religious" than average was reinforced when my father-in-law died. Knowing that his condition was terminal, he had given specific instructions to my mother-in-law to pay as little as possible for the (socially mandated) Buddhist funeral and not to pay a single yen for a posthumous Buddhist name. Immediately after his death, Keiko's mother went to the local *o-bo-san*, who happened to be a priest of some rank, and requested a discount for his services in chanting the *sutras*. (The words of the Buddhist texts, which came to Japan via China, are, incidentally, totally unintelligible to all but a small number of genuine believers.)

My mother-in-law gleefully reported that the man was so flabbergasted at the unprecedented demand that "he gave in after the second cup of tea." In her house, there is a family altar, which includes the photographs of Keiko's father and her older sister, who died some years ago of cancer. Whenever we are there for a visit, we light incense sticks, strike the small bell, and bow our heads, hands pressed together, as we pray for their repose. Our children, brought up as Catholics from their earliest years, have no more qualms in doing this in front of a Buddhist altar than has their mother. Whatever objections I might have are mitigated, oddly enough, by the thought that she is no more a Buddhist than they are. When the body of my sister-in-law was brought home from the hospital, her mother was adamant that Keiko should avert her eyes. She warned her that the child she was then carrying might be marked by the vengeful spirit of the deceased. (This essentially animistic belief was quite impersonal, having nothing to do with the character of the deceased, who had always been very kind to our children.) When Keiko, who had never heard of such a thing, indignantly refused to comply, her mother pleaded with her to wear a mirror of some sort, explaining that such would mitigate the danger. Again, Keiko dismissed the very idea as superstition. Six months later, when I called her mother to announce the birth of her grandson,

David Hiroyuki, she immediately asked whether there was anything wrong with him and was greatly relieved when informed that he was quite a normal baby.

For more than two hundred fifty years in Japan, the practice of Christianity was punishable by death, and even today less than one percent of the population professes it. Yet among today's young people, gold and silver crosses on necklaces and earrings have become immensely popular. On television, one hears "Amazing Grace" and Händel's "Hallelujah Chorus" used to advertise everything from diamonds to toilet-bowl cleansers. Commercial Christmas has long been almost as big a holiday in Japan as in America, and in recent years it has become fashionable for young (unmarried) couples to spend *hori-ibu* (Holy Eve) in a love hotel.

Keiko celebrates Christmas by bringing in our evergreen tree from the garden plot, decorating it with candles, baking German Stollen, and listening to carols. She also cheerfully attends Christmas Eve Mass with the rest of us. Yet while readily acknowledging the sense of wonder and warmth that the holiday inspires, she deftly deflects any attempt on my part to discuss the Incarnation. She also goes along to Mass with some regularity and has many friends among the faithful, but when I suggest that she go to instruction, at least to sort out her own beliefs, she says she cannot be bothered.

Already by the end of our years in Hawaii, I knew that I wished at last to become a Catholic. Looking back, I wonder only why I had been so slow in coming to that realization. By way of speculation, all I can say is that the barriers were far more cultural and social than doctrinal. What I suppose I wanted was what C. S. Lewis called "Christianity and . . .": Christianity and socialism; Christianity and the mind-set of most of my unbelieving friends and acquaintances; Christianity and the endless freedom to hedge and equivocate.

Providentially, I was helped along the way by utter disillusionment with the secular and liberal world of academia and post-1960s culture as a whole. Casual observation of the professoriat's personal behavior, abysmal even by the standards of the New Morality, convinced me that if this was the vanguard of the future, we were all in deep trouble. The worst of the lot were, it was equally apparent, the politically engaged: socialists fuming at capitalist greed, even while defaulting on alimony and child-support payments.

Among my immediate peers, youthful radicalism was yielding to guilty yuppyism. Belief in God was untenable — or at least unfashionable and utterly private; apocalyptic pronouncements about overpopulation and the ozone layer were not. I found myself rereading C. S. Lewis's *That Hideous Strength* and remembering the oft-cited comment attributed to Chesterton about the utter credulity of apostate man.

What I later realized was another turning point came one day as I was watching the local television news. A Catholic priest was being interviewed by a young reporter, who asked him a pointed question about abortion rights. To this, he replied firmly but calmly: "The Catholic Church teaches — and rightly so — that abortion is just another form of homicide." I bristled at his bluntness. Yet suddenly I realized that any rebuttal I might offer was in the language of an ideology I had abandoned. I sensed that his words had stung me because they were true. In the same instant, I saw the mask of journalistic objectivity fall with a crash from the face of the media spokeswoman, replaced by an expression of undisguised hostility. Months later I happened to meet that same priest and summoned up enough courage to speak to him about what I had seen. This time I felt no ambivalence and remarked that I thought he had done very well in the lion's den of the liberal media. He grimaced and said of the TV reporter: "She was a real snake in the grass."

The Journey Home

Our days in Hawaii were meanwhile coming to an end. In mid-1978, while writing my doctoral dissertation, I heard of a teaching position at Chiba University in Japan and applied for it. News that I was the candidate selected gave me a strong incentive to finish my work, and so it was that at the end of September, I successfully defended my dissertation.

Some months later, having settled into my new position at Chiba University, I was asked to teach an English literature course in the international division of Sophia University, a well-known Jesuit institution in Tokyo. Among my students was an extraordinarily conscientious Italian nun, with whom I sometimes chatted during the breaks.

One day I took a deep breath and told her that I had long been drawn to the Catholic faith. She told me that she would be meeting an Irish Columban priest living in Chiba and would be happy to introduce me. So it was that the following week I first met Father Denis Curan, with whom I rode the train back from Tokyo.

The next crucial leg of my journey was completed in fitful bursts. My conversations with Father Curan were always most enlightening and enjoyable. Eventually I began to attend Mass. Then, for no other reason than the various distractions of day-to-day life, I would resolve on Saturday to go to church the next morning, only to lose heart or to find some excuse or distraction. Yet the day came when my sense of drifting was no longer endurable. Despite my embarrassment, I telephoned the ever-patient priest and arranged to see him. I told him that I wished to become a Catholic, and so it was that on Holy Saturday of that year, I was finally — to my great relief and joy — received into the Church.

Between January 1979 and March 1984, Keiko and I were blessed with the birth of three children, two daughters and a son. From 1986 to 1988, we lived in America, where all but the youngest went to school and acquired a good command of English. The children's first language is Japanese, and their primary cultural identification is with Japan. As Catholics, they have had to contend with social pressures, both similar to and different from those felt by their European and American counterparts. In particular, the enormous demands made by Japanese schools and the overall influence of "education-alism" have meant that attendance at Mass and involvement in church activities are easily relegated to "optional" status.

As a Japanese mother and as a non-Catholic, Keiko inevitably has had different priorities than I, though in all fairness and honesty, I must give her credit for trying to strike what she has seen as a reasonable balance. Often when I have been tempted to blame her for giving the children leeway I think they should not have, she has merely been coping as best she can with the power of a teenager's will.

Japanese Catholics themselves refer to *kyokai-banare* (drifting away from the Church) among the young, particularly during the years when they are facing entrance examinations, as though it were an inevitable phenomenon. My own feeling is that there is a measure of self-fulfilling prophecy in such talk, but as my own house clearly has a larger glass component than I would wish, I am in no position to preach.

Over the years, I doubt that I have become any more virtuous or any less foolish, but my mustard-seed faith has grown, even if only so slightly. I confess I find it ever more astonishing how anyone could live without it. Yet I have also come to see that faith is truly a gift. While one can reason and cajole — and even attempt, however badly, to set some sort of example — it is not something that can be copied or cloned. As impatient as I become with those who would explain away Christian convictions with simplistic pseudo-psychology, I must also resist the temptation to think that if only I could formulate my thoughts more skillfully and persuasively, the thick walls of unbelief would come tumbling down.

For a person such as myself, a word-obsessed linguist, it may be particularly difficult to learn that mere talk has its limits. Moreover, the fact that my conversion to Catholic Christianity came at least as much from the head as from the heart makes the illusory hope of dialoguing others into belief seem all the more tantalizing. I must learn to wait.

Afterword

Easter Week at our church is shadowed this year by the sadness of recent events, including the passing of a much beloved lay leader and the death in a house fire of a fourteen-year-old boy we have known since his birth and baptism. "What is death?" Keiko asks me. We both know the question is rhetorical. Yet, in spite of myself, I try to speak once again about the great mystery of the faith we celebrate this week: that even the Son of God could grieve, that even the Son of God could die, and that he lives and, with him, the hope of our own eternal life (cf. John 14:20).

O Crux ave, spes unica — "Hail O Cross, the only hope." I can only pray that one day Keiko, too, will know — and more fully than her unworthy husband — that awesome and joyous truth.

Chapter 4

The Making of a Fool

by Justin Case

I felt like a deer in the headlights: fascinated, terrified, and paralyzed. It was as though I had never seen this Scripture verse before. What really disturbed me was that I was sure I had read the passage hundreds of times and yet never considered the ramifications. "If I am delayed, you may know how one ought to behave in the household of God, which is the church of the living God, the pillar and bulwark of the truth" (1 Timothy 3:15). For years I had looked only to Scripture; I had never even considered that the Church could be the pillar of the truth.

That is how my journey home to the Catholic faith began. A childhood friend of mine, Carl, whom I hadn't seen in years, had come over to visit. As we shared the latest and greatest in each of our lives, I told how I had come to faith in Jesus Christ, and that I was now enrolled in an evangelical seminary. He then told me about the tremendous renewal of faith he had in his own life. Being alerted to the fact that my friend was Catholic, I thought it necessary to bring his renewal to completion by setting straight the errors of Catholicism. I was completely unprepared for what followed.

From the first time my wife, Julie, and I listened to my friend defend the Catholic faith, it was as if the road we had been on together suddenly came to an intersection where I went one way and she went the other. After Carl left our house I turned to ask my wife what she thought of his explanations of Catholicism. She immediately wheeled around and said, "It's hard for me to imagine anyone who would have the audacity to try to defend the Catholic Church," and "How you were so taken by his argumentation is beyond me." What I found disquieting was that she could tell that his arguments were in fact disturbing to me. Actually, disturbed is much too inadequate a term to describe my feelings. Horrified is probably more accurate. At the same time I was excited, and that was also frightening.

I have read a lot of conversion stories and I'm always amazed at how long it has taken some people to finally come into the Catholic Church after first being confronted by her. For me, the truth of the Catholic Church was an arrow in my heart. The blow that struck me in that first conversation with Carl pierced to the depths. Of course I did a lot of research, and left no stone unturned by the time I came into the Church, but I knew almost instinctively that Carl's statements were true, even when I tried to deny them. Julie had picked up on this, and almost immediately a wall went up between us. As Julie was aware, many of the controversial topics that Carl and I addressed that evening had bothered me for a long time. However, neither Julie nor I would have expected to find answers in the Catholic Church.

My whole life as an evangelical, I see in hindsight, was filled with ambiguity. As a "Bible only" Christian, I was certainly frustrated in trying to put together a systematic theology that could gain the unanimous consent of Christians, as I believed the New Testament demanded. Over time, I began to do what so many of my evangelical teachers and friends had done: relegate the controversial topics to the "nonessentials" category.

When I was confronted with the truth of the Catholic Church, it was as if someone had removed a giant weight from me. I felt as if I had just gotten off a bicycle and onto a rocket ship. The intrusion of joy in my heart at hearing the voice of the Church was frightening, but at the same time invigorating. To describe it another way, my experience was like being a juror in a capital case. All the way through the trial it appeared that the evidence was pointing to the guilt of the defendant, in this case, Catholicism. But then, at the eleventh hour, a key witness came rushing into the courtroom demanding to be heard and proceeded to correct the misunderstandings, providing conclusive proof of the defendant's innocence.

Julie had always trusted my judgment, for the most part, when it came to matters of doctrine and faith. Many of our friends also would defer to me on these matters. People were always approaching me with questions about the Bible, since I had earned a reputation as someone who was well studied. Interestingly enough, when I started to take Catholicism seriously, these were the first people to oppose me, but none more aggressively than Julie. She was outraged that I could find any semblance of sanity in the Catholic Church. She constantly brought all of the stereotypical objections to my attention. If I tried to respond, we would end up in a terrible argument.

In the beginning of my journey, I would bring books home and sit on the couch at night reading, consumed with finding out more about Catholic teaching. I knew this bothered her, but I believed I couldn't just stick my head in the sand and ignore the claims of Rome. I felt all the more compelled, since my studies in the seminary were to prepare me for a life of telling people what they ought to think about these things. I didn't want to step into a pulpit every week without integrity in my heart. My dilemma was that the more I read, the more Catholic my thinking became.

Only a few weeks into my study of Catholicism, Julie told me that she didn't want me to read in the house any more, that she could no longer tolerate me bringing "that garbage" into our home. She begged me to stop reading these other books and concentrate on reading the Bible only. I would try to tell her that most of my reading was constantly referring me back to the Scriptures, and that even now I had found a whole new appreciation for them. This only made her angrier. However, I complied with her request and instead made frequent visits to the coffee shop at the end of the street to get some time to read. Julie chastised me about not being home and neglecting my family obligations. This was the most difficult thing for me to manage. It may have been different had Julie agreed to allow me some time to pursue my investigation, but she was unwilling to allow for that. She immediately accused me of sneaking around, continuing to pursue this thing that I knew was so offensive to her. It seemed I couldn't win.

Her reactions against Catholicism made me furious. I would ask her how all of a sudden she had become such an expert on Christianity, the Bible, and history. She had never made any serious attempt to become what one might call theologically astute, even in regard to her own faith. I was disappointed and angry that she was so unwilling to put aside her presuppositions and one-sidedness. When she would start to criticize the Church, I would often get upset and pose questions to her that she was incapable of answering. I would not let up until we were yelling back and forth at each other.

My heart was broken. I couldn't believe how my wife was reacting. I felt misunderstood, abandoned, frustrated, and angry. It is so hard to relate the emotions that I felt. Pain was mixed with joy at finding my homeland in the Catholic Church. Bittersweet would be a profoundly inadequate way to describe it. It was the most turbulent experience of my life. The most frustrating element was her feeling the same way, but at the opposite end of the spectrum. We were seemingly incapable of discussing these things in a civil manner.

Julie and I, like any couple, had had our share of difficulties, but we had experienced nothing like this. We had a good relationship. We would take time away on romantic weekends when we could afford it, and always remained open to ideas and activities that would enrich our marriage. Each of us wanted to continue to grow in our love for one another and we both made efforts to invest in and refresh our relationship. Now suddenly, it was as though all the lines of communication had been severed.

Julie desperately tried to find anyone who could show me the errors in Catholic thinking. I would come home from work to find that she had arranged for me to speak with some expert about why the Catholic Church was wrong. I willingly took part in all of these discussions, but I always came away feeling even more convinced of Catholic claims. I tried to be docile; I wanted to guard against becoming defensive. I was willing to be embarrassed if I was wrong in defending Catholicism. I'm sure Julie would claim otherwise. Anytime I would rebut whomever she had invited to speak with me, she would become frustrated and complain that I was not hearing what was being said. Again, this led to arguments that generated a lot more heat than light. Before deciding to come into the Catholic Church, I must have had at least twenty of these discussions, including a phone call from a prominent anti-Catholic apologist Julie had asked to contact me.

The stress of trying to balance my responsibility as a husband and father versus the need to be obedient to Christ was becoming unbearable. As the resolve in my heart grew stronger regarding the rightness of the Catholic faith, I felt I could wait no longer. I felt Christ calling me to abandon everything and trust him. I could not anticipate Julie ever being sympathetic to my becoming Catholic. She was staunchly opposed to even discussing it. I felt that there would be no "good" time and that getting it out in the open now would force her to deal with it. I was prepared for a negative reaction, but didn't think that Julie would take any drastic measures. I needed peace. I needed to drop my nets and follow Christ. I was baptized as an infant in the Catholic Church, so my returning was a matter of receiving the sacrament of reconciliation and once again taking my place in the Church.

If what my wife and I had been through already wasn't

enough, it got that much worse with my return to the Church. It is difficult to describe what living together in those times was like. I felt that I was walking on eggshells even to get a cold drink from the refrigerator. Julie's unwillingness to allow me even to read in our home had made it possible for us to get along only in silence. We would pass hours in front of the television, avoiding any discussion. Inevitably something would be said that would begin an argument. Sunday mornings were the worst. As I tried to silently get showered and ready to go to Mass, Julie and the children would be milling about getting ready to go to church. Often, before I would get out the door, she would begin crying and beg me to reconsider. I would try to explain to her that maybe it would be better if we just allowed each other to follow the dictates of our conscience. We could focus on the things we held in common, trusting that God would provide answers for us. This was unacceptable to her. In her mind, the Catholic Church was an instrument of the devil and by my participation in it I made myself an enemy of Christ. I would love to tell you that I handled these situations with great tact and diplomacy, but I didn't. More often, my emotions would get the better of me and I would lash out in defense, challenging her again to defend her arguments with substance rather than intolerance.

These outbursts would happen on a weekly cycle. On Sunday nights we would usually apologize to each other and then sit on the couch watching more television. Throughout the week the tension would build until the next Sunday morning showdown. At times it seemed to me that we were getting along very well. I grew hopeful that we would be able to continue to live together in peace. It was at one of these times that I arrived home from work to find a note on the counter telling me that she and the children had left, and that she could no longer live with me as a Catholic. I was devastated. I fell on the floor racked with emotional pain. I thought my head would explode from the anxiety and panic that gripped me. I desperately picked up the phone and called friends of hers to find out where she was. They wouldn't tell me. I'm glad that I was on the phone with these people, and not in their physical presence, because I would have hurt them. Later that night no one would even take my phone calls, and I was left alone crying on my kitchen floor.

After three days, my wife finally called and told me again that we could not live together. I begged and pleaded with her to not stay away, but she was adamant. At last I talked her into coming home. Our children are all very young, and so it was not possible for them to stay in one person's home for any great length of time. I told Julie that it wasn't right for our children to live out of boxes in strange places, and that, if she would come home, I would leave.

We separated for a month. I still have no idea how we got back together, because she hadn't changed her feelings toward my being Catholic at all. Even before she left, I had promised her that I would not try to force her to become Catholic, and she had always made it clear that I was not to attempt to proselytize our children, otherwise she would leave. I had kept those promises, and, upon going back home, recommitted myself to them.

We decided to try counseling. I agreed to meet with a mutual friend, a pastor at the church we used to attend. My agreement to meet with Dan was on one condition: I was not going to debate apologetics. I wanted someone to help us figure out how we could learn to tolerate and respect each other's differences in order to keep our family together. This proved frustrating as well, but not because Dan didn't agree to my terms. Actually, I think he did a good job of facilitating discussion. The problem was that for Julie there could be no compromise. I was given an ultimatum. Stop participating as a Catholic for six months, with the only reading material allowed being the Scriptures. If at that time I was still convinced of the Catholic position, that's when she would start separation proceedings. I refused. First, I would have refused simply on the basis that I had gone back to the Catholic Church with my eyes wide open. I had counted the cost and relied on the grace of God to help me pay the price. But secondly, I was offended that I was being asked to abandon my faith while she was not being required to do anything except sit and wait for the outcome.

Over the next twelve months, the cycle of "argue, apologize, and watch television" continued. We made repeated attempts at seeking counsel, but it seemed always to end in a stalemate. Even though things were very rocky, I thought that maybe we could weather the storm and eventually learn to live peacefully. Julie had other ideas.

At the start of summer, she told me that she was setting a date of August 1 for me to make a decision to renounce Catholicism. This shocked me because I had been feeling again that things had been going rather peacefully. We were getting into arguments only about once a month rather than once or twice a week. Throughout the summer I hoped and prayed that she would back away from her decision. In July I told her that I was willing to go to the Catholic friends I had made and tell them that I could no longer meet with them socially, or even casually. I told her that I would not so much as say hello to them if I saw them. I told her that I would get rid of all the Catholic books I had gotten. Also I vowed not to teach or speak at my parish. In a nutshell, I told her that the only thing I needed to have freedom to do was go to Mass on Sundays and on Holy Days of obligation. She refused, and by August 1 she had already done the legal work necessary to force me from my home.

Many people have asked me why I didn't fight this legally, why I didn't fight for the custody of our children. My reasons for not doing so are both practical and diplomatic. Julie had arranged for a flexible agreement that would not need to be drawn up in court as long as we agreed concerning visitation rights and financial terms. These terms were acceptable to me and I didn't want to take my chances with a court making them more restrictive. I also am very confident of Julie's parenting skills. She is much more capable of taking care of our children than I, since I work every day and would have to find childcare for them. I moved into an apartment about a mile away from our home and continue to hope that this will only be temporary.

Of the many issues between us over the last year and a half since my coming into the Catholic Church, the one that I misunderstood and failed to address the most was Julie's emotional struggle with this. In other words, especially in the beginning of my inquiries, I failed to recognize how she perceived this as a personal attack against her. She repeatedly told me that I had no right to act independently of her, and she constantly appealed to a subjective line of argumentation. She equated my desire to become Catholic with a rejection of everything she was. Even though I knew how much this was affecting her, I couldn't help but appeal to the rational apologetics that had convinced me to become Catholic. I would try to tell her that this was not about my feelings toward her, or toward any of the wonderful blessings we received together as evangelical Protestants. I think that had I just stopped long enough to consider her perspective and her emotional ordeal in the beginning, if I had taken her in my arms and let her know how much she meant to me, and how I needed her help and support in investigating these things, maybe it could have turned out differently. By the time I caught on to this, she thought I was only saying things I thought she wanted to hear.

Over the months, Julie had poured her heart out to me in letters regularly. I was frozen as to how to react to them. The reasonableness of Catholicism had so revolutionized my faith, that in reacting to her arguments I didn't listen to her heart enough. Her arguments were not at all threatening in their theological content. Actually the very thing that frustrated me about them was their naïveté and ignorance. I was very comfortable debating the scholarly arguments posed against the Catholic faith because the arguments were structured and focused, and the topics were individually investigated and dissected. Julie's letters were from a wounded person who felt betrayed. In her mind, by becoming Catholic I was now rejecting as counterfeit the evidence of the grace of God we had clearly seen in our lives as evangelicals. Mixing this rationale with a steady diet of stereotypical anti-Catholic misinformation, my wife would write me letters to which I was at a loss as to how to respond. When I responded with logic, she saw it as cold rationalism. When I would try to tell her that my becoming Catholic was in no way a wholesale repudiation of the experiences of faith we had as evangelical Christians, she would dismiss that as impossible. She felt abandoned. In my excitement of discovery and exploration into the Catholic faith, she saw herself and our children suddenly placed at the bottom of my priorities. I couldn't even have imagined her feeling that way, partially because of my excitement and also because I assumed some things about her own spirituality that I shouldn't have.

We had never really discussed truth in a philosophical vein. Our lives together reflected the idea that the truth we received, even recognizing the fallible aspect of Protestant teaching, was all we would ever need. Actually, my inability to communicate my fascination with my pilgrimage to Catholicism was rooted in something else. This was my unwillingness to communicate throughout our married life just how frustrated I had been by the lack of doctrinal absolutes in Protestantism. I had told Julie of my frustration, but I always knew that she had lost no sleep over these things as I had done. I firmly believe that Julie's emotional attachment to the evangelical community, plus the fact that there is a great degree of truth taught in Protestantism, is why she found my journey so repulsive. Of course, earlier in our relationship I had talked quite a bit about these frustrations. Again, with no foreseeable answers in sight, these complaints of mine were considered by both of us to be the longings of the finite human mind that would just have to wait for Jesus to clear up in eternity.

In my growth as an evangelical, I started to complain less vocally about these things for that very reason. That certainly didn't mean that I didn't think about them — I just didn't think out loud. And so, as Cardinal John Henry Newman has so eloquently said, I lived my life the "safe man."

If I had the opportunity to start my journey to the Catholic faith over again, I would start by making sure that Julie understood just how frustrated I was. I could have gone back to the many things she knew bothered me and reiterated them before moving on to apologetics and what so compelled me to become Catholic. Waiting to tell her until after the journey had gained momentum in my heart just added insult to injury. She not only felt that I had abandoned her in our faith, but that I had hidden my ongoing struggles from her. This clearly was never my intention, but I never really thought about all these dynamics until I had to try to put the pieces together to see how we could have avoided our present circumstances.

I'm hoping that I might help someone in a similar situation to learn from my shortsightedness. I wish that I'd read something like this early in my journey. As the insightful reader may suspect by now, I was afraid to show weakness in the early stages of my investigating Catholicism. I felt that before I could really let my wife in on the struggle, I needed to provide answers, not anxious questions. My pride did not allow me to be a "fool," although I believe now that this was dead wrong. The innocent passion I had as I began to discover the Catholic Church could have been the very thing that allowed Julie to see my heart more clearly. If you are now reading apologetic works with a mind to becoming Catholic, and preparing for the onslaught of argumentation you anticipate from your spouse and friends, put down the books. They will be there tomorrow. Perhaps by displaying in true humility your heart for truth, you will have someone to share them with. That is my hope.

Hindsight is twenty-twenty, the saying goes, and if I had

a nickel for every time I felt the need to say that, I would be a wealthy man. I do not regret becoming a Roman Catholic. On the contrary, I have no greater boast, nor comfort. I would do it again under worse circumstances if I had to.

I have attempted to bare my soul in the hope that my experience might help others. The one caution I would give to anyone embarking on this path is not to expect it to be easy. It wasn't meant to be. In my coming home to the Catholic Church I was labeled a fool by my wife and friends. You, too, after reading this, may think some of my reactions and decisions foolish. I agree. The comfort I have now comes from knowing that Christ has chosen the foolish things of the world to shame the wise. My goal is to daily become a greater fool for the Lord, and in so doing, trust that he will reunite me to my Julie and my children.

(*Editor's Note:* The last I heard from Justin, Julie was divorcing him, and he was in great emotional pain.)

Chapter 5

Different Timetables

by Bruce Sullivan

"Look, Sharon, if you or anyone else can convince me from the Bible that the Catholic Church is the church established by Christ, I'll be a Catholic tomorrow!" With this bold challenge I had hoped to goad my devout Catholic friend into a serious, evangelistic Bible study. Instead she presented me with a copy of Karl Keating's *Catholicism and Fundamentalism*, and so began the end of my career as a Fundamentalist preacher.

I was raised in the South as a Southern Baptist. Attending services three times each week was standard fare in our home. However, it was not until I went away to college that I began to explore what I believed and why I believed it. To make a long story very short, my theological inquiries eventually led me to a relatively small denomination that calls itself the Church of Christ (also known as "Campbellites" by their detractors). However, while the denomination itself may be small, its impact on my life was enormous.

The impact of the Church of Christ was felt in at least two areas of my life — the theological and the sociological. Theologically, the members of the Church of Christ introduced me to the biblical basis for believing that Christ established a visible, identifiable, and institutional church (a decidedly Catholic concept). Sociologically, they introduced me to my wife, Gloria!

Gloria was raised where we presently reside, in south central Kentucky (a Church of Christ stronghold). We met through the campus ministry of the Auburn Church of Christ while pursuing our education at Auburn University in Alabama. I had long looked for a woman such as described by St. Peter in his first epistle: one characterized by "reverent and chaste behavior" and whose adornment subsisted in "the hidden person of the heart with the imperishable jewel of a gentle and quiet spirit." In Gloria I knew that I had found such a woman. We were wed upon graduation from Auburn in June of 1986.

From Auburn we went to Lubbock, Texas, for a two-year course of study at the Sunset School of Preaching. We chose Sunset because of its reputation among Churches of Christ for being a school characterized by exceptional missionary zeal. In fact, it was there that we joined with others in forming a mission team bound for Brazil. We targeted Brazil partly because we believed that Catholics, more than anyone else, stood in desperate need of the *true*, uncorrupted Gospel of Jesus Christ. While the mission team later disbanded, this conviction regarding the condition of Catholics simply grew stronger. Hence, years later we arrive at the scene with which I began this story: the challenge I laid before my Catholic friend, Sharon, in an attempt to rescue her from the clutches of Roman Catholicism.

I accepted Keating's book from Sharon's hand with great eagerness (I considered it to be an indication that we were finally getting somewhere). A quote from Sheldon Vanauken on the book's back cover greatly amused me. He said, "I strongly advise honest Fundamentalists not to read this book. They might find their whole position collapsing in ruins." Indeed! Vanauken's "warning" served only to bolster my determination to read the book and expose its manifest errors! After all, what could be easier to debunk than Roman Catholicism, right?

As it turned out, Vanauken's words were prophetic. I did read the book and, consequently, I did see my position collapsing in ruins. In the interest of brevity, let me simply say that the Holy Spirit used Keating's book to cut through my preconceived ideas about the Catholic faith while exposing the inadequacies of the presuppositions underlying my own. Indeed, the ball was finally rolling . . . just not in the direction I had originally intended — thanks be to God!

That was more than five years ago. From the start it has been a journey that Gloria and I have undertaken together, even though at the time of this writing she has yet to be formally received into full communion with the Church. It could even be said that she began the journey slightly ahead of me. After all, it was Gloria who first discovered and brought to my attention the Church's teaching on artificial means of contraception. She saw beauty and continuity in the teaching; I initially saw only a papal plot to ensure a burgeoning population of Catholics. And it was Gloria, in her personal desire for answers, who encouraged me to dig deeper into the issues after I first read *Catholicism and Fundamentalism*. However, I don't think she realized at the time just how quickly this slow-moving train would gather steam.

We came to our study of Catholicism with pretty much the standard package of objections and misconceptions. We did not understand, and therefore had strong objections to, Catholic beliefs concerning Mary, the papacy, the communion of saints, and the Eucharist. But this is not surprising, since neither one of us had ever read a book about Catholicism written by a Catholic. Up until then virtually all of our information on the Catholic faith had come from non-Catholic (most often anti-Catholic) sources.

We initially faced the same fears and apprehensions. We both had — and, I might add, still have — strong convictions regarding the nature of truth, the reality of judgment, and the existence of hell. We believed, and still believe, that only the true Gospel of Jesus Christ can bring men to salvation and were, therefore, sobered by scriptural admonitions to be on guard against the treachery of false teachers who ruin men's souls by corrupting Christ's Gospel. And yet we now found ourselves giving serious consideration to what we had thought to be the greatest corruption of them all — the Catholic faith.

It was a time for mixed emotions, to say the least. The fear of damnation weighed heavily upon our hearts and minds. Especially troubling was St. Paul's warning to the Thessalonian Christians regarding the "strong delusion" that God would send upon those "who did not believe the truth but had pleasure in unrighteousness" (2 Thessalonians 2:12). On the other hand, the cogency of the arguments in favor of the Catholic faith propelled us into deeper study, and the deeper we went, the greater grew our excitement and anticipation. Yes, anticipation. It was as if we could sense that we were on the brink of a great discovery: "the faith which was once for all delivered to the saints" (Jude, v. 3)! Yet, even then, we sensed the irony of the situation: a "discovery" that had already been the familiar experience of millions of Roman Catholics throughout the centuries.

As stated earlier, we began our journey in unity — a unity of purpose that has never faltered. Nonetheless, it did not take long to realize that we were approaching our journey with different degrees of intensity. The flexibility of my job at the time afforded me ample opportunity to study, pray, and reflect in a relatively peaceful atmosphere. Gloria, on the other hand, faced the constant demands of being a stay-at-home mom — demands that were intensified by her commitment to homeschool our children. To be sure, she was deeply interested in finding answers to the numerous questions that were being raised. However, she simply lacked the time and opportunities for study that were afforded me. The result was that very early on I began to run on ahead of Gloria. My "running on ahead" was not, of course, by design. I wanted very much for us to go step by step together. However, it just seems that in many ways it simply was not possible. I had time on my hands, a "bee in my bonnet," and an insatiable desire to resolve the issues facing my family. I also realize that this produced some nervous moments for Gloria. Yes, she wanted answers, too. But she was also concerned that I not be too hasty in coming to any final conclusions.

The ensuing year was an interesting one, to say the least. Hardly a day passed without Gloria and me spending at least some time discussing various points of Catholic teaching. We formed an invaluable friendship with Father Benjamin Luther, a convert from the Church of Christ, who kept us indescribably inundated with study materials. I attended a retreat of the Coming Home Network with Father Luther, where I came face-to-face with the Mass for the first time. And one of my former instructors from Sunset flew in from Texas in an attempt to salvage my faith. Yet, during that same year, I went on a mission trip with the Churches of Christ to Haiti and preached frequently to local congregations. We even attended a meeting convened by a group attempting to organize a Church of Christ mission team for Brazil. In other words, we found ourselves in something of a spiritual "no man's land" and were not especially eager to burn any bridges until we were sure of where we were going!

Finally, in August of 1994, we came to a mutual decision: it was time to leave the Church of Christ denomination. For a couple of months prior to this decision, I had been attending an early Mass on Sunday mornings by myself before going to services with my family at the Church of Christ where we were members. By August neither one of us felt comfortable in our old denomination; and even though Gloria was not yet ready to become Catholic, she knew that I was. I was formally received at the following Easter Vigil (1995). Now, at this writing, Gloria believes she is ready to be received as well.

Obviously, this brief sketch of our journey hardly does it justice. There were many long walks in the woods behind our house, during which I debated aloud arguments from both sides and poured out my heart to God in prayer. At times I found myself able to argue the issues both ways — which only heightened my feelings of anxiety. I felt the crushing weight of my responsibility to lead my family in the right path but felt frustrated in that responsibility by the seeming lack of clear-cut answers. And I wasn't alone in this: Gloria was facing these same struggles. However, due to the circumstances already described, my approach was to bury myself deeper in further studies, whereas Gloria's recourse was to give things time.

Many will not be able to appreciate the significance of the decision we made on that lonely day in August of 1994. Gloria had been raised in a sect that believed, for all practical purposes, that they were the sole proclaimers of the true Gospel. However, Gloria had come to the point where she no longer believed that she had to be a member of the "Church of Christ" in order to go to heaven, but that did not mean that she was yet certain she could arrive there as a Catholic! She was far from feeling comfortable with Catholicism. Her decision was, in actuality, a tremendous step of faith. The light of faith often leads us into the foreboding domain of the unknown. For many there is no apparent light at the end of the tunnel. Instead, there is only a flickering lamp that illuminates just the next two or three feet of the path. The temptation to turn back and seek the security of familiar surroundings is enormous. But accompanying the temptation is the realization that to turn back is to risk losing that light altogether. So we take the small steps that faith requires and, thereby, find ourselves advancing toward our heavenly home.

During the years that have elapsed since the time of our leaving the Church of Christ in 1994, I have often had to remind myself that Gloria's apparent reluctance to formally enter the Church did not constitute a request for additional "information" from me (that is, "sermonettes" in the kitchen). Rather, it was a reflection of her need for time . . . time to acclimatize. For example, she had come to see that seeking the intercession of the saints in heaven made sense, but that did not mean she was ready for the Rosary! There comes a point where the emotions must catch up with the intellect, or there exists a deeply unsettling tension within. What was formerly strange and offensive requires time to become familiar and appreciated.

During those years of struggle we shared certain frustrations. We had fully expected our brethren in the Churches of Christ to write us off as "moonstruck" and eternally lost, and those expectations were not disappointed. What was disappointing was the lack of appreciation that many Catholics seemed to have for the spiritual battle that was raging in our souls. They seemed unable to relate to the fears that held us back. Our society's pluralism has crept into the Church and fostered a prevailing mood of indifference. As a result, many Catholics appear to be perplexed when they witness firsthand a person on the pathway to conversion struggling as if eternal salvation hung in the balance. Correspondingly, as our journey progressed, our growing enthusiasm for the faith often met with disbelief from Catholics. It was in these confusing circumstances that we derived consolation from the lives of the saints and the many faithful Catholics that God brought into our lives.

Yes, the struggles were great, but the graces that God supplied were even greater. And that, of course, is the bottom line. Grace is the key. Without God's graces we would have never cut through the "hodgepodge" of erroneous ideas and ingrained misconceptions. With God's grace, the fears subsided, the path was made straight, and the light of truth scattered our darkness.

This recognition of the role of grace is the key when one spouse converts ahead of the other. Argumentation accomplishes little. In fact, it is impossible to simply argue someone into the kingdom of God. If it were, conversion would be reducible to a merely intellectual exercise. However, conversion, while involving the intellect, is essentially spiritual and, therefore, is primarily the work of the Holy Spirit.

Given her love for Christ and her openness to the truth, I

knew that Gloria would eventually be Catholic, but I knew it would take time. I also knew that I had a God-given part to play: the part of prayer. Prayer is the primary means that we have of opening the floodgates of heaven, and yet we so often neglect it. We are, in fact, called to persevere in prayer, but how easy it is to become discouraged and give up. Remember, our Lord desires that we should pray at all times and not lose heart (cf. Luke 18:1).

One evening, about two months ago, I was working at my desk when Gloria poked her head around the corner and said, "I guess I'll have to become a Catholic this year." That was all. No big discussion. No elaborate explanations (none were needed). I did not draw this statement of intent out of her in the context of a heated debate or while presenting an apologetical lecture. It was her intent, stated in her words, given when the time was right for her.

At last our unity of purpose has, by God's grace (and in God's time), culminated in a unity of faith. Now we both look forward to the day when we will share a unity of experience when Gloria receives, for the first time, the body and blood of the Lord Jesus Christ in Holy Communion. Amen.

Chapter 6

Love Compelled Me to Wait

by Paul Thigpen

"Why do we have to go to the Catholic Church, Dad? Why?" Tears were spilling off my daughter's face onto her dinner plate. "I don't know anybody there," she went on. "The way they do things is so weird that I can't understand what's going on. They don't dance and shout like the charismatic churches we've belonged to. And week after week, nobody says a word to us when we go. Why do we have to become Catholic?"

My wife, Leisa, sat across the table in an angry silence that echoed my daughter's protest. How could I do this to them? Our family's spiritual home had always been a major concern for us; most of our life together had revolved around the church. I'd even been a pastor! But now I'd brought chaos into our home by insisting I had to become a Catholic.

Leisa and I had always agreed that a husband and wife should belong to the same church; if a couple couldn't meet on theological fundamentals, how could they possibly agree on anything else of importance? Having a religiously "mixed marriage" was simply out of the question for us. But for Leisa, becoming Catholic was out of the question as well.

Working on a doctor of philosophy degree in historical theology, I'd had the high privilege of reading Augustine, Aquinas, Newman, Chesterton, Merton, and a host of others whose arguments and personal example had pressed me, over a period of years, closer and closer to the Catholic Church —

until finally I felt I had nowhere else to go. But Leisa had spent those same years caring for our kids and for me and serving in the congregations where we'd made our spiritual home, with precious little extra time to read the heavy old tomes on my shelves. Without our realizing it, we'd drifted apart theologically. But the distance hadn't been apparent for a long time because we'd remained close spiritually: that is, we'd continued to pray together, worship together, have fellowship with the same Christian friends, rear our children in a friendship with God, and minister to others together in practical ways.

But now the hidden shifts in the tectonic plates of my theology had built up so much pressure underground that an earthquake was inevitable. The surface of my everyday religious practice was at last feeling the tremors, causing panic in my family and forging an unfamiliar landscape for us all. I had begun attending Mass, saying the Hail Mary, praying to the saints, and making the sign of the cross. In my office at home I had placed a little statue of St. Joseph on my desk and a crucifix on the wall. My wife and children thought all this new behavior was strange, and they chided me about it — first gently, then with increasing anxiety.

In my times alone with God, I wept, I struggled, I interceded; I asked the help of St. Joseph (the patron saint of families), St. Anne (the patron saint of homemakers), and the local parish. In the occasional quiet moments when Leisa and I could try to lay aside our emotions and talk rationally about the issue, I laid out my reasons for taking this new direction. But nothing seemed to be working. We were at an impasse.

I felt as if God had put me in an impossible dilemma: I believed it was His will for me (and my family) to become Catholic. But I also believed that He wanted me to care for my family, to hold it together, to protect it from the devastation that would result if I parted ways with them theologically. Could the Lord possibly want me to "divorce" my wife and children spiritually — to head for Rome and abandon them?

The struggle stretched on for weeks, and the weeks became months. Leisa said one day that if I became Catholic, she would leave me. I didn't think she would actually carry out the threat; even in the worst of times before, we had always considered our marriage vows inviolable. But her words were a cry of pain that told me just how deeply the battle was hurting her and the kids.

At last I came to a difficult decision: I would wait. I told Leisa and the children that, for the time being, we would take no more steps in the direction of the Catholic Church. They were visibly relieved. Though I didn't promise them that I would never become Catholic, I said I wouldn't fight them or try to drag them down that road any longer, and I wouldn't tear the family apart.

For the months following, I stopped attending Mass and retreated to my prayer closet to ask for wisdom and grace. Throughout this difficult period, I wrestled with all the theological issues again. Was it really necessary for me to associate with the institution? Couldn't I simply pray to the saints in private, attend Mass occasionally, wear a crucifix under my shirt, and be a closet Catholic? I even tried to forge some kind of compromise with my wife in which we would plant a new congregation that would draw liberally from Catholic sources for its belief and practice — similar to the high Anglican tradition — without actually being Catholic.

During these months, we rarely attended church of any kind; wherever we might visit on Sunday morning, no place seemed right. We gathered as a family every Sabbath to read Scripture, sing, and pray. But it felt as if we were simply playing at church, and I could see our spiritual life withering. I kept praying and trying to be patient. But I knew we couldn't survive spiritually if we remained long where we were.

In the meantime, no matter how I twisted and turned, I couldn't escape the conviction, once again strengthening its grip on me, that the Catholic Church was the Church Jesus had established through his Apostles. No compromise, no middle way, was possible. And I began to hunger for the Eucharist as never before.

Then, one day I received word that an old family friend had a terminal illness. I asked myself, "If you, too, discovered that you only had a short time to live, what would you do immediately and without fail?"

The answer leapt to mind: I would join the Catholic Church. At that moment I knew that even if I were in the best of health, I couldn't wait any longer.

January and a new year had just rolled around, and Leisa knew as well as I did that our family's spiritual life had to change. I don't remember who first brought up the subject, but I do remember the look of resignation in her eyes when she asked me: "You'll never be happy outside of the Catholic Church, will you?"

I shook my head. "It's becoming a matter of conscience. I feel as if I'll be disobeying God if I don't."

The calmness of her reply shocked me. "Then I guess you'd better go along with your conscience. But I just can't take that step myself."

We talked awhile longer, and we each made concessions that we believed were reasonable and loving. The Rite of Christian Initiation of Adults classes would begin at the local parish soon (they had a rather short course of instruction), so I would start attending them and Mass with the firm intention of entering the Church at Easter. Leisa agreed to attend with me and to keep an open mind, but she was making no commitments. If I would not pressure her to come along on this road, she would stand aside and let me proceed.

The local priest who directed the RCIA classes was a Christlike, Christ-centered man — just the person my family needed in this new, close encounter with the Catholic faith. He led us gently through the basics and gave Leisa the freedom to attend without making any commitment until close to the class's conclusion. By the time my preschool-aged son began greeting the priest with a warm hug, my hope had grown that, by some miracle, Easter would see us all in the Catholic Church.

I was not disappointed. In less than three months, Leisa had passed from resignation to interest to conviction, if not enthusiasm. She read, prayed, asked countless questions. She left some things on the shelf for the time being. ("Even if I'm Catholic, I may never pray to Mary," she once said. I just smiled.)

So much that was Catholic still seemed alien to her, yet she was finding a home in the Church nevertheless. And the children, with that marvelous flexibility God graciously gives to youth, were coming around as well.

On Palm Sunday eve — the day we entered the Church — Leisa still couldn't bring herself to "pray to Mary." But she took her leap of faith with grace and even a sense of peace that passed her understanding. The children took their part excitedly, happy to be settled at last in a spiritual niche that felt surprisingly comfortable.

Ever since we took the plunge together (a year and a half at the time this was written), God has done more for us than I could have dared to ask. When we had to move to another state so I could do my dissertation research, I asked St. Joseph to pray that we would find a parish where we could grow as a Catholic family. We had much of our theology in place, but we needed Catholic friends who could show us how to pray the Rosary as a family, teach us Catholic table blessings, tell us how to celebrate our children's confirmations. We needed up-close models of godly Catholic manhood and womanhood, people for whom practicing the Catholic faith was so natural that we could learn from them just by watching.

That's exactly the kind of parish we've found in our new home. The community is warm, the liturgy is magnificent, the theology is orthodox, and the pastor is wise. Several families have befriended us and helped us learn the everyday practices of Catholic family life. We've become Eucharistic ministers; Leisa and my daughter are helping out with sacristy responsibilities; and the two of them have just helped to found a new sodality in our congregation for young girls and their mothers.

During Lent, God gave Leisa a deep hunger for spiritual reading. I was amazed to see how much she grew in a few short weeks as she devoured biographies of the saints. Ever since then, her conviction has been fired with enthusiasm as well; sometimes she's the one pulling me farther down the road, exploring new paths of Catholic tradition and introducing them to me.

Meanwhile, my daughter's perspective has been transformed as well. I could tell she was enjoying herself in church, but my heart almost broke with joy on the day when she came to me quietly and said almost in a whisper: "Dad, I'm so glad we're in the Catholic Church now. I have such a sense of peace in the Church that I never had anywhere we've been before. When I go to Mass, I can feel the presence of God and a spirit of worship in the people."

I weep even now to realize how far we've come so quickly. In fact, at times I find myself wishing that I hadn't delayed entering the Church, that I hadn't wrestled through those long months till my family was ready to consider joining me. Think of how much farther along we might be by now if I hadn't hesitated! And think of how terrible it would have been if one of us had died while I was waiting!

And yet . . . it seems to me at the same time that the timing was all in God's providence. I suppose I could look back and conclude that my hesitation reflected weakness or cowardice on my part. But even if those were truly factors in the situation, I know for sure that at the heart of my decision was an overriding pastoral concern, a desire to lead my family without bludgeoning them, to allow God to woo them to the Church as He had wooed me. If I had walked over my wife and children to get to Rome, they might never have followed me; bitterness might well have sent them running the other way instead.

Above all, I know now that it was love that finally enabled us to conquer our dilemma. The very fact that the issue was so explosive for our family indicates how much we cherished one another: we simply couldn't bear the thought of being separated, spiritually or otherwise. It was my love for my wife and children that gave birth to my patience; and it was their love for me that pressed them at last to risk letting go of me so that I could find peace.

Perhaps much of this story sounds all too familiar to you. Perhaps you, too, are caught in a demoralizing battle with your family over your conviction that Rome is home. If so, I want to encourage you that the most important thing you can do just now is simply to love your spouse and children. God may want you to wait for them, or He may not; that depends on the details of your situation. Only you and He know. But whatever God calls you to do, He wants you to do it compassionately, gently, and sensitively.

I can't help thinking that our Lord is more than willing to honor such love by working out all the messy details in spite of us. In any case, of this much I'm certain: whatever my family may have lost in those months of uncertainty, when love compelled me to wait and compelled them to let go, we have more than regained in the glorious days that have followed, and our love for one another is stronger than ever.

Chapter 7

Converting One at a Time

by David K. DeWolf

Priscilla and I had been married twenty-two years when I began thinking seriously about becoming Catholic. We met in a meditation group in Orange County, California, back in the early 1970s. I had just graduated from college and had moved to Southern California because a friend of mine from college had told me about a meditation group that he was attending. I had a lot of respect for him, and I was in between assignments, since I had turned in my draft card the last year of college and was waiting for the draft board and/or the United States Attorney to decide what to do with me. I expected to go to prison eventually but didn't really know what was in store.

I didn't fall into any immediate line of work, so I wound up working for a temporary agency, with a long-term assignment at a pharmaceutical company in Long Beach. I rose in the morning early enough to do some yoga and meditation, packed a huge lunch for myself, and rode my bicycle about forty-five minutes to the industrial part of town, then came home to a vegetarian dinner. On the weekends there was a class in the theosophy-type meditation course entitled "Nature of the Soul." Class lasted about three hours and featured a limited amount of socializing afterward. There was also a class on Tuesday nights called "Corrective Thinking," and it was taught in Orange County. I decided to try to get to that class when I could. It was a fairly strenuous bike ride, but I made it. I've long since forgotten the class, but I met a woman there with a Mickey Mouse T-shirt who caught my eye—it was Priscilla. I ran into her at a weekend class and we got to know each other. Early in 1972 we got better acquainted and in September of that year we got married under a bough of flowers in the backyard of one of the meditation group members.

Priscilla sewed her own wedding dress (practically made of polyester cloth at my suggestion, so she could wash it after what we thought would be subsequent uses — it never emerged again from the closet), and as a portent of many years to come of my poor taste in clothes, I combined a Mexican wedding shirt with white pants and black wingtip shoes.

We exchanged vows Quaker-style, and invited those in attendance to join us in saying the New Age equivalent of the Lord's Prayer. After about forty-five minutes of silence, the guests made a beeline for the punch bowl. Priscilla's father thoughtfully provided some alcohol for one of the punch bowls (as vegetarians and teetotalers, the thought hadn't occurred to us), and it was gone in a twinkling. After making sure that friends and family who had come a long distance were squared away in our rented house, Priscilla and I spent the night in an orange tent in the backyard. Having practiced, um, New Age morals up until that point, it was no big deal. The next day we left with a surprise guest from Germany to spend a few days camping in Yosemite.

Our happiness with New Age philosophy continued for a couple of years, but as we watched many marriages spring up and then wither like the seed sown on rocky ground, we knew that there was something impermanent about New Age philosophy. In 1974 we moved to Boulder, Colorado, and began attending Quaker meetings there. Something about the Christian origins of the Society of Friends was attractive, and there were some impressive academic types who seemed to add gravity to the somewhat countercultural atmosphere. I had been raised in a pious Methodist household (my father was a Methodist pastor until his retirement in 1982), and I was very much at home with Christian theology. But I carefully avoided its more Fundamentalist aspects.

After two happy years we left Boulder so that I could go to law school in New Haven, Connecticut. We were sad to leave the Boulder Friends Meeting and the fellowship we experienced there. In our new location we'd go to church on holidays or special occasions, but the demands of school and work took over. In the fall of 1979 we moved to Boise, Idaho, and there we started going to a large Methodist church. The pastor was educated and outgoing, and the congregation was respectable and sincere. I loved the hymns of my youth and began to take a Bible study course. I think I might have gotten more involved except that I knew we weren't staying in Boise. A year later we moved to Spokane, Washington, where we found a Presbyterian church with a somewhat similar demographic profile.

Our first two children were born in 1982 and 1984, and then we moved to Oklahoma so that I could start teaching. There we wound up in a Disciples of Christ Church, which was more florid and emotional than we were used to, but it was reasonably satisfying. Even its more Fundamentalist leanings had its appeal. There was something attractive about the angular quality of Fundamentalism — its willingness to be "out of step" with reigning fashions — that helped prepare me for a similar quality of Catholicism.

As time had gone on we were becoming more conservative, both politically and theologically. Having children and running a business gave us a perspective on the need for bedrock principles. It was frustrating to begin searching each time we arrived in a new location — which we seemed to do every two years or so. In 1987 we moved back to California, and then in 1988 we were able to move back to Spokane. By that time we had our third child, this one with Down syndrome. Shortly after arriving back in Spokane, Priscilla discovered she was pregnant with our fourth child. We had always been pro-life, but we were surprised at the concern of the doctors who wanted to be sure that Priscilla had "genetics counseling" — which told her she had a five-percent chance of delivering a second child with Down syndrome. We weren't particularly worried. Sure enough, our Peter is now an all-too-normal ten-year-old.

I came back to Spokane to teach at Gonzaga Law School, a nominally Catholic and Jesuit institution. I say nominally because much of the university had by that time lapsed into secularism. (As I write this there are reasons to hope that this trend has been reversed at Gonzaga, but it is a long struggle.) Ironically, even before coming to Gonzaga, I had described myself as a "closet Catholic."

What I understood of Catholic doctrine I tended to like. I felt more at home with the consistency and high intellectual content of Catholic teaching. Compared to the mainline Protestant denominations, which had given in to the culture on many of the social issues, the Catholic Church fearlessly preached the truth. The Fundamentalists, on the other hand, who were good on the social issues, couldn't connect their heads with their hearts. Occasionally the two would be combined in an admirable individual — a pastor or a teacher — but this disjunction prevented us from getting firmly attached to any church body.

Upon returning to Spokane, however, we tried once again. Having journeyed from New Age to Quakers to nothing to Methodists to Presbyterians to Disciples of Christ, we thought we had returned home, ecclesiastically speaking, by joining the Presbyterians down the street from our home in Spokane.

But two things intervened. One was my eldest brother, who had lived in Japan all of our married life, whom we had seen only intermittently. He had become a Catholic convert shortly after he married, which was the same year that we married. He didn't talk too much about his faith, although he was very well read philosophically and theologically. Once we both discovered e-mail in the early 1990s we began a pretty regular correspondence and the discussion often turned theological. My frustrations with the Presbyterian Church, particularly on social issues, provoked him to say at one point, "Then how can you remain a Presbyterian?" I didn't have a very good answer. The other thing that happened was that a student of mine from Alaska heard that I was one of the few actual Christians teaching at the law school, and made an appointment to see if there were any cure to her sense of isolation. When she said she was Catholic, I said jokingly that I described myself as a "closet Catholic" which piqued her curiosity as to why I used that term. I explained that I often found myself defending orthodox Catholic doctrine in debates with nominal Catholics — and sometimes with priests. She groaned with recognition and said she would give me some literature and some tapes that would show how consistent and satisfying Catholic doctrine was. I thanked her and said I looked forward to it.

Over the next six months I became a project of hers and I looked forward more and more to her visits. At one point her mother came for a visit, and we invited the two of them for dinner at our house. It was a memorable evening. Mother and daughter were clearly in love with their faith and were delighted to have an opportunity to share it with people who were receptive but didn't yet know much about it. And as orthodox Catholics, they were also embarrassed by the unwillingness of some nominal Catholics to accept the fullness of their faith. They were as grieved by the prevalence of "cafeteria Catholics" who were no better, and in some cases worse, than the Presbyterians with whom we went to church, selecting those portions of the faith that were convenient. There was also something bold and exciting about people who were willing to be different, and who didn't mind upsetting those who were more anxious to be accepted by the world than to be faithful.

During this period Priscilla remained interested but non-committal. Her primary challenge was dealing with a tragedy involving her father, Russ. Shortly after the birth of our fourth child, Russ had suffered a freak accident, which resulted in a broken neck. After weeks of hovering near death he was released from the ICU as a quadriplegic. Eventually he was transferred to a veterans' hospital on the Hudson River in New York. While Russ lay helpless in a hospital bed, Priscilla tried to negotiate the transfer of his limited possessions to suitable quarters, but it was complicated by the fact that Russ had just separated from his second wife. Priscilla also agonized over how to keep in touch with him over the long distance. He was in a considerable amount of pain; even though he had lost the ability to use any of his limbs, the involuntary muscle contractions were excruciatingly painful, a condition that was relieved only when the tendons were surgically severed.

Priscilla could only visit her father once a year at best, and yet she thought of him constantly. His pain was mingled with her own at the sense of loss and futility at not being able to do anything at such a distance other than to pray. In addition, many other painful memories from her childhood and adolescence surfaced at this time (her own struggle with survival as a severe asthmatic as a child, her brother's polio, her mother's early death due to rheumatoid arthritis, struggles as a stepchild). At one point she sought relief through the counsel of a psychologist, who after one visit told her she needed a divorce. Thankfully, she did not take this advice but rather struggled to keep her head above water and maintain order in a very busy household. During this time we opened our home at different times to a homeless family of refugees, exchange students from both Germany and Denmark, two nieces—one from Japan and one from California— and a grandniece who lived with us from age two to age five. Needless to say, this time of needing supernatural strength when our emotions were fragile (particularly in the case of Priscilla, who was unable to discuss her father without unleashing a torrent of tears) put us on a path of deep inner searching.

As I began to explore the possibility of conversion more

seriously, I had sharply conflicting emotions. On the one hand, it seemed that I had finally found a kind of home, although it wasn't entirely to my liking. One thing I had to get used to was the fact that I only really liked a small number of people that I met in the Catholic Church. That is, I was only attracted to a certain mind-set about the Church. Most of the people I had known as Catholics, and whom I continued to encounter, were frankly unattractive. Many were uneducated; many were heretical; many were irritating in one way or another. Whereas a Protestant can choose a denomination that is comfortable in terms of its intellectual content, social class, and taste in music and dress, Catholics were all over the lot. Although Priscilla would grouse from time to time about the Presbyterian Church, she enjoyed the high quality of preaching that we got on Sundays; the music was superior; and we'd made a number of friends whose general life experience and outlook were compatible with ours. Most important to Priscilla, our children were going to church without resistance. They either went to Sunday school or stayed with us in church, but it was a relatively easy routine for us on Sunday. In previous years, one or more of the children was either too old or too young to sit quietly in church, and Priscilla refused to put them in a Sunday school class unless they wanted to be there, which they typically did not. As I drew closer to thinking that the doctrine of the Catholic Church was actually true, I wondered how I could ever persuade Priscilla to fix what, to her, wasn't broken.

A related problem was that I began to wonder whether my inclinations were just part of a midlife crisis. I was forty-five years old; I had just gotten tenure, and thus had job security and lots of leisure. I couldn't help wondering whether my fascination with Catholicism was just an unusual form of looking for novelty. Would I convert, and make this serious commitment, only to discover that the grass was no greener on the other side of the fence, and that the flaw lay not in the church I attended but in myself? I couldn't resolve this issue, but it made it all the more difficult to share these things with Priscilla. I didn't want to convert and wind up in a different church, but I also felt that I couldn't be of much help to Priscilla in sorting out what ought to happen to the rest of the family. I was in this helpless sort of drift when I got the wake-up call from my brother Charles, mentioned earlier. How could I remain in the Presbyterian Church given my knowledge that it did not contain the fullness of the truth?

I decided that I should sign up for an RCIA program and put myself on the road to an official decision, but I didn't know where to do it because I wasn't really connected to any church. Most of what had attracted me to the Catholic Church was what I read, my conversations with the student from Alaska and her family, and e-mail communication with my brother. I thought the best thing would be to go through the RCIA program at Gonzaga; it fit my connection to the university and my lack of connection anywhere else. When I signed up, it was suggested that I find a sponsor who would attend the classes with me. Although I knew several people who might be willing to do this for me, my first choice was the student who had first nurtured my interest in the faith. But I was simultaneously reluctant to impose upon her, particularly because she was still a student. In the end I decided just to ask her, and she immediately said yes. So Monday nights I dutifully attended the class, and most of the time my sponsor was able to come.

The RCIA class itself was symptomatic of much of what is wrong with the Church today. It was taught by an assistant in the campus ministry program, a nice enough fellow who traded a career in the U.S. Air Force as a navigator on B-52 bombers for more peaceful pursuits. Once or twice we got a visit from the Director of Campus Ministry, a priest, who seemed anxious to make us feel comfortable. The first few weeks featured some student assistants, one of whom was the campus militant for gay rights. At one point I expressed my surprise that the book we were using to learn the fundamentals of faith (what in an older era would have been a cat-echism) referred to Old Testament dates by giving the date followed by "BCE" (rather than "BC"). "What's the meaning of that?" I asked. The assistant patronizingly explained that it meant "Before the Christian (or Common) Era," in order to be more respectful of our Jewish and Muslim brothers and sisters. I again expressed surprise that this kind of politically correct thinking, which I had encountered elsewhere in the secular academy, should have permeated a book that was presumably designed to explain the Lordship of Jesus Christ over all of history. Perhaps because of this and my other in-temperate remarks, the student assistant found other ways to occupy his time on Monday nights. Almost all of the other students in the class were students at the college, many of whom were preparing to marry Catholics and were happy to accommodate their spouses by accepting the religion of their loved ones. Others seemed drawn by some social aspect of the faith. The message they received was that this was indeed a neat religion, and one that would make them feel at home.

I reported my experience to Priscilla and also the fact that my sponsor took the time after each class to correct the obvi-ous errors and cover the kinds of things that should have been covered in the class. It hardly whetted her appetite for con-version. I also began to feel more nervous about the fact that my primary lifeline to what was beautiful about the faith was my sponsor. It began to feel more like a midlife crisis and less like something that was of God.

Fortunately, at the end of October, I was able to go for a four-day Ignatian retreat outside of Phoenix, Arizona, with a wonderfully gifted priest, Father Donald J. McGuire, S.J. There I felt a sense of community with people whose passion for their faith was similar to mine. I also encountered a priest to whom I could happily entrust my spiritual guidance. I made my first confession, said my first Rosary, and spent time in adoration of the Blessed Sacrament. Finally the yearning of my heart was met with a true community of kindred spirits.

Priscilla now says that I came back from the retreat walking on air. I had turned the corner in my determination to enter the Church, but I was still dealing with an environment that was hardly hospitable to her. Moreover, the children had no idea what I was up to. While Priscilla tolerated, and to some extent encouraged, this exploratory venture, it was mine rather than ours, and I could not see at that point how I would ever be able to make it ours together. However, I also knew that it was useless to try to persuade her to do something I was still only contemplating doing myself. And if I attempted to make my conversion contingent upon her wanting to convert at the same time, it might bog down in endless complication. I had to follow my own light, as selfish as it might seem. As Easter finally approached, Priscilla remained neutral; she neither encouraged me nor put up resistance. She came to the Holy Thursday confirmation ceremony, and afterward we went out for a little party with our Catholic neighbors and friends, my sponsor, and an earnest Protestant friend of ours who was himself searching. As we drove home, Priscilla said to me that I should not expect her to convert to Catholicism in order to please me. She was going to do so, if at all, for her own reasons. I interpreted this at the time as a healthy form of candor, and it proved to be a very wise insight on her part.

Although Priscilla was understanding, my mother was not. I had talked with her by telephone along the way and was somewhat lighthearted about the whole thing. She was hoping that I would simply think better of the whole thing, but as the time approached she became more insistent about knowing why I was taking this unusual step. I got a letter from her that politely complained about the fact that by becoming Catholic I had in effect repudiated the lifework of my father, who had retired some years ago from almost forty years as a Protestant minister. I wrote her a reply that was as diplomatic as possible, but I still felt wounded. (This reply, incidentally, has been published, in a slightly edited form, in the February 1998 edition of *This Rock*, entitled "Dear Mom, I'm a Catholic.") For reasons I did not understand at the time, I began to spend regular time saying the Rosary. I left early in the morning to walk through the woods near my house and say the five decades of the Rosary while I walked. While doing so I began to see how much I needed my Blessed Mother, in part because my earthly mother had been unwilling or unable to salve some deep wound. I recognized that one of the things that appealed to me about my sponsor was her reflection to me of a kind of holy femininity, which I craved as desperately as a refugee from institutional food craves a home-cooked meal. I also realized how lucky I was to be married to someone who, though she wisely refused to try to fill the gaping holes in my psyche, recognized some basic goodness that managed to maintain itself.

I asked our Lady's special help in finding some avenue for Priscilla's conversion. By praying for her I also recognized how much she needed me to be a better person, not only that she might sense the value of the faith, but because it was only through a massive infusion of grace that this dream could become a reality. Luckily, I was greatly aided by the generosity of my sponsor's family. When they came for their daughter's graduation, they extended an offer to send Priscilla an airline ticket to Alaska for one of Father McGuire's retreats. I had tried to get her to go to the retreat in January of the preceding year, but she thought I was more than slightly crazy for wanting her to go to Alaska in the dead of winter. Another retreat was scheduled for Labor Day of 1995. At the time Priscilla was still dealing with her father's physical decline. She might never have considered a retreat if my sponsor's family had not made her an offer she couldn't refuse.

I felt reasonably confident that the retreat would be a success, since Priscilla had always demonstrated a natural spiritual gift; after all, we met in a meditation class. I was also reasonably confident that Father McGuire would appeal to her in much the same way he appealed to me. But nothing was guaranteed. Despite the awkwardness and novelty of being the only Protestant and having to observe silence as a retreatant, Priscilla dutifully attended all eleven conferences, daily Mass, praying of the Rosary, and stations of the cross— all new experiences made all the more special by the transcendent beauty of Alaska with moose cavorting around the retreat center and Mount McKinley visible in the distance.

As always on Father McGuire's retreats, the Holy Spirit was very active. From the first night Priscilla knew she had found her spiritual home. By the end of the retreat she was bursting with newfound enthusiasm. In her private conference with Father McGuire she asked two questions: what do I do with our children, and where to find a parish? He said to let both things work themselves out with patience and prayer. Indeed, I had just discovered a wonderful parish in Spokane and met the priest, the Rt. Rev. Adrian Parcher, O.S.B. I was confident that Priscilla would be able to make a reasonably smooth transition from Father McGuire. When I asked about an RCIA class, Abbot Adrian said that he preferred to do the instruction on an individual basis, since he rarely had more than a few candidates at a time and he preferred to have more flexibility in designing an appropriate program of instruction.

It turned out that the abbot was a wonderful shepherd for Priscilla. He had two qualities that I believe are essential in such a situation. First, he was extremely knowledgeable about the faith, and able to answer difficult questions about Church doctrine. What makes the questions of an adult convert difficult is not so much that they are theologically hard, but that they require an ability to relate what the convert already knows to what is new and puzzling. Converts usually have an easy time with some aspects of the faith, and a difficult time with others. That raises the second important quality, which is a strong pastoral insight into the condition of the soul presented to the priest. The convert often has mastered some steps along the path of faith (in many cases well beyond those of a cradle Catholic). But other steps are surprisingly difficult. The pastor has to discern which steps the convert is ready for, and which to postpone for a later day. On the one hand, a convert should be expected to embrace the faith wholeheartedly, not with reservations. At the same time, there may be things that will become clear in time, as long as the fundamental disposition is correct. The pastor's love for souls and his delight in pastoring them is essential to making the convert feel wanted and appreciated in his or her own right, and Priscilla could not have asked for a better guide. During the time of Priscilla's instruction we attended an early Mass (powerfully centered on the Eucharist and with no music) followed by the Presbyterian Church where the preaching and the music were skillfully done. Our children also began to be introduced to both forms of worship. Although Priscilla still found much in the Presbyterian service that was nourishing, it became clear to her that something important was missing. Despite the earnestness of the preacher and the musicians, something was being withheld; it remained more performance than worship. Despite the recent impoverishment of Catholic liturgy in many parishes, it had a kind of authenticity that was missing in even the most heartfelt Presbyterian service.

And to return to a theme touched on earlier, there is in Catholic liturgy an acceptance of human suffering, a sanctification of that suffering, that makes other worship pale in comparison. In the Presbyterian Church there was always a weak spot when it came to an appreciation of suffering. Priscilla felt that many people wanted to avoid admitting difficulty in their own lives or in someone else's because in their minds a true Christian never really suffered; one's faith should always triumph over any apparent misfortune. It had a kind of Christian Science quality to it. By contrast, Catholicism seemed to her to recognize more clearly that the cross is at the heart of the miracle of salvation—a truth poignantly demonstrated by the last six and a half years of Priscilla's father's life. Russ was not a religious man, but he accepted the cross that was handed to him with astounding equanimity, grace, and even humor, which increased over time. Russ died on December 12, the feast day of Our Lady of Guadalupe and the day before Priscilla's forty-ninth birthday.

It was not long before we knew that Priscilla had passed the point of no return. She was reluctant to call an end to her instruction, in part because it was so enjoyable and in part because she hardly felt that she had mastered what she needed to know. But, as she said, if she waited much longer she would be "one awfully thirsty communicant." So she arranged to be received at Easter Vigil in 1996, only a year after my own conversion, and of course my joy was indescribable. Not only had we put aside the divisiveness of two different faiths, but we had done so in a way that Priscilla felt was on her own terms. Miraculously, our prayers for our three younger children were answered. They were received into the Church less than a year later. Our oldest child, a son just finishing high school, will occasionally ask questions about Catholicism but is too involved in Young Life and other youth groups to seriously consider a change. Occasionally we feel guilty about blithely accepting our separate status and not exerting more influence for fear of exacerbating an adolescent rebellion, which was well on its way at the time of our conversion. Despite our concern that he's missing out on the graces that flow from a sacramental life, we have to trust in God's timing.

Having narrated the story of Priscilla's conversion, I cannot resist the temptation to offer advice to those who identify with my position in the early parts of the story. The first piece of advice during the conversion process itself is to try to identify those aspects of your attraction to Catholicism that represent some wounded quality of yourself. That is, to what extent might I justifiably be accused of a form of escapism? Of course, this is not a disqualifying feature; St. Augustine described our condition as being restless until we rest in God, so that all human longing can be seen as a path by which we eventually find God. But our religious life may reflect less admirable motives. Church may be a place where we can feel self-important or escape unpleasant relationships that dog us in other contexts. Or it may be a simple case of boredom; as the saying goes, the grass frequently looks greener on the other side of the fence. An honest self-assessment serves several purposes. For one, it alerts us to areas where we are vulnerable to criticism from our spouse or from others who question our motives. Even if our accusers do not themselves have the best of motives for their criticism, we need to have a reasonable answer for them. As a corollary, identifying the suspect motive gives us an assignment to demonstrate the redemptive power of our newfound faith. When Christ restored sight to the blind or hearing to the deaf, he produced many converts. If our faith leads us to demonstrate true love for our spouse—obedience toward our husband, sacrificial service of our wife—then that miracle may very well bring about the conversion we seek. Alas, it is often the case that our discovery of the one, holy, catholic and apostolic church leaves us wanting to spend more time at church, on retreats, and in pilgrimages, and less inclined to spend time at home. Or we love our spouses conditionally—to the extent they share our faith. It can't be helped that we need to go to a different church, often at a different time from the rest of the family; but that should be more than made up for by the fact that in all other respects we are a much better spouse and parent. As important as it is to be obedient to the Magisterium of the Church, the greater challenge for most converts is to display humility and loving service toward their spouse.

A second piece of advice is at the risk of being obvious, but it is to offer our marriages up in prayer, and to request heavenly assistance, especially from our Lady. Not only will she obtain for us the grace to transform us into spouses who make our faith more attractive, but she will prepare everything else that is necessary. The Rosary in particular should be relied upon. I would recommend the seven-day scriptural Rosary, which includes not only the three traditional groups of mysteries (joyful, sorrowful, and glorious) but also four others (healing, Eucharistic, salvation, and consoling) that add to the richness of that devotion.

A final piece of advice would be patience. In some ways I lack standing to make this recommendation, since my wish was granted almost immediately, compared to many conversion stories. However, from the time I first began drifting toward Rome, until Priscilla's entry into full communion, seemed like a long time. If I had known that the condition was only temporary, it would have eased a lot of the anxiety. But no matter how long it takes, by eternal standards everything is temporary. Priscilla was wise enough to know from the beginning that if she were ever to convert, it had to be on her terms, not mine. It wasn't my job to convert her; it was my job to deepen my own conversion. Learning to treasure our spouse without preconditions is the quickest way to marital harmony, whether or not it includes sharing the faith.

Chapter 8

A Protestant's Prayers

by Karen Peterson

Am I being naïve to think that Jon could become a Catholic and I could stay Protestant? The dilemma is that even if I accept his quest, I want our family life to stay much the same. Maybe it would be better for me to just go along with Jon, since I am not strongly against him becoming Catholic, but I'm afraid I could never become a Catholic just to keep the peace. As an adult, I need to decide what I truly believe. Although I might have just gone along with our last church change, I feel I would have to draw the line at Catholicism.

I do believe people can live together with different beliefs. A Catholic and a Protestant should be able to live together because we have more similarities than differences, especially if neither one is very insistent about it toward the other. We need to be accepting and respectful of each other.

We've been married nineteen years. At first, Jon didn't have strong opinions about religion. On the other hand, I grew up in a charismatic church and it was a large part of my life. Jon joined me at the church I was attending, and worshiping together became very important to us.

Then about eight years ago, Phil, a friend at work, got Jon thinking about why he was choosing one church over another. Jon started making his faith his own, and I was glad that he wanted to learn more about Christ. However, his reading and studying began to seem very unbalanced, since he was concentrating almost exclusively on materials about the Reformed faith, also known as Calvinism. Phil supplied Jon with a steady flow of books, tapes, and even occasional videos. I sometimes resented this. I tried not to, because I knew he wasn't forcing these things on Jon, but Phil didn't realize how disrupting this was to our family. Jon was spending every spare minute reading, and we would argue as he pressed his new beliefs on me. It seemed like he was trying to convert me as if I weren't already a true Christian.

After several years of his reading and our fighting about it, Jon announced to me, the week after Christmas, that after the first of the year he would be attending the Presbyterian church. He said the kids and I were welcome to go with him, or we could stay at our church. I chose to join him so that we could all continue worshiping together, but it was extremely difficult for me to leave my comfort zone of thirty-five years. For a more gradual change, the kids and I continued to attend the mid-week service at our charismatic church for another year, partly because I didn't want to leave, but also so that I could finish teaching a children's class I was committed to.

I tried to make the most of a new church and a new situation. I learned and thought more about doctrine; this church was much more intellectually inclined. The focus was more on worshiping God and not just on what he could do for you today — what a breath of fresh air! I learned about the Protestant Reformation, which it seemed I had not even heard about in the other church. And of course, I met wonderful people and formed new friendships. Still, I missed the worship choruses; at the Presbyterian church we sang mostly hymns.

A few years after we switched churches, Phil, Jon's spiritual mentor, joined the Catholic Church. I'm not sure exactly what Jon felt at the time. I think he was surprised, having thought that Phil was perhaps going to become an Episcopalian. I said to myself, "Well, so much for Phil's one true religion of the Reformed faith." At church, I assured people that Jon had no intention of becoming Catholic. I honestly think that was true right then. But before long, Jon came home with a couple of big, thick Catholic books under his arm — courtesy of Phil. I got a sick feeling in my stomach — I certainly did not want to go through more fighting and family disruption.

The Catholic turns in the road have been only in the last two or three years. Jon's new interest made me anxious because I thought, "When is this going to stop? Maybe he'll find that Catholicism is the truth; then he'll settle down. But what if he just keeps searching forever?" Although I realize that I'm not very knowledgeable in this area, his becoming Catholic is not the worst thing that could ever happen. What I feared is that he might never settle in, that he would keep searching and get so confused in the end that he'd reject everything. I found myself wondering, what if Jon becomes a Catholic, and finds that's not good enough? And then what if Jesus isn't good enough? What if he has to go back as far as Judaism? What if he wants to try Buddhism? How far back in history does he want to go? But I'm not seriously worried about that; it's just where my imagination can take me.

Jon is passionate about discussing Catholicism, but nobody else in the house is. We've had some fights about it, although it seems to me we fought more about the last church change, from charismatic to Presbyterian. I would say, "Why are you pushing me about this? Let me find out about it on my own!" Of course there are many things about Catholicism that I don't understand, but Jon reads so much more than I that I can't possibly refute what he says. I might ask him about a Scripture verse that occurs to me, but I don't do it to attack, mostly just to clarify. I think I'm fairly open-minded, and I hope Jon agrees.

I wonder how many people feel torn apart by this kind of conflict. I sometimes ask Jon not to even talk about it, because even without fighting, it is a source of tension. As a couple you want to think alike, and when one of you is going a different direction it's uncomfortable. We have established our family, and this is upsetting to all of us. But at least we are dealing with something good — our faith. It's not like Jon's disrupting the family with drinking or excessive sports, or immoral things. He is genuinely searching, so I want to recognize that and be grateful for a husband who is concerned about truth and goodness.

However, the children are upset about our discussions, saying things like, "We don't have to become Catholics, do we?" But they don't know anything about Catholicism, really. For them, the last church change was almost like changing religions, it was so different: a different culture, an unfamiliar style of worship. They often say that they wish they were back at the old church. It may be because when they hear us discuss it, although we aren't usually angry, Jon gets worked up about it, and starts gesturing with his arms. Then we all groan, "Here he goes again!"

Perhaps because we don't have many problems other than this, I don't like even thinking about it; I would rather that life go along as usual. But what can I do? Jon is an adult; he can make his own choices. On the other hand, I don't want Jon to pressure me. It's doubtful that I'd ever become a Catholic, but I won't say I *never* would, because we don't know the future. (And I might have time to read some day, too.) Right now I don't worry about what it will be like if Jon converts. I prefer to take things as they come, so I can wait and see about Catholicism. If he ever becomes a Catholic, I wouldn't like it, but I could accept it.

Jon and I have quite different perspectives on religion. He has a strong desire to know the truth, and to see the bigger picture. He wants to be part of the Church that's truly the Church. I've come to realize my view of Christianity is very simple. My goals are to love, obey, and serve God — to live a Christian life. I don't really care if my doctrine isn't perfect. I know that drives Jon crazy.

I've said that I just haven't had time to read, study, or discuss these things. I realize, though, that I don't have much motivation; I don't want to change. If I had the drive that Jon does, I would be devoted to learning more. But I am really content with the way we are; I'm satisfied to believe what I have always believed. I know the truth is important, but I feel like I already have it, so I'm not searching.

One thing I have resented is that Jon wouldn't read the books I would get him, for example, about parenting. I might as well have rewrapped them every Father's Day and given them to him again, yet he can find the time to read all the Catholic materials. I respect Jon's search, but I am concerned that it takes him away from us.

I admit I am jealous and offended, because he was so involved in reading when we last changed churches, and now it's a whole new set of materials for Catholicism. Audiotapes have been especially irritating. At first, if Jon was going to do the dishes, he would put in a tape to listen to, and then if we tried to talk to him, he'd run over and stop the tape so he wouldn't miss anything. When I complained about that, he got a small tape player with headphones. I would start to say something, and he wouldn't even hear me. It wouldn't hurt him to read a book I choose now and then, because he could use a little help. Of course, it's easy for me to see how Jon could improve his relationship with us; it's more difficult to see my own shortcomings.

So that's part of the tension; I want Jon to spend more time with our family. But he has a full-time job, works on the side with his dad, and has to practice the music for church services. He doesn't have a lot of leisure. Our children are going to be grown sooner than we imagine. If he could put off his search, they would be grown, and then he could go more peacefully into the Catholic Church. But for now he needs to be fully involved where he is.

Sometimes he reads things and decides he won't be able to wait even two or three more years to become Catholic. He still gets plenty of reading material from Phil, who is a walking library. I just wish that *nobody* would give Jon all this stuff.

I don't resent Phil personally; it's just that he's a very persuasive individual. I used to believe that Jon might be thinking this way just to please Phil, whom he respects and trusts. But as I said, I know Jon is an adult, and he can make his own decisions. He says possibly the Holy Spirit is using Phil to bring people into the Catholic Church. But I'm concerned that when Phil believed in Reformed theology, Jon thought that was the truth; now that Phil is Catholic, Catholicism must be true. I realize that if he draws the same conclusions as Phil, he's not necessarily just following. After he reads the material and understands it he really believes it. Nonetheless, when Phil converted to the Catholic Church, the kids said, "Does that mean we have to go, too?"

I used to think that if Jon started going to the Catholic Church, he should go to Mass on Saturday night and still go to our church with us for a while. I don't know if I would want to stay at our church without him being there. I'm there now because we're together, but I disagree with some of the teaching. I certainly love the people, though, and it's hard to change groups and start all over to make friends.

I know I couldn't suddenly start going to Mass with Jon on a regular basis, anyway, especially because of my mom and my extended family, who would all think I was absolutely crazy. I guess that shouldn't matter so much to me, but it would. We are in an awkward position right now, with Jon looking seriously at the Catholic Church, and the kids still wanting to return to our previous church. I worry especially about our teenagers, since adolescence can be an extremely confusing stage. If their parents are a little confused, it's not a stable situation for them. I believe that's one reason Jon is delaying his decision. He says the more he reads the sooner he wants to become Catholic, but at the same time, he wants to wait for the sake of our unity. Then there's the baby — I don't like wondering whether he will be raised Catholic or Protestant.

After attending our current church for several years, we

recently became members. We wanted our baby to be baptized, but that didn't require that we join, so I was surprised that Jon wanted to become a member now, when he seems to be so seriously considering Catholicism. Perhaps it's that there is much more to read before he can make a decision; it could take years. Also, since making that membership commitment, he will not change his mind very lightly. In this denomination, the church leadership takes the responsibility to keep us on the "straight and narrow." If a member of the flock seems about to stray, the pastors will counsel, rebuke, and discipline in order to save him from his error. It's a protection Jon chose for himself, and it may at least slow him down.

I would resent it if he were in a great hurry. Catholic Mass is so different that I can't imagine myself rushing into it. If, in conscience, Jon wanted to become a Catholic and honestly couldn't wait, I don't know how we would deal with the children. How can parents predict what a decision like this is going to do to their family?

Another concern is the wrong ideas that the kids pick up elsewhere about Catholics and then repeat. If Jon becomes Catholic, I don't want them thinking those things about him; he is their dad. They might end up considering him a traitor, having gone over to the "other side." Twenty years ago, I didn't think I would ever have to face such complicated questions.

Growing up, my contact with Catholicism was very limited. I had a Catholic friend in high school and went to Mass once or twice with her. I remember attending a Catholic wedding with Jon, shortly after we were married. Growing up in an Assembly of God church you don't drink or smoke, dance, or play cards. I was about twenty-three when Jon and I went to his friend's wedding, and there was a keg of beer at the reception afterward. Even the priest in his Roman collar was drinking. I thought, "What kind of church is this? He's drinking!" It certainly reinforced my ideas about those "worldly Catholics."

I have a few Catholic relatives, but we didn't have a lot of contact. Unless I was very sure the Catholic Church was the one true religion, it would be very hard for me to convert, especially because of my mom. When you grow up in your parents' church your whole life, it's hard for them to see you change. My mom is seventy-nine, and I don't want to hurt her. I know she has Catholic friends who watched out for her when my dad died. Even now she meets with them once a month for Bible study. But when I was young, I would hear her say little things— for example, that the Catholic Bible has extra books— and I would say to myself, "That's wrong, because you're not supposed to add anything to the Bible." I didn't realize that Protestants were the ones who took them away, and I would like to read them sometime.

I feel that both Protestants and Catholics are focused on Jesus Christ, but I wonder about the conversions between Catholics and Protestants. Yes, there are Protestants becoming Catholic, but there are also Catholics becoming Protestant. Who knows which side has the truth? Perhaps there are a lot of Catholics becoming Protestant because they don't actually understand their own Church's teachings. Certainly as a Protestant I have many questions.

For instance, I don't go along with honoring Mary and praying to her. I know there is the Scripture, "All generations shall call me blessed," so that's fine. It is important that she's the mother of Jesus, but to me she seems to be overemphasized. I don't understand saints very well either. I have heard it explained that we are asking them to pray with us, not that we are praying to them, and if they are strong in a certain area, they can help us where we are weak. That doesn't come easily to me, although I like the idea that they are still part of the body of Christ.

I hear Protestants object to Catholics calling priests "Father," but that doesn't bother me. After all, Jesus didn't mean that we couldn't even call our own fathers "father." I actually have more of a problem with Protestants calling ministers,

"Reverend," because we revere Christ and God, but we don't revere men.

Confession I have only seen on TV. I believe accountability is good, but if the priest says, "Go say fifty Hail Marys," I don't get it. Perhaps it's to put your repentance into action, but sometimes it looks like a punishment. I can see it as an act of repentance that depends on the heart condition of the person; so I suppose a priest has to be part psychologist to know how to give the person a meaningful action to perform.

We Protestants don't believe purgatory is biblical, but now I realize that the Catholic Church also depends on Tradition. I don't know how this particular tradition came about, so I don't have a firm opinion on that yet, although I assume there is a connection to the early Church beliefs. Protestants supposedly stick with the Bible only, but they still can create their own traditions and even make a new religion out of them, so perhaps they shouldn't criticize tradition quite so fiercely.

What about liturgical worship? My kids say, "Why would you want to listen to a man who wears a dress?" We answer, "It's not a dress, it's a robe. And it has a lot of symbolic meaning." Although I don't understand a lot of the symbols, I do know that Catholicism kept these symbols alive for fifteen hundred years before the Reformation, and people who couldn't read learned through the symbols, the stained-glass windows, and by hearing the preaching. They couldn't go home and read their Bibles; Bibles were very rare, even among those who could read.

I appreciate it that the Catholic service is filled with meaning; you're not doing things just because somebody arbitrarily chooses it. I prefer a certain formality to church service, but I also enjoy a more intimate part of the service where the focus is on God and not on people. The emphasis should certainly not be, as it is in many churches these days, "Come to our church and see what God can do for you today!" So in a Catholic church, if you know the meaning behind the standing up and kneeling, and other liturgical actions, you can worship God more reverently.

I was in high school when I last attended a Catholic Mass. The kneeling was new to me, and I remember that I wasn't allowed to take communion. The people giving memorized responses to what the priest would say was different. I'm sure that can get boring, especially for children—mine always say how boring church is. Our former church had candy and donuts for them, dramatic productions, and lively singing. I have to remind them that we are not in church to be entertained. No matter how prevalent that mentality is in our society, they have to get that out of their heads; we are there to worship.

For years, I had no idea that Catholics believed Christ was received in communion as really present. The first time I heard of that was about fifteen years ago in a pamphlet by Keith Green, and the way he explained it sounded incredibly disgusting. Since then, I have heard the Real Presence explained by a Catholic speaker, but it just didn't sink in. I would have to study and know more.

If Catholics believe their Church is the one true Church, do they think Protestants are going to make it to heaven? I've heard that we are seen as separated brethren, still part of their Church in a way. But it's hard for me to see how the Catholic Church could believe you are part of their Church without being baptized Catholic. It does make sense that not just anybody can give the Lord's Supper. It's partly historical, the way it has come down through the ages, and that's appealing to me. The idea of apostolic succession, that the authority of the apostles has been handed down without interruption, is very attractive to me. I know there was a lot of corruption at times in the Church, but I don't believe the corruption would make everything else nil down the line. I have to give some more thought to the idea of one true Church. Besides, there were various schisms through the centuries, which complicates things.

I see the Pope as a great person who does have authority

on earth. Perhaps a lot of Protestants maintain that the Pope is the antichrist. But anyone can see that he is doing good, and passing on the Word of Jesus Christ; so I don't believe he could be.

I respect the Catholic stand on abortion and family planning — children are a gift from God. People don't question families having many children if they are Catholic. I wonder why Catholic families are not as large as I remember when I was growing up, but I don't think the Catholic teaching on birth control is ever going to change, and I admire that immensely. Children are important! If you do need to space your children, abstinence is a discipline. And there's plenty of need for discipline and self-control in marriage.

Jon talked about Catholicism extensively with our pastor, and they would go back and forth over all the arguments. However, that pastor moved away and the newly arrived pastor is unaware of Jon's interest and reading. We had a pastoral visit last week, which meant that the pastor and a church elder came to our home. But nobody mentioned anything about Catholicism, even though the elder knows about Jon's interest. So I hope we're going to leave it like that for a while — it's better if Jon studies this quietly because if people find out you're studying it, they seem to attack you. At church, a friend gave Jon a book about how the papacy is corrupt. To me, Catholics are real people, and I can't stand it when they are put in a category to hate. I realize that our church is somewhat anti-Catholic, so as I consider it, I can see why it would be almost impossible for Jon to continue attending there. If people knew he was also going to Mass, it wouldn't be fair to him because everybody would try to argue with him about it. Even if it's from their sincere concern for a person's salvation, a lot of Protestants act like Catholics aren't going to heaven.

My hope for our family is that we will continue to serve and worship God together as Protestants. But since Jon will probably convert to Catholicism eventually, I hope that we can live together in harmony. Jon could easily create an atmosphere of constant tension by continually trying to persuade me to become a Catholic. I trust he wouldn't put Protestants down or try to argue a lot. It wouldn't bother me if one of the kids wanted to go to Mass with Jon. I wouldn't mind going along occasionally, either, and would try to be supportive about it, since Christians shouldn't be set against one another. Even though Sunday morning worship would change, and it would be very sad not to worship together, I hope the rest of the week would not change much for our household.

This is my prayer: that Jon and I will learn to accept each other where we are spiritually. May we focus not on our differences, but rather on loving, obeying, and pleasing God, loving others, and becoming more Christlike. May he help us each to love and serve him by living a Christian life and being godly, loving parents. And may God bring our children into a deep and lasting relationship with him, full of trust, obedience, and joy.

Chapter 9

A House Divided

by Michael J. Bolesta, M.D.

I do not remember October 24, 1954, and it would be forty-four years before I would thank God for that special day. On that day, the firstborn son of a young Roman Catholic couple was born of water and the Spirit. I was baptized at the Church of St. Peter in Kirkwood, Missouri. My father, Edward, eldest of three, was raised by a poor Polish coal miner and his Lithuanian wife in Pennsylvania. He embraced his faith and matured under the Jesuits of St. Louis University. A quiet man, he lived his faith in the loving way that he raised his family of five, and practiced dentistry. My mother, Mary (née Lorenz), youngest of three daughters among ten children, was raised by two Austrian immigrants who farmed the rich land outside of Fargo, North Dakota. Her faith formation was strong throughout her childhood.

My parents were faithful in attending Mass every Sunday and holy day. I cannot recall other parish activities, but in those days the laity was not as prominent as today. Along with the older of my four siblings, I attended parochial school. As was the custom at the time, I received Christ in the Blessed Sacrament for the first time in first grade and was confirmed in the second. While I have a dim recollection of the Latin Mass, by the time I could serve at the altar (we were still called altar boys), Vatican II had permitted worship in the vernacular, so I learned the responses in English. My other involvement was a long stint in the parish Boy Scout troop.

My parents had concerns about science education in the parochial school, so they decided to move their five children into the public school, delaying my crossover one year so that I could complete eighth grade. I am grateful for the eight years of catechesis, but unhappily, it abruptly ceased once I entered high school. While I continued sacramental life with my parents and four siblings, there were no high school CCD (Confraternity of Christian Doctrine) classes or youth group.

In high school, my thirst for meaning and purpose grew. I recall reading eastern mystics and dabbling with yoga, though I felt no attraction to Hindu deities. Though I would not have quoted him at the time, the words of St. Augustine aptly described my state: "You have made us for yourself, O Lord, and our hearts are restless until they rest in you."

Early in my senior year I met a small group of evangelical Protestants. One young woman told me that she and her mother had left the Catholic Church. When I found myself romantically attracted to her, I was told that Christians were not to be "unequally yoked together with unbelievers," referring to St. Paul's proscription in 2 Corinthians 6:14; she did not consider me to be a Christian. Not understanding, I asked for an explanation and was given a booklet entitled "God's Plan of Salvation." On October 23, 1972, I read the tract, checking references in our Catholic family Bible. As a Catholic, I held the Sacred Scriptures to be the very Word of God. The verses I now read seemed to support the Protestant notion of salvation. This message was different from what I had been taught, but seemed to be true. That night I asked Christ to be my personal Lord and Savior. He and his work were more alive to me than ever before. While I was overjoyed, my parents were not. I shared the tract with them, but they rejected it, forbidding me to speak of such things with my sister and brothers. I was forced to find solace in the small group at school. They were of different Protestant denominations, but held to basic core beliefs, knew the Scriptures, and, most importantly, they knew and loved Christ. To the eyes of a teen, this was a stark contrast to many I saw within the Catholic Church. I was grieved by my perception that I had never heard the Gospel, at least not clearly. And many at Mass seemed only to go through the motions. I could not see Christ in their lives. An idealistic youth perceived not Jesus in them, but hypocrisy. I had become a Protestant.

Nonetheless, I loved my parents, and sought to honor and obey them. My father nearly disowned me, but Mom reconciled herself to my change, finding solace in that I still had faith, albeit different from hers. I think that she clung to the Vatican II teaching that Protestants are separated brethren. Once I left for college, I split my time, attending Saturday evening Mass and worshiping on Sunday with my friends at an Evangelical Free Church. My major involvement was in Intervarsity Christian Fellowship on the campus of the University of Missouri. Through these loving Christians, I learned the disciplines of daily Scripture reading and study, and private prayer. I also met a staff member of IVCF whose family, like mine, was Catholic. It was clear in his experience, and in mine, that one could be Catholic and Christian. Many Catholics would laugh, if they did not become angry, to hear that many Protestants believe that Catholics are not Christian. I did not believe that the Catholic Church was the healthiest or easiest place to be Christian, but it was certainly possible. This small concession was the start of the long journey home. As I attended Mass, I recognized how much Scripture is laced throughout the liturgy. I could worship at the Eucharist even though I denied myself the Bread of Life. At that point I much preferred the Protestant worship service, and I prayed that my parents and siblings would be saved.

As time passed, my attendance at Mass became infrequent, occurring only when my parents visited or when I returned home to St. Louis. My church membership was in the Evangelical Free Church in Columbia, Missouri. In that congregation's singles group I met Sharon Farris, a godly woman who grew up in a Southern Baptist church.

Shari's mother grew up in a Brethren church in Kansas. This small Protestant denomination sought to pattern its simple worship upon the descriptions of the early Church found in Acts and the Epistles. They held to *sola fide* and *sola scriptura*, viewed through the lens of dispensational theology. Faith, not works, saves a person. If they could not find something in the Bible, they would not accept it as Christian. There were no ordained clergy and no sacraments. Elders, men of the congregation, would read a passage of Scripture, and then speak on it. Baptism and the Lord's Supper were observed as ordinances of Christ, not as means of grace. The people of these congregations are typically pious, industrious, and sincere. Most would view Catholics as trapped in superstition and hopelessly attempting to earn salvation.

Shari's father grew up in a small Baptist church in rural Kansas. They had ordained ministers, but like the Brethren, they had only the two ordinances, baptism and the Lord's Supper. People were baptized after they made a profession of saving faith in Jesus Christ. In their belief, it is felt that this profession leads to rebirth and salvation, and that baptism does not bestow grace or rebirth. It is simply an act of obedience. The Lord's Supper is seen not as Christ's body and blood, but as a memorial service, commanded by the Lord. Like the Brethren, Baptists believe in the classic Protestant concepts of *sola fide* and *sola scriptura*. They ask people to make decisions to follow Christ by publicly walking the aisle to profess faith. This occurs during what is called an altar call, though altars are not for the holy sacrifice of the Mass, but simple tables to hold the Lord's Supper.

Shari's father became a veterinarian, serving in the European theater of the Second World War. After this, he and his wife settled in Morristown, Tennessee. They joined the First Baptist Church, where they were devoutly active for fifty-three years. Shari was their only child. In those days before the Second Vatican Council, Protestants and Catholics tended to keep to themselves, not considering one another as true disciples of Christ. Furthermore, Catholics were in the minority in the Bible Belt. But they were not absent; Shari recalls seeing a group of nuns in the old, traditional habits, and wondering what sort of people they were. When John F. Kennedy was assassinated, she remembers a childhood friend pulling out her rosary to pray for the repose of his soul. This friend and Shari both evangelized another child who did not attend church, one sharing the Church, the other sharing the Bible. While Shari was solidly Baptist, she was intrigued by the mysterious Church with its ancient rites and traditions.

She studied elementary education at Stephen's College in Columbia, Missouri. In the turbulent 1960s she was one of the few who worshiped on Sundays, visiting a variety of Protestant churches. She dated, but did not join the sexual revolution. After graduation, Shari taught second grade for one year in Atlanta, but returned to Columbia where she taught first grade for eight years. I was finishing medical school when we met. We quickly bonded, becoming engaged after a brief courtship. I was out of Columbia on medical externships for several months, so much of our relationship developed by letter and by telephone. Both of us had prior broken engagements, so we knew what the pitfalls were, and what to look for in a mate. On December 26, 1980, we decided to marry, but did not tell anyone for a while, lest they think we were rash. Yet our plan to marry in June forced us to share our joy with surprised family and friends. Shari's parents were initially concerned about my Catholic background, but were assured that I was a strong Christian. I did not consider myself Catholic in any sense. My parents quickly accepted Shari. We married on June 6, 1981, in the Columbia Evangelical Free Church. Interestingly enough, we asked the minister to let us celebrate the Lord's Supper, something that is not routinely part of Protestant weddings. Perhaps we subconsciously desired to receive him who blessed the wedding in Cana so long ago, though we did not believe in the Real Presence at the time.

After our honeymoon, we moved to Durham, North Carolina, where I spent six years of residency in orthopedic surgery. We sought a church of Bible-believing evangelicals. After a brief time in a Christian and Missionary Alliance church, we joined a Presbyterian church. Our son was born and dedicated there. Though Presbyterians practice infant baptism, we held to a belief that baptism should occur after the age of accountability was reached and a personal profession of faith was made, and we were accommodated. Later I became a deacon, a lay position in that denomination. But all was not well. The denomination had some liberal tendencies that we did not think were biblical and the pastor seemed to be acceding to the hierarchy rather than to Scripture. We spoke at length with him, but had to part ways, agreeing to disagree. This grief was heightened when another Presbyterian pastor failed to accept us into his congregation once he learned of our ties to the first Presbyterian church.

My training then took me to Case Western Reserve University in Cleveland, Ohio. We looked for a church where we could heal during my one-year fellowship. Many of the congregations representing the major Protestant denominations seemed liberal and dead. One nondenominational church, meeting in a high school auditorium, was alive and biblical; but it was a long way from our home, and I kept falling asleep in the comfortable seats during the lengthy sermons. In desperation, Shari suggested that we visit an Episcopal church located a few blocks from our rental home. Shari fell in love with the Anglican liturgy. At last she felt that she could worship and not be limited to a sermon bracketed by a few songs. As the Episcopal worship service shares many similarities to the Roman Catholic rite, I had an eerie sense of *déjà vu*. That church was a perfect place to heal, and we found ourselves on the Canterbury Trail. I ended up staying on the Case Western faculty for five years and we moved to another Episcopal church, where we taught Sunday school and where on December 31, 1989, Shari was confirmed. I was received into the Anglican communion, and I served as lay catechist and vestryman, the latter position akin to that of a parish council member. Our son was baptized there and we were quite happy.

It was not perfect, however. Shari's parents took her to task. Though Episcopalians are Protestant, their worship is Catholic in form, and that disturbed them. They never approached me, but suspected that I was to blame for this apparent apostasy. She assured them that the decision was mutual and that she chose to be Episcopalian. Nonetheless, the Protestant Episcopal Church of the United States was hard to defend. It was busy ordaining women and those actively engaging in homosexual practices. Many practiced contraception and accepted abortion. Renegade Episcopal bishops and priests defied church law by blessing same-sex relationships as they would a marriage. Frustrated, we joined a group that supported and promoted historical orthodoxy. Having tasted liturgy, we could not return to sermon-based worship.

When we entered the Episcopal Church, I had been Protestant for fifteen years. My theology and worldview remained solidly evangelical. Entrance into the Anglican communion put us on the *via media* and we were curious whether there were other evangelicals among us. Being avid readers, we turned to books. Perhaps the author most celebrated by both evangelicals and Anglicans is C. S. Lewis; a hero to evangelicals, they seem to forget that he was Anglican and that he accepted the Catholic dogma of purgatory. Anglicans loved his beautiful prose. If this scholarly, wise man was Anglican, then so could we be.

From my Intervarsity days, I knew that John R. W. Stott and J. I. Packer were Anglican. As for converts there was Robert Webber. We greatly enjoyed his *Evangelicals on Canterbury Trail*, a collection of testimonies by evangelical Protestants who had discovered the wonders of worshiping God through ancient liturgy. We resonated with Thomas Howard in his *Evangelical Is Not Enough*. As we read, we found that we were not alone, that it was quite respectable to be Anglican, even if all Anglicans were not evangelicals. However, we found it curious that Thomas Howard did not remain an Episcopalian. In fact, Ignatius Press, a Catholic apostolate, published his book. In the epilogue to *Evangelical Is Not Enough*, he reports his reception into the Roman Catholic Church. Though we were at home with liturgical worship and weekly communion, I could not fathom such a move. The Tiber might as well have been the Pacific. Shari, though, could see the day when we might be Catholic or perhaps Orthodox.

Michael, our only child, has no recollection of attending the Presbyterian Church. He came to faith in Christ through the Episcopal Church. Since he was not baptized as an infant (something Shari and I agree we would do differently now), he needed to take that step before he could receive communion. On May 17, 1992, he was baptized and received his first communion in the Episcopal Church. It was incredibly moving to hear our eight-year-old personally renounce Satan and all his works, and affirm the Apostles' Creed. He loved the liturgy and looked forward to communion. Transubstantiation is not widely accepted among Episcopalians; those who consider the matter at all probably hold to consubstantiation. Some may even see the communion as no more than a memorial. During our time as Episcopalians, Michael, Shari, and I came to see Christ present in the Eucharist. As I progressed in my reading of Roman Catholic Church teaching, I learned that the Anglican schism broke the apostolic succession (something the Anglican communion denies) and hence the Church does not recognize their orders and sacraments, save baptism, as valid. Nonetheless, communion is something Michael cherishes. Even before I reverted, participating in Catholic Mass was problematic because he wanted to go forward to receive. Having him read the guidelines from the Catholic bishops of the United States, reprinted in many missals, was of little help. The practice of most Episcopal parishes is an open table. That is, any baptized Christian is invited to communion regardless of the person's understanding of the sacrament. While Catholic practice is perfectly logical given the Real Presence, it rankles many Protestants, especially egalitarian Americans and teenagers.

Some twenty years had passed since my Protestant conversion. My changing perspective had softened my heart. My prayers for my parents were answered, but in a way I had not foreseen. I wrote a long Father's Day letter to my father, thanking him for both spiritual and physical life, for a foundation of faith that was finding maturity in his eldest child. Happily, we could reconcile after two decades of pain, and before his untimely death a few months later, in the fall of 1992.

In June 1993, our family moved to back to Columbia, Missouri, for a year. We were still committed Episcopalians, and options were limited in that small community. So we did visit a variety of other churches. There was a lively Catholic parish that we visited on occasional Saturdays. Although we had visited Catholic parishes in Cleveland, it was a rare event. In Columbia, we became more comfortable with Catholic liturgy. We continued this practice even after we left that community.

When we arrived in Dallas in 1994, I wanted to find an Episcopal parish that was orthodox. While Shari shared that goal, as a mother of a child approaching the teen years she saw the need to find a congregation with a solid youth program. She put that ahead of denomination, so we visited a wide variety of Protestant congregations, including nondenominational Bible churches. I appreciated some of the teaching from the pulpit, but the worship itself was nothing even close to the grandeur of a Eucharistic celebration. I did not need to protest, because Michael let us know that we were Episcopalian and needed to find an Episcopal church. That was part of his identity. Happily we found an Episcopal parish with a good youth program. We became quite involved and happy in this Episcopal church for several years. Shari and I taught Sunday school; I served as a lay reader and chalice bearer. Shari developed a network with several women. Michael was an acolyte and choir member. He was confirmed there on October 27, 1996. Active in the Scout troop sponsored by the parish, he advanced rapidly. In June 1997 he completed his Eagle Scout project by fingerprinting many of the children of the congregation. We were unaware of the storm clouds gathering on the horizon.

We kept reading and praying. The "communion of saints" came to be a favorite phrase in the Nicene Creed. For many Protestants there is a huge gap in Church history between the Book of Acts and the Reformation. We took great comfort in the mystical union with our ancient sisters and brothers. This led me to delve into Church history. I found to my surprise that liturgy appeared very early in the Church. Indeed, the more I read the more the early Church looked less and less like a nondenominational Protestant church and more like the Catholic Church. And these histories were written by Protestants! Professing the Nicene Creed week after week implanted it in my soul. It came crashing into my consciousness . . . "the one, holy, catholic, and apostolic Church." What was the meaning of that adjective, "catholic"? It means universal, and I knew Christ's body to be universal. Yet could it mean Catholic, as in Roman Catholic? I shuddered. Historically such a notion made sense. Intellectually it made sense. In contrast, Henry VIII's break with Rome over his unfruitful marriage was scandalous, despite the gloss of Anglican historians. As John Henry Newman put it, "To be deep in history is to cease to be a Protestant." It is to be Catholic.

Another factor in my journey was unity. Our Lord's high priestly prayer "that they may all be one" (John 17:21) struck a chord within. At one time, I celebrated the Reformation as a great moment in history. I came to view it with profound sadness as a tragedy that must break the heart of our heavenly Father. Our Savior must weep at this calamitous divorce. As I delved into the historical and theological foundations for *sola fide* and *sola scriptura*, I was chagrined to learn how untenable they were.

Our reading brought us to others besides Thomas Howard who had crossed the Tiber River. We read Scott and Kimberly Hahn, Peter Kreeft, and Steve Ray, to name a few contemporary converts. I also read works by Cardinal John Henry Newman, the brilliant British Anglican of the nineteenth century whose quest to discredit Catholicism convinced him of its truth.

Thomas Howard testifies that he read himself into the Church. I resonate with that, but he adds that many had been praying for him. Community, the communion of saints, is a mighty tool and gift of God. It was our Lord who then brought people directly into our lives. Shari was good friends with the Palm family of Columbia, Missouri. David Palm, a graduate of Trinity Evangelical Seminary, shocked his parents by converting to Catholicism. Early in 1997 Shari telephoned him and obtained his e-mail address. David and I began an electronic dialogue. Shortly thereafter, he asked if his wife, Loreen, and child, Christopher, could stay with us in April. They wished to attend a seminar sponsored by the Young Serran Community of Dallas. It was a dialogue between Protestant and Catholic scholars, discussing *sola fide*, *sola scriptura*, and meaning of the Eucharist. We were delighted to entertain the Palms, and attended several of the events together. Shari and I thought that the Catholic apologists clearly had stronger cases. She still had reservations, but I was convinced.

After that visit, David and I continued our correspondence. He patiently answered my questions and prayed for me. My prayer and reading intensified. I found the *Catechism of the Catholic Church* to be a masterpiece, in which I found wondrous treasures. Shari became a bit uneasy. She wanted me to slow down. Before, she had been far ahead of me, seeing Catholicism in the future, but in an undefined way. She felt no rush. Her parents were aging, and to her there was no point in upsetting them any more than they had been by the move to the Episcopal Church. Before, it was I who could not see us as Catholic. Now I could clearly see that the Church the Lord Jesus founded was and is the Catholic Church. Historically, intellectually, emotionally, and spiritually I was persuaded. To me, not to revert was inconceivable. Loyalty to Christ demanded action. To quote Jerry Rouse, the Protestant minister who had married us, "Delayed obedience is disobedience."

On the feast of the Assumption, August 15, 1997, I contacted Father Gerald Hughes, rector of St. Rita Catholic Church, the parish Shari and I visited most often for Saturday evening Mass and the one I intended to join. I thought that he would counsel and question me, offer the sacrament of reconciliation, and receive me back into the sacramental life of the Church. I was shocked when Father Hughes suggested that I go through the Rite of Christian Initiation of Adults program. I gently demurred, pointing out that I had already been baptized and confirmed in the Church. I recalled that David and Loreen Palm had simply been received without the RCIA. It did not seem fair to me or to Shari, when I shared my disappointment with her.

Father Hughes was acting as my shepherd, in a sense as Christ's surrogate. He wisely reasoned that my eighteen years as a cradle Catholic were with a child's faith. He wanted me to develop an adult faith. Later I recalled the words of J. I. Packer as he spoke to my Intervarsity Christian Fellowship group on Mark 10:17-22, the encounter of Jesus and the rich young ruler. "It is Jesus' privilege to make special demands of certain people." So I obeyed.

At Advent, the RCIA group made the initial commitment to enter the Church. On the advice of our deacon, the RCIA program director, I stopped receiving communion in the Episcopal Church. That added some strain to our family relationship that was diffused by my going to the rail to kneel with them, even though I did not partake of the elements. Our pattern was to attend the Saturday evening anticipatory Mass and on Sunday the Episcopal liturgy.

For me, Advent was good, but Lent was profound. My hunger for the Blessed Sacrament grew, and I bonded with the RCIA group. What I learned intellectually through the RCIA could have been learned more efficiently through books and articles. Something wonderful did come out of the RCIA, though, and that was my integration into the community. Many Protestants enjoy strong and wonderful fellowship, but the emphasis on personal salvation combined with rugged, American individualism can lead to a private "Jesus and me" religion. The time of learning and sharing together, sharing rites and worship, going on retreats, being sponsored by a mature parish member — all of these things combined to graft me into the community of St. Rita. It was difficult not to partake of the Blessed Sacrament once I knew who it is, and had made the decision to revert.

Holy Week transported us, and we walked with our Lord in his last week. My mother and a brother from St. Louis joined us for the Triduum, the three days before Easter. Another brother, from Tyler, Texas, came for the Easter Vigil. Shari and Michael, along with my relatives, shared our joy that holy night. We were joined by a friend from our Episcopal parish who presented me with a rosary that she had bought in Jerusalem earlier that year. There was a special joy at the Easter Vigil, April 11, 1998, in joining the newly baptized catechumens and the freshly confirmed at the Table of the Lamb. I would not trade it for the world.

But what of Shari? Our time before and during the RCIA was like being on a roller coaster. As I indicated, she had been ahead of me on the trail to Canterbury, and from Canterbury toward Rome. But she was not prepared to cross the Tiber yet. She still has a few lingering questions, mainly about our Blessed Lady. And she wished to honor her parents, to avoid hurting them. As I began the RCIA, she confronted me, saying, "I thought we were one." Indeed, by the biblical norm of

Genesis 2:24, endorsed by our Lord (Matthew 19:5, Mark 10:8) and affirmed by St. Paul (1 Corinthians 6:16, Ephesians 5:31), we are one. I could have countered that as spiritual head of the family I could insist that she and Michael must become Catholic with me (Ephesians 5:22-24). Of course St. Paul goes on to instruct husbands to love their wives as Christ loved the Church (Ephesians 5:25), a standard that I routinely fall short of. Our answer was one of mutual love and respect (Ephesians 5:21-33). I would not impose the conviction of my conscience upon Shari, and she in turn would give me the freedom to obey the prompting of the Holy Spirit. I gave her the freedom to wait while she did not impose on me her desire to wait.

It was not without struggle, however. As the RCIA progressed and my resolve to enter the Church increased, Shari cried once again that we were one and asked why I could not wait. At the same time, we were struggling with problems in our Episcopal church, so I did not hesitate to offer her the "solution" of joining me. Michael was having a conflict with the Boy Scout troop sponsored by the Episcopal parish. The leaders of the troop would not approve his promotion to the rank of Eagle Scout. The rector of the Episcopal parish was either unwilling or unable to help us through the painful ordeal. Despite our prayers and appeals, doors shut at every turn. Providentially, Shari and I seemed to suffer more than Michael. Finally, late in 1997 we confronted the rector with our disappointment in the Boy Scout troop and in his handling of the affair. I told him of my intent to reenter the Catholic Church. We planned to worship as a family at both St. Rita Catholic Church and in the Episcopal community. Shari and Michael would remain members there because the youth program was meeting Michael's needs. This proved to be a temporary settlement.

Our split arrangement continued through the spring while I completed *mystagogia* (Greek for "initiating into the secrets"), part of the RCIA program. I did stop going to the communion rail at the Episcopal parish, and both Shari and Michael accepted this as appropriate. After Pentecost, another change occurred. The youth program slowed for summer. Shari was feeling more and more disaffected with various aspects of the parish, so I accompanied my family on Sunday visits to various Episcopal parishes. It has not been easy to find a good fit. One large parish has a majestic service, reminiscent of the old High Mass, which Shari gravitates toward; but the youth group's schedule conflicts with Michael's Scout troop meetings. Another parish has a strong youth group, but the Eucharist is "low church," not to Shari's tastes. Though it is some distance from our home, Shari and Michael saw the latter congregation as the better choice.

Our prayers about the Scouting problem, including many a Rosary, were eventually answered. Michael joined another troop and was awarded his Eagle rank on July 16, 1998. In the fall of that year, I began teaching in the St. Rita CCD, so I stopped attending the Episcopal service. That is a mixed blessing. I miss worshiping with my family, but must admit that I felt growing uneasiness with liturgy outside the apostolic succession, alienated from Mother Church.

Also at this time, the next RCIA series began. I suggested that Shari "give it a try," But she was not ready. We both have had to forgive one another in love. In Scripture, it is common for a person or event to prefigure or model someone or something to come. For example, King David is a type of Jesus, circumcision is a type of baptism, and Esther is a type of our Lady. There is a sense in which our family is a type of the tragic Reformation split between Catholics and Protestants. It is difficult to bring Michael to Mass because he still wants to go to the altar for communion and I have to remind him that he is a separated brother, even as I go forward. Wisely, his mother takes him aside to light a candle before our Lady. I yearn for my family to come home to Rome. I cannot say how the story will end, though I have hope. Much prayer, mutual submission, love, friends, and God's grace — all these things have brought us this far, and grace shall bring us home. In the meantime, there is great consolation in being home, in receiving our Lord in the Blessed Sacrament, in being united with that great cloud of witnesses, *unam, sanctam, catholicam, et apostolicam Ecclesiam*, "the one, holy, catholic, and apostolic Church." May Jesus Christ be praised!

Chapter 10

As Christ Loved the Church

by Barbara G. Brown

In the summer of 1996 I began working as a proofreader for the publisher of *Sursum Corda* magazine. The first issue I proofread contained the story of the conversion to Catholicism of Tom Woods, the magazine's managing editor. Although I found his story interesting, I immediately took issue with his comparison of Protestant tradition to the hidden knowledge of Gnosticism. Pointing to the plethora of Protestant sects that have arisen since the time of the Reformation, Woods claimed that Protestant "attacks on ecclesiastical authority left the common man with no way of discerning which was the true Church and which were false ones. Only those with a strong theological background — akin to the Gnostics' 'hidden knowledge' — possessed a basis for judging whether they belonged to a church that could lead them to eternal life. Without a visible Church and hierarchy, how can the well-meaning but uneducated layman decide between a host of competing and often abstruse theological claims?"

Although I attempted to forget Woods's article, I was to find myself repeatedly confronting the same theme in the course of the next few months. By February of 1997, it was distressingly clear to me that the Lord seemed to be leading me to the Catholic Church. After several pointless and unsatisfying conversations, I had given up my attempts to discuss questions of church authority or sufficiency of Scripture with my Protestant friends. No one could answer my questions satisfactorily and my failure to accept unsatisfactory answers seemed to arouse suspicion and even anger. Many of my Protestant friends regarded Catholics as heathen and derisively referred to the Catholic Church as a "cult." I felt increasingly alone, as I realized that I was undergoing a conversion of heart and mind that was beyond my ability to explain.

I had read of the Coming Home Network in a back issue of *Sursum Corda* and had finally found the CHN web page on the Internet. On February 11, I reached Kenneth Howell by telephone and talked to him for over an hour. He reassured me that I wasn't losing my mind or my faith in Christ. We talked about my husband, Bruce, and my reluctance to tell him that I wanted to become Roman Catholic. I didn't know what his reaction would be, since I realized that he had little idea of the inner turmoil I'd experienced as I'd wrestled with the issues of church authority and Christ's Real Presence in the Eucharist. I hadn't meant to conceal from him my quest for truth, but the crisis had come upon me slowly and then with a certain relentless inevitability. I seemed suddenly to reach the point of no return and didn't know how to explain how I'd arrived.

My concern for Bruce was that the possibility of my conversion might damage his reputation as an elder in our Presbyterian Church in America congregation and perhaps even cost him his job at a local Presbyterian college. Kenneth encouraged me to find a good time to talk to Bruce and he promised to pray for us both. When he asked if I would allow him to share my name and e-mail address with a lady who had recently returned to the Church after several years as a Presbyterian, I readily agreed. At the end of the phone call, I felt relieved and yet apprehensive. I had finally confessed out loud that I wanted to become Catholic. It was as though I had crossed a boundary of some sort. A few days later, the first letter from Lynn Nordhagen, the lady Kenneth Howell had mentioned, showed up in my e-mail in-box. Lynn's correspondence became my lifeline. My letters to her allowed me to pour out the cries of my heart. Her prayers for us and her wise and gentle responses to my questions and my account of each day's struggle brought me much grace and gave me strength to stand firm in the Lord.

Almost two weeks after my first conversation with Kenneth, I still had not found an opportunity to break the news to Bruce that I was considering becoming Catholic. I knew that Lynn and Kenneth were both fervently in prayer for this, and I prayed for the fortitude to take this step.

I chose my moment when Bruce and I were driving back from the grocery store. Our children were at home, and, for once, we were alone in the car. After stammering and struggling to bring the conversation to the point, I finally just blurted out, "I don't know how to tell you this, but I think I want to become Roman Catholic." Bruce always thinks deeply and carefully before responding in conversation, so the silence that greeted this announcement wasn't unexpected. I tried to explain how I had become convinced, almost against my will, of the truth of the Catholic Church's claim to be the Church founded by Jesus Christ and possessing the full truth of the Gospel as preserved in Scripture and the Apostolic Tradition. It was a lot for him to take in all at once.

Later that evening he began to tell me what was in his heart. His reaction was neither anger nor fear, only a deep sadness. He was grieved that after so many years of walking in unity in the Lord, it appeared that I was beginning to travel a road that he might not feel led to follow. He had no strong prejudice against the Catholic Church, but he had never considered it as a destination. It was so very unusual for us to have any major issue in which we were not in agreement. I realized that this must seem so sudden to him, and I attempted to explain how I had been led down this road and why, until now, I had remained silent about the conflict I'd experienced.

Bruce and I had married in 1972, but had divorced in 1977. After our separation, we had each become Christian and had reconciled and remarried in a Protestant church. Our relationship from the time of our remarriage was one in which we strove to live according to the standards of the New Testament, each of us trying to love and serve the other in submission to Christ. We rarely had any conflict, and the few issues of contention that arose between us were soon resolved. We had experienced several major changes over the years, but we had been in nearly perfect accord in our decisions for almost twenty years. We regarded our family and our marriage as a gift from God, knowing what a disaster our life together had been when we had attempted to live apart from Christ.

Now, I had introduced a severe strain into our relationship, an element that threatened the bond between us. How could I embrace a belief that contradicted the Reformed faith that had become our foundation? Would we, like other mixed-faith couples we knew, simply have to "agree to disagree" and pretend that there was no real difference in conflicting truths?

Although it was the issue of church authority that had catapulted me into the search that led to the Roman Catholic Church, it was the belief in the Real Presence of Christ in the Eucharist that had won my heart and filled me with the longing for the consummation of the sacrament of Holy Communion. Could a love for Christ and a belief in his work of redemption be enough to hold us together if we could not agree on whether or not Christ could be truly present to us under the form of bread and wine in the sacrament?

How could I have come this far — to a point at which I felt there was no turning back — without having confided in the one with whom I had shared everything for the past twenty years? I could sense Bruce's hurt at having been shut out of my mind and my heart as I'd grappled with something so momentous; but as I described to him my frustration at not being able to discuss my questions with anyone we knew, receiving only unsatisfactory answers tinged with anger and suspicion, his sadness was for me.

I hadn't kept silent about my quest for truth from a desire

to deceive him, but rather from a desire to spare him the pain and frustration I'd known. When I'd first begun to question the assumptions we'd both taken for granted about our Protestant faith, Bruce had still been employed in a position that had become increasingly stressful for him. I had begun to fear that the stress of his job might eventually result in a heart attack, and I had prayed earnestly that the Lord would help him in his search for a better employment situation. It didn't seem right to add to his stress by telling him of my doubts about the foundations of our faith. I was still looking for the answer that would show me the fatal flaw in the claims of the Catholic Church. I didn't want to believe that the Catholic Church was truly the Church of Jesus and his Apostles, and I was hoping that I would find something that could restore my sense of confidence in the writings of John Calvin, who claimed to be following in the footsteps of Augustine, Athanasius, and the other early Christians.

By the time I'd read enough of the writings of the early Church to realize that the Church they described was found today in the teaching of the Roman Catholic Church, Bruce had begun his new job at a nearby Presbyterian college. The new job was wonderful, and I just didn't have the courage to dash it all to bits at the outset by bringing up the claims of the Catholic Church as a topic of dinner conversation. All the while, however, I could sense the struggle within my heart as I wrestled with my own obedience to God. If this was the Truth, why wasn't I following it? Having reached a point of personal crisis, I had no choice but to break my silence and shatter our peace. Bruce's reaction to me was so typical of his Christian character. He didn't threaten to divorce me (as I had feared more than once on sleepless nights), nor did he rail at me and denounce the Catholic Church. Deeply grieved by the thought that we might somehow lose the sense of unity that we'd known for so long, his response was to pray that wherever the truth was to be found, God would show us both.

His immediate concern was for me, for our marriage, and

for our relationship to the Lord. When I said that I didn't want to damage his reputation as an elder in our church by embracing doctrines that were antithetical to the Westminster Confession, he replied that he was not worried about his reputation — he wanted only for us to know and to be obedient to God's will. Since my desire to unite with the Church came to me only because I felt that God was demanding it of me, I prayed that he would show Bruce as clearly as I believed he'd shown me the direction we should take.

The next month was a time of wild fluctuation for us. At times Bruce seemed almost confident that the Lord was leading us into the Church. The second morning after I'd first spoken to him about the Catholic Church, he awoke with a Scripture from John 10 running through his mind. "My sheep hear my voice. I know them, and they follow me" (John 10: 27). He said at that point he could believe that our becoming Catholic could be truly the leading of God. He had had a long talk the day before with Ray Clark, a professor at the college who had served as an interim pastor at a church we'd attended for several years. Kenneth had suggested that Ray might prove to be a sympathetic counselor for us as we tried to discern our direction. On Ray's recommendation, Bruce and I had decided to read and study together the new *Catechism of the Catholic Church* so that we could know for ourselves what the Church teaches and the basis of her teaching. Only a few days later, Bruce returned home from an exhausting day at work and told me that he was deeply afraid that he would discover that he could never accept the teaching of the Catholic Church and that he would lose me as I proceeded on a journey that he could not join. The enemy always seemed to strike when we were likely to be tired or ill or somehow at a low point, bringing to the surface all sorts of untruths and distorted fears about the Church.

By God's grace, my response to these attacks was to pray harder and more often instead of resorting to argument. The Rosary had become a daily mainstay in my life, and I usually prayed five decades for Bruce as he took the forty-five-minute drive to work each morning. My prayer was always that God would lead us both into his truth and not allow us to remain in error or to be led astray.

Although by this time there were many people praying for us from a distance (mostly Catholics), very few people in our immediate proximity were aware of our investigation. A young man in our church called on the telephone one evening while we were at a Saturday evening Mass. When he asked my daughter where we'd gone, she replied that she didn't know. (At that point, we had not shared our questions with our children.) When we returned his call, he was very curious about where we'd been. Bruce told him that we'd been to the Catholic Church, and the young man replied that he had once been Catholic and would like to share some literature about the Catholic Church.

On Monday evening, Bruce came home very upset by the material that our friend had given him. It was a pamphlet that claimed to compare the truth of the Bible with the claims of the Catholic Church. I had recently finished reading Karl Keating's *Catholicism and Fundamentalism* (published by Ignatius Press), a gift from my Catholic employer. As I read through the pamphlet, I was struck by its similarity to the anti-Catholic materials described in Keating's book. The author made his charges against the Church by stating certain assumptions as though they were proven truths and then listing a number of Scripture references that seemed to agree with his assumption. Other charges were made by taking certain sentences and phrases from the *Catechism of the Catholic Church* completely out of their context and juxtaposing them so that they seemed to imply something quite different from their original intent. We read through the pamphlet together, comparing the citations to the actual quotations from the *Catechism* and to Scripture. It was obvious to us both that the author had badly twisted the citations in order to make his charges against the Church seem like the truth. Instead of being persuaded by the arguments in the pamphlet, our faith in the *Catechism* was strengthened because we understood for ourselves how the statements had been distorted. Although Bruce was once again at peace, we sensed that this was only the beginning of the opposition we'd experience.

When Bruce approached our pastor and the other elders to request a leave of absence so that he could, in good conscience, reevaluate his standing in regard to the doctrinal tenets of our denomination, they responded with anger and accusation. They unanimously regarded the situation as a "headship issue," and their primary instruction was that he should never have allowed me to bring Catholic materials (the magazines that I copyedit) into the house. They reminded him of his position as spiritual head of our household and told him that he should simply tell me that he wouldn't allow me or any member of his family to become Catholic. Bruce replied that our relationship was not based on domination, but on love and respect. His concern was not to control my thoughts but to obey God. He told them that I was submitting to him in asking him to pray and study with me. Reluctantly, they allowed him to step aside from his duties in serving our congregation so that we could have more time to read and study together and pray for discernment.

We had met Father Hepburn, the parish priest at the Catholic church nearest us. He had graciously offered us books from his own library that he thought we might find of interest. Although he had counseled us not to allow our investigation to consume our lives, our reading and study kept us preoccupied. All of our conversations seemed eventually to return to the Real Presence in the Eucharist and its centrality in the life of the Church of the Apostles and the early Fathers. In the meantime, we did share our questions and our search with our three children. We told them they should feel free to ask us anything or to tell us if they thought we were really missing the truth.

We also asked them to come to us if anyone tried to question them about our intentions; we did not want our children to be the targets of misplaced evangelical zeal. They began reading some of the books that had been given to us, and our daughter began her own study of Scripture, using a concordance that she borrowed from a friend.

One Saturday morning Bruce said that he wanted to apologize to me. He said that, although at the beginning of our study together he had wanted to discern the truth, at some point his focus had changed and he had begun looking for something in our reading that would show me that I was wrong. He said that the Lord had showed him his error and he asked my forgiveness. I was humbled to realize what a rare man my husband is, one who truly loves his wife as he loves his own body and as Christ loves the Church. I had promised him that I would not seek to join the Church on my own until he told me that he was certain that he could never join with me, and I wouldn't join if he felt that he couldn't allow it. I had thrown my hope of uniting with the Church on the mercy of God, trusting that he would somehow bring things right for us both. At that point, I still had no assurance that Bruce would want to join the Catholic Church, but I knew without a doubt that he would never deliberately hurt me, and that he would do whatever he believed God asked of him without attempting to salve his pride or protect his reputation.

Even though I thought that any resolution would be a long time coming, I was prepared to wait and pray. Many of the stories I'd read of converts to the Roman Catholic Church seemed to have transpired over a period of years. It had been less than a month since Bruce and I had had our first conversation about the Church, although we had been so intensely involved in our study of the *Catechism* that it seemed much longer. It must have seemed much longer to the elders of our church as well, because they began to hint that they thought Bruce had had enough time to convince me that I was wrong. They began bringing us new material to read to prove that the Catholic Church was apostate. Their insistence seemed to push Bruce to the point of resolution.

On March 16, Bruce decided that we could no longer hesitate between the Protestant and Catholic churches, as we were no longer in agreement with the doctrinal tenets of our denomination. Our reading of the *Catechism* and the Bible served to show us the beautiful truth of the Catholic faith. We didn't understand every point of doctrine, but the Lord had convinced us that the fullness of truth was to be found in the Catholic Church.

We arranged a meeting with Father Hepburn to ask him to instruct us for reception into the Church, and Bruce spent a good portion of the week composing a letter to our former pastor and the other elders announcing our decision to unite with the Roman Catholic Church. The question of when to deliver the letter to the elders was problematic. Our pastor had already told us the week before that he had had trouble writing the Sunday sermon because he had cried for days over our spiritual condition. We didn't feel that it would be fair to add to his grief late in the week when his congregational responsibilities were at their height. Bruce chose to wait until after the close of the morning service on the following Sunday.

On Palm Sunday, after most of the congregation had left, Bruce presented all of the elders with his letter announcing our decision to join the Catholic Church. The next day was the beginning of Holy Week. Our family attended all of the services for the Easter Triduum, culminating in the Easter Vigil Mass. As we watched the catechumens receive confirmation and First Holy Communion, our hearts were filled with joy to know that someday soon we, too, would be anointed with the oil of chrism and receive the true body and blood of Christ in the Eucharist.

The elders of our former church read Bruce's letter aloud to the congregation on the Sunday following Easter and publicly called us to repent for having abandoned the "Gospel in its biblical purity." Our prayer has been that we will be able to walk in true humility and that God will grant them the grace to see the Truth.

Father Hepburn gave us instruction throughout the summer of 1997 and on September 14, 1997, the feast of the Triumph of the Cross, all five of us were confirmed and received into full communion in the Catholic Church. For us, the journey into the Church has given us far more than we could have imagined or asked for. Like other converts before us, we are overwhelmed by the sense of having come home at last to find our place in "the one, holy, catholic, and apostolic Church." *Deo Gratias.*

Chapter 11

Joy and Sorrow

by Maxine Smith

Joy describes my new relationship with God. I feel I have abandoned myself to God in a way that is far beyond my previous level of commitment. By no means have I become perfect, but I now strive to be faithful in all things. Sorrow describes my disappointment in the fact that my husband, Bill, finds my conversion a bitter pill. I am deeply sorry to have caused him concern and embarrassment, but since I firmly believe my first commitment is to God I believe if I am to be faithful I have no other choice. The joy does indeed overcome the sorrow. It is like the Light that overcomes the darkness. I continue to hope that either Bill will eventually see the same message from God that I have seen, or that he will at least become reconciled to my faith. Nevertheless, if I must walk this current path for the rest of my life, I will. Even if the feeling of joy should disappear, I will remember it and continue to strive for faithfulness.

In consideration for the feelings of other family members I believe it is best to write anonymously even though my strong preference would be to write this openly.

My conversion really took place over a number of years, although I only became aware of it in the last few of those years. During this time of more intense searching I listened and talked with others, read and researched, pondered many questions, probed denominations, and fought hard against each answer that drew me closer to the Catholic Church. My search was made more urgent by the increasing liberalism I was encountering in our denomination and heightened awareness that lack of unity among Christians seriously eroded our Christian witness to the world. By the time I was received into the Church I was in my fifties.

I think one of the reasons my conversion took so long was that I simply wouldn't allow myself to consider it while I had young children. Nor could I have found the time to be mother, full-time employee, and do the necessary reading. I reasoned that if my husband were to convert to something I had no inkling of when I married him, and he tried to bring the children with him to that new faith, then I'd be understandably irate. I felt that part of the fidelity I owed to him was to raise our children in the faith that we'd both agreed upon from the beginning. I sometimes tried to discuss my concerns of deficiencies in our congregation and denomination, but while Bill might have shared my concerns he simply accepted things as they were. When the children had left for college, not only did I have more time to finish my search, I also felt freer to make the commitment.

I have heard his complaints regarding my conversion and I know he believes that having the children reach any particular level of maturity is not the real issue. The issue as he states it is that he didn't agree to marry a Catholic. He didn't agree to have his wife feel subject to a different religious system than his own. He didn't agree to go to church without me and to face the embarrassment of seeing his fellow parishioners who know his wife used to sit beside him in the familiar pew but is now at that Catholic church down the block. For him this is pain. For me there is an agony in knowing that it has caused him pain, but because I believe I owe my greater allegiance to my God, in my opinion it is really out of my hands.

Key factors in my search were my increasing inability to evangelize for my denomination for two reasons. First, they were moving in an increasingly liberal direction. For several years they had been ordaining women. Now the national church was enduring pressures to ordain practicing homosexuals and had recently been embarrassed by the release to the press of an interim report on sexuality that went far beyond the traditional stance in issues of accepting divorce, living together, and homosexual unions. They also sidestepped controversial issues like abortion. These were discussed, then the answer was simply left to individual consciences. At about the same time there was discussion about one pastor's proposal for modernizing the names for the Trinity. Although our pastor assured us this couldn't be passed, if it could be discussed, I wasn't so sure. All of this made me feel that my husband's church, which I'd willingly adopted early in our marriage, was abandoning the very principles that had made me believe it represented a firm faith.

Second was the lack of unity among Christians. I was accustomed to listening to evangelical coworkers discuss which denomination was right and how to properly interpret the Bible. They represented independent churches, which weren't part of a larger denomination. Sometimes such independent churches would band together with others to produce literature, support a church camp, support missionaries, etc. Yet these alliances were often realigned when disagreements developed and splits occurred. Such factionalism disturbed me and it was not unusual for new Christians to get annoyed with the divisiveness and drop out. Amid all of this I wondered how to invite a friend or new neighbor to my church when that person would have to pass the local Baptist and Catholic churches or Presbyterian and Episcopalian churches to get there. If I gave reasons why they shouldn't go to these closer churches instead, I was afraid I would be smearing my neighboring Christians and certainly wouldn't display the kind of Christian attitude that was likely to draw anyone to my church. On the other hand, I had difficulty trying to focus on an outstanding positive trait that I could use to attract them. Were we the most friendly? Did we have the best choir? Did our pastor give the best sermons? Did we have the best Sunday school, or the most convenient schedule, or any other distinguishing desirable feature? My mouth would go dry. This was difficult for me because I was raised with the expectation that Christians evangelized. As a child this was easy. We would simply invite someone to come one Sunday and hope they liked it and wanted to come back. In my childhood neighborhood there were three churches: Methodist, Baptist, and Catholic. We knew the Methodists and Baptists were both Protestant and the Catholics were different. Now as an adult there were seven denominations within a half-mile. Anyone on my block would pass two or three churches on the way to my church.

When I would try to discuss some of my frustrations with Bill, he might acknowledge my frustration, but he was a man with a strong dislike for disagreements and could not see that this meant we were in a flawed religious system. He was also someone who would rather enjoy life than get bogged down in trying to figure it out. I believe that, in his opinion, some of these issues were unfortunate, even upsetting, but that we weren't the ones in control so we shouldn't make waves by trying to fix the problems. In a nutshell, we were the followers, not the leaders.

My Christian upbringing emphasized learning God's truth and following it as faithfully as possible. This has always been my challenge and my call. When I was unable to align my denomination's new decisions with biblical teaching, I first reviewed both the biblical teaching and the denominational stand. Next, finding the alignment lacking, I looked at other denominations to assess their alignment. I didn't find good alignment until I finally looked at the one remaining Christian body — the Catholic Church. At first I thought it, too, was lacking. Then I realized my areas of disagreement were not points of liberalism or a lack of belief in the Real Presence (as with conservative Protestantism) — my problems were with the more specifically Catholic doctrines. Now, with trembling for fear that my findings might push me into the Catholic Church, I began to investigate the basis for these teachings. In the end I had to agree that these doctrines had a reasonable basis. This — taken in combination with my disappointing findings for the various Protestant denominations and my increasing appreciation for the teaching authority found only in the Catholic Church — convinced me that I had at last found truth. At this point there was no question in my mind that my only acceptable choice was to follow that truth. I could not continue to call myself Christian if I tried to accept a partial truth, and so at this point I really had no alternative but to join the Catholic Church.

When I began to see that by some strange coincidence the Catholic Church was the answer to many of my concerns, I tried to share these thoughts with Bill. He would get bored. It was too early or too late for a deep topic. He was too tired or had too much to do. In earlier days when the Catholic Church posed no threat to his household, he had always been more cordial toward Catholicism than I had been. When I saw it wasn't possible to talk to him, instead I talked with a close friend. Eventually I talked with Sara, my daughter and walking companion. At this time both she and her brother James were in college. When I saw myself being drawn closer and closer to the Catholic Church, I spoke with both children before speaking with Bill again. They were supportive, but when I spoke to Bill he made it clear I would be doing this without him.

I remember he laughed, "You? A Catholic?" His tone suggested, "This won't last long." He knew nothing of what I'd already discovered and simply saw the Catholic Church from the perspective of jokes and half-truths. Perhaps I was as much in my cocoon as he was in his. I naïvely thought, "Surely he'd join me within a couple of years. If he takes one look at what the Catholic Church really is, his conscience won't let him stay away." It's been five years now since I began the RCIA program and I'd say he is further from the Catholic Church than he's ever been.

At first he encouraged me to go to the RCIA and see how foolish the Catholic religion is, and to get the *Catechism* and just try to make sense of it. His knowledge of the Catholic Church was from the media or from complaining or ridiculing coworkers. He was convinced that the Catholic Church would disprove itself to anyone. I was already aware that there were formidable thinkers in the Catholic Church, both today and over the centuries. Whatever my decision was to be, I wasn't ready to dismiss the Catholic Church so lightly.

When I began reading books by Catholics, I saw a very different perspective than the media presented. Given the fact that I believed there were insurmountable problems with the doctrine and administration of our denomination, I was cautiously open to listening to what the Catholic Church said about various doctrines and practices. I was profoundly respectful of their position on abortion and what seemed to be a cautious approach to modernization. In learning more about the Catholic Church's pro-life position, I began to see that this was part of a whole fabric on marriage and family, human sexuality, the human psyche, and human society. All of this fit together masterfully in God's plan for us. I listened to what the Church said about purgatory. This also fit together well. Now I could no longer be sure of my former position.

One of the things that had deeply troubled me about our denomination was its manner for deciding issues of doctrine and practice. Deciding these issues in voting sessions seemed to me to only guarantee the will of the majority, not necessarily the will of God. If the Holy Spirit was guiding each Christian in each denomination, how could sincere, devout Christians end up in so many different denominations? The pieces simply didn't fit! I began to envy the clarity of the direction of the Catholic Church. Had it not worked well for all those years? I looked again at more issues that separated Protestants and Catholics. Was Mary conceived immaculate, and was she assumed into heaven body and soul? Long before I settled these issues I became scandalized at the faint treatment she was given throughout Protestantism. Didn't Scripture say, "All generations shall call me blessed"? How biblical was the Protestant position? If the Holy Spirit was not effective in guiding all the Protestant denominations into truth (and how many "truths" could there be?), might the Spirit be effective in guiding a single leader, the pope?

In the end it came down to what I was capable of knowing and understanding. When I finally believed I had found the truth, and had discussed it with my immediate family, I was convinced that I would have to answer unfavorably to God if I didn't follow my conscience. I was prepared to accept any consequences for the promised peace of God. I told my siblings of my plans when I was in the RCIA. They basically said that was my choice. Some of Bill's' siblings have tried to help him accept my decision. He will occasionally admit to me that they tell him he just has to accept the fact that I'm Catholic, but then he will say he can't do it.

Shortly before I began the RCIA program, for personal reasons Bill joined a different congregation and took their six-week instruction class for new members. He constantly reminded me that most members of the class were former Catholics. I asked him how many were divorced. He said most of them, maybe all of them. I countered that I felt this meant they were choosing this denomination as a matter of convenience, not necessarily as a matter of conviction.

One source of constant agitation for my husband was an evangelical coworker and seminarian. He was a sincere Christian, but he constantly challenged Bill to reclaim his position as a Christian husband and head of the household and require me to be obedient, that is, leave the Catholic Church. Sometimes the coworker would supply Bill with tracts, videos, and cassette tapes that "disproved the Catholic Church." One such video attacked (1) the Real Presence, (2) the "idolatry" of praying to the saints, (3) Mary, "the fourth person of the Trinity," and (4) papal infallibility. Since Bill believes in the Real Presence he found their first argument to be totally absurd. Nevertheless he cheered the other three issues, insisting that the tape must be right about those issues or why would they have said it!

As a brief aside, I did discuss several doctrinal differences with the coworker. As you might expect, no one really won. I believe, however, that I opened his eyes to the fact that there was a lot more in the Bible to support Catholic doctrine than he had been aware of. I also noticed that during the UN Cairo conference, he recognized and appreciated that, due to the Catholic Church's unique position of holding a small piece of land that made the Church a political state, the Church was able to send a representative to this conference. Thus the Church alone was able to argue the Christian position on abortion and birth control, which also concerned my spouse. I think he now has a small measure of respect for the Catholic Church.

Bill and I have had many arguments about religion. Unfortunately I felt that his aim wasn't to understand my position better, or even to challenge me with facts, but rather to try to use some peculiar quote or method that, like magic, would simply break the spell that the Catholic Church had placed upon me. Whenever he lost ground in these discussions his retort was to claim I'd been brainwashed. It is challenging to face criticism that is simply goal-oriented. The intent isn't to discuss and know, or to find the truth, but simply to disprove you by whatever means it takes.

I think he was either denying to himself that I would really become Catholic or he simply believed his own words, that the Catholic Church would disprove itself. He was patient while I attended the RCIA and he often joined me for the weekly *Catechism* program taught by Bishop David Foley on EWTN (Eternal Word Television Network). Up until a couple of weeks before the Easter Vigil he seemed to think I would back out. Then he panicked. He wanted us to meet with one of the priests.

I called the rectory to make an appointment. It was suggested that we meet with the priest who was himself a convert, since he might have a better understanding of Bill's position. At that meeting Bill pleaded with me not to join the Catholic Church. I was unable to comprehend how a follower of Luther, who had claimed to rely on his conscience to guide him in his break with the Catholic Church in the sixteenth century, could now insist that I not follow my conscience. Although Father suggested that I might want to wait a year, I felt a strong urge to complete my decision. Somehow I felt that God had work for me to do that required that I be Catholic. That evening Bill reluctantly gave me his permission.

When the evening of the Easter Vigil arrived, he could not believe I would really do this. I left the house with his bitter words ringing in my ears. I don't recall his exact words, but I believe he said that if I loved him I would stay home and not do this. From the time I had told God I would accept this as his will, I had felt an immediate lifting of the burden I'd carried during many months of indecision. Had I not felt this I cannot say whether I would have continued. I was very concerned over Bill's reaction, but felt I should fulfill my commitment to God.

Sara, home from college for Easter, came with me to the Easter Vigil, but James's college spring break had been earlier. By the time we arrived for Mass I had buried my emotions as best I could. We had rehearsed earlier and I knew what to expect. The catechumens and candidates sat in the front pews on both sides. Sponsors sat in the second pews behind their candidates. The evening proceeded according to plan, but I was somehow numb. It was as if I were observing this from a high balcony rather than actually being there. By the time my daughter and I left for home, the Easter Vigil seemed somehow anticlimactic. It had happened and I was satisfied, but there were no fireworks. It had been a quiet evening with great ceremony and meaning, but I hadn't caught up to it yet.

Easter morning arrived and while I knew that the Vigil

Mass had fulfilled my Sunday obligation for Easter, I never-theless dressed for Sunday Mass. Bill and Sara were going to their Protestant church. Not being one to be satisfied with meeting minimum requirements, I, too, set out to celebrate the glorious Easter morn in worship. I arrived about ten minutes early and discovered the church was already quite full, but I found a mid-pew opening in about the eighth pew from the front and took my seat. More and more people were arriving and we were all squeezed closer together. I sat among total strangers but felt I was amidst a vast throng of fellow worshipers. For months I had sat against the side wall and remained in my seat during the distribution. Then at the Easter Vigil, along with the other candidates, we had been given Communion separately. But now when the usher came to our pew and people rose, I felt an inner glow as I got up, too. Now I was part of the People of God. How beautiful! It was on Easter morning that my feeling caught up with the events.

I have reflected many times on whether I made the best decision. I cannot know where I'd be with my faith nor where my relationship with Bill would be if I'd waited a year. I do know it would have been a year of agony for me. I had been open to discussing this from the time I first mentioned my concerns a few years back. Whether or not it was smart or right for me to proceed when he was obviously opposed I cannot say. I only know that the door had been open for discussion for a long time. In fact I tried to encourage discussion. I believe he felt that I'd been doing all this religious reading and he didn't stand a chance in dissuading me so there was no use talking about it. When the time came for me to move forward, he wanted to call a time-out. My response was to say we should have talked earlier.

Bill told me I was a fool to leave our little congregation where I had many friends. How could I find friends at a church with over two thousand members? I agree that friends are nice, but I didn't join the Roman Catholic Church for friends. As far as I could tell then, he was probably right that finding friends would be difficult. I've often heard it said the way to meet people is through your children. Mine were grown, so my prospects might be dim. I did, however, have a drive to be an active member of the parish. My first activity after joining the Church was to attend the monthly Nocturnal Adoration Society. This has become very dear to me and I rarely miss. When fall came, I joined the small Tuesday evening Bible study group. I soon became close friends with a couple of other women. Later I was involved with Renew and in this small group setting I got to know another circle of people. Now I know enough people that it's not unusual for me to be still standing out front talking to friends by the time people begin arriving for the next Mass.

Bill followed my reception into the Catholic Church with a long siege of comments. He said he felt betrayed. He was especially angry that we could no longer commune together and he insists to this day that the Catholic Church has come between us, that we are no longer truly married. He claims that to be married we must be one, and he asks, "How can we be one when we can't commune together?" His logic escapes me, but I recognize that he feels he has lost something very important.

I have tried in many ways to bridge the gap, but he usually rebuffs my attempts, although there have been a few isolated successes. Most of the time it has been I who have gone to his church functions with him. I think that he believes that I will be drawn back to my former congregation through some combination of fellowship, friendship, familiar hymns, seeing the old church again, and feeling drawn back. I have attended a few classes with him on such subjects as strengthening marriages, living wills, and a congregational discussion on their denominational document on sexuality. I have also attended Vespers and Sunday school frequently during the past year.

In return Bill has attended Mass a couple of times a year and a couple of one-session meetings or events over the four-year period. Perhaps twice he has made favorable comments. Usually he has negative comments. I thought he might sit in on the Bible study of Sirach, just to see what it was about, but he seemed offended that I asked; after all, he didn't consider Sirach as part of the Bible. His choice of which things to attend is not predictable from my perspective.

In the first few months after my conversion I thought that Bill might be adjusting to my being Catholic. He was bitter for a couple of months, and then he improved. After a few more months the bitterness returned. I said, "I thought you'd gotten over the bitterness." "I'll never get over the bitterness," he replied. I think it can be a little like having a serious illness that goes into remission. Life is beautiful again for a time, then *wham*, the sickness returns. One problem with this is that I have a tendency to anticipate the next cycle. This is something I have to work on because it can give me a negative mind-set even when everything is going fine. The bitterness can invade normal daily activities in a way I was unprepared for. I had been accustomed to discussing needed home or car repairs. During one of his bitter periods, I asked Bill to reach a decision on a particular repair. He refused. When I asked him to cooperate, he responded, "Why should I cooperate when you won't cooperate?" I asked what this meant. "You know," was his response. It meant that if I came back to my former denomination, then he'd discuss the repair. I can't remember how we solved the impasse, but it wasn't by his suggested method.

I'd like to think that these ploys are all in the past. I simply don't know. Right now all seems pretty normal and I'm beginning to hope that maybe we won't go through the bitterness again. Maybe I'm learning how to be more understanding. Maybe he's learning what can be changed and what cannot be changed. One thing grown children are good for is to keep parents informed of their missteps. As painful as it has sometimes been, I am truly in debt to my offspring for pointing out to me several times when I have needed an attitude adjustment. And I'm afraid I've sometimes become defensive and sulked before recognizing their wisdom.

I know Bill's great concern is that our children may join the Catholic Church. I feel this is a decision that they must make for themselves. Our daughter is still Protestant. Having attended a Catholic college she goes to church with her dad when at home. I believe James has written off all western religions. I'm not even sure if he has a real interest in eastern religions, or perhaps just in knowing what's there in case there appears to be something worth borrowing. Bill has even admitted he'd rather see our son in the Catholic Church than totally away from Christianity. From all he's said since my conversion, this is a very big statement!

Periodically we have watched EWTN together. We used to watch Mother Angelica regularly. When she would mention Mary, other saints, purgatory, etc., Bill would argue back at her, denying her comments.

Currently we are watching Marcus Grodi's program, "The Journey Home." Bill says he wants to see what makes a person convert to the Catholic Church. After several weeks of either missing half of the program while we discussed something that came up early on, or trying to watch the whole program and then discuss — only to find that we couldn't recall something exactly — we now tape the programs. Now we can pause the tape and discuss, then finish the program. Unfortunately his recent response has been that watching the program reinforces his reasons not to be Catholic.

Bill had also asked me to write to Father Peter Stravinskas, editor of *The Catholic Answer* magazine (published by Our Sunday Visitor), to ask him to specifically address whether either I can take communion with him or he with me. His sister insists that several Catholics now receive communion at her church because their priest told them this is acceptable, but that the Protestants may not receive at the Catholic Church. This makes no sense to me and I feel it is clearly a case of the priest being mistaken, or the people not understanding. Nevertheless, Father Stravinskas has received yet another letter on a previously discussed topic (although with a slightly different twist) and I have no reason to believe that he will want to take up space with the answer. From my perspective, this is one of those times when the issue is not worth the argument, so I've simply done as asked.

Sometimes I have said to my pastor that I don't understand Bill's refusal to come to terms with the fact that I'm now Catholic. He says he understands. I believe he means that he's seen it before, that he knows the tenacity of anti-Catholicism, that he knows the irrationality, the depth, and the breadth of the emotion. I think that he also knows that sometimes people aren't aware they have a sore spot until they are poked.

If you ask whether I would I do it all over again, I'd give you an emphatic yes! Not, of course, because I love living on the defensive, and certainly not because I love to torment my husband (as he sometimes insists). My reason is purely and simply because I believe I am doing God's will, and in so doing I have received a peace and joy that transcends the turmoil I've endured. I pray that Bill will one day join me in experiencing this peace and joy, but it would be an improvement if he were to accept my decision and try to work together in Christian harmony.

If I were to give advice to others, I'd suggest trying to push harder to communicate together prior to the decision. This is something you must gauge for yourself, since only you know the peculiarities of your situation. However, if the decision is made and there is a closed mind on the part of your spouse, then pray for guidance and do what you feel is right. Making a conversion against your spouse's will is not for the faint-hearted. If your marriage survives, you will learn much about forbearance and hopefully also about prayer. A well-grounded faith is a necessity, and a good sense of humor is nearly indispensable, especially one that permits you to occasionally laugh at yourself.

On the other hand, I cannot imagine a relationship with

God unless it is honest — one in which we are willing to accept all on God's terms and then simply follow him as faithfully as possible. I cannot imagine a closer walk with God than in following where he leads, and this has brought a joy to my heart that is greater than anything I've ever known.

Chapter 12

The Two Shall Become One

by Tim and Mary Drake

Courtship

HER SIDE OF THE PEW

Growing up, I attended Catholic schools, and everyone I knew was Catholic. So, when I began dating in high school I didn't give the faith of my boyfriends much thought. As for marriage, I hoped to find someone who was Christian. Tim was one of the first Lutherans I had met, let alone dated.

We met and began dating as freshmen in college. At the time I had a poor understanding of my faith. I felt that there were more similarities than differences between our churches. We both believed in the Trinity and in Jesus Christ. We could share the "Our Father" as a common prayer. We both believed in the importance of church attendance and in raising our children to be Christians.

My mother expressed concern over Tim's denomination. Although she didn't specifically say so, she was worried about how we would raise our children, and feared that I might leave the Church. I explained to her that although Tim was Lutheran he cared about his relationship with God. In that sense he was unlike any of the Catholics I had dated. They were Catholic in name only. Tim, however, took his faith seriously. He attended church regularly, he prayed, and he and I were able to have serious conversations about our faith and morals. These were conversations I had never had with previous boyfriends.

I was baptized, raised, and confirmed in the Lutheran Church. Through the example of two faithful parents I came to know and believe in Jesus Christ, his mercy and redemption, and the power of prayer. Little did I know where my relationship with Christ would lead, and that my journey would take me someplace I had no intention of going.

I grew up surrounded largely by Lutherans and was seldom exposed to the ideals of Catholicism save for an occasional Catholic wedding. I remember finding the wedding Masses long, the kneeling odd, and the church decorations ornate. Over the years I acquired the usual prejudices toward Catholicism. I thought that Catholics worshiped Mary. I could not understand papal infallibility, and confession seemed very strange to me.

At the age of ten, standing in a hallway on my first day in a new grade school, I met the first Catholic I ever truly got to know. Mark and I quickly became best friends. At that age religion wasn't something he and I discussed; however, as our relationship developed, we couldn't help but recognize the differences in our lives. Mark and I spent as much time as we could at each other's houses, and on a few occasions attended each other's churches. One night while I was staying over at his home I discovered a laminated prayer card from Italy sitting on his nightstand. It was a prayer card of St. Joseph. I found the artwork and the prayer to be quite beautiful. I told him how much I admired the card, and he gave it to me.

After high school, Mark, the prayer card, and I journeyed to the same college. As I had in high school, I called upon St. Joseph in times of special need. As an intercessor he never seemed to fail. Sometime later during college I misplaced the card and feared I had lost it.

At college I met the second Catholic in my life, Mary. She and I became friends in our freshman year; we lived on the same floor of the dormitory. We enjoyed going on walks with each other, talking for hours on end, and simply being with each other. By the end of our freshman year we began dating.

Our courtship lasted four years. In Mary's junior year she decided to live off-campus in the Newman Catholic Campus Ministry Center. Partly in response to her, and partially out of my own desire to learn more about my faith, I decided to live in the Lutheran Christus House.

During my junior and senior year of college I lived in the Christus House with a group of four to five fellow resident peer ministers. We held Bible studies and weekly Wednesday night worship services for Lutheran college students.

Once a year the Newman Center and Christus House would host a joint ecumenical retreat. These retreats and the daily practice of our faith fostered a mutual respect between Mary and me. It also opened us up to discussing more seriously matters of faith. Our discussions covered everything from the inappropriateness of living together before marriage to contraception and abortion. I was as committed in my Lutheranism as Mary was in her Catholicism.

I was often a visitor in Mary's home. I found the faith of her family, their devotion, and traditions particularly inspiring. They were truly a holy family and this showed in their faithful attendance at Mass every Sunday and in their praying together before bed each evening. Not only did I find myself drawn to attending Mass and praying with them, but I also found myself falling in love with Mary and with her family.

Engagement

HER SIDE

Prior to and following our engagement in November of 1988, Tim and I began to talk more seriously about our respective faiths. We took a premarital inventory and went through a marriage preparation course in the Catholic Church. This forced us to address issues such as NFP (natural family planning), finances, churchgoing, and raising children.

I was thankful that Tim respected my desire to use NFP in our marriage. However, he did have a hard time understanding the Church's desire that couples raise the children as Catholic. I worried about our children and wondered what church they would attend. We talked through every conceivable option available: my converting, his converting, us both converting to a third denomination, raising our children all Lutheran, all Catholic, alternating with each child, raising them Episcopalian, or letting them decide for themselves. I feared having our children going back and forth between both churches, thinking that they would consequently grow up with a weak faith. In our hearts we knew that raising them in one church was the answer, but we weren't sure what we were going to do. So, since we were childless, we put off making a decision and hoped that something would make sense to us when we did have children.

His Side

As an interdenominational couple, we struggled with the questions all such couples struggle with. What church would we attend? How would we raise our children? We found comfort in our similarities. We both believed in the Father, Son, and Holy Spirit. We often prayed those prayers that our denominations held in common, such as the "Our Father," bedtime prayers, and meal prayers. We wrestled with issues such as the Rosary and abortion, and occasionally we argued, but slowly we began to realize that we could, if we remained respectful, work through them all.

During marriage preparation the priest asked us if we were willing to raise our children Catholic. This promise was one I found difficult to understand. I felt slighted, as though my denomination were somehow inferior or less important. I thought to myself, "What if I don't want to?" I certainly didn't want to agree to something I wasn't sure about. Begrudgingly, however, I said yes to the promise. Although we didn't have all the issues worked out, we were married in July 1989.

Marriage

Our wedding was about a month after graduating from college, on July 8, 1989, an extremely hot day. We had an ecumenical ceremony at St. Eloi's Catholic Church in my hometown of Ghent, Minnesota. We decided not to have a Mass so that Tim's side would not feel left out. It was the second mixed marriage in our family, so no one in the extended family said anything about the lack of a Mass. Tim's Lutheran pastor from college and our parish priest both participated in the ceremony.

I particularly remember the "Our Father." Tim and I were near the altar, in a circle holding hands with our wedding party, the pastor, and the priest. Father Bernie Schreiner asked that to show our unity, everyone should hold hands, even across the aisles. A college friend sang a moving rendition of the prayer. Toward the end, overcome with emotion, Father Schreiner shouted, "Everyone!" and together we sang, "For thine is the kingdom, and the power, and the glory, forever. Amen." There wasn't a dry eye in the place.

After our wedding, as before, we would sometimes attend our churches separately. At other times we would attend one or the other together. Sometimes we would even attend both churches each Sunday. We both found it difficult to do this. Although I had attended Catholic grade school, I didn't know my own faith well enough to be able to explain to Tim why I could not omit Sunday Mass. Out of a sense of fairness I often attended the Lutheran church with Tim. I found it frustrating that Tim's church usually received communion only on the second and fourth Sundays. If Tim skipped going to his church it was often weeks or months before he received the Body of Christ. This concerned me, and I worried about his soul.

We continued to struggle with attending both churches until sometime in 1993. We had just moved into our first home in St. Paul, and Tim found it more convenient to attend St.

Columba Catholic Church just three blocks away from our home.

I began praying for Tim's conversion. I didn't know if this was the right thing to do, and so I would pray, "Lord, I don't know if this is your will. If Tim would be converted, that would be great. Whatever you think is best, Lord." I prayed this way because while I loved my Church and knew it would be easier if Tim were Catholic, I felt guilty. I knew that Tim loved his faith and probably hoped I would convert as much as I hoped he would. It didn't seem fair that Tim should have to be the one to convert.

His Side

The day we married was so hot that one of my memories is of standing in the Catholic school's walk-in-freezer with my brother and Mark, my best man, as a way to keep cool prior to the service. But what really struck me about the day is that it would be one of the few times in our lives when all our loved ones would be gathered together to help us celebrate our love for each other.

After our marriage we struggled with Sunday services, vacillating between attending Mary's church, mine, or both. I found it frustrating to attend both of our churches each Sunday morning. Often the Scripture readings would be identical at both churches. It was painful to watch Mary receive the Eucharist while I remained behind in the pew. Occasionally I would cry, thinking about what it would one day be like to watch Mary and my future children go to communion without me.

One part during Mass particularly bothered me. When the congregation said, "Lord, I am not worthy to receive you, but only say the word and I shall be healed," I felt that because I was Lutheran I was not deemed "worthy" to receive that which Christ offered for all.

However, over time I grew disillusioned with the Lutheran parishes we attended. The messages or teachings of the church seemed to vary greatly depending on the pastor. For convenience I started attending church with Mary, and forgoing a Lutheran Sunday service, reserving Lutheran services for only special occasions such as Christmas and Easter.

In 1993, an Evangelical Lutheran Church of America task force released a draft of its report on human sexuality that I found particularly troubling. Four years in the making, the document accommodated what until then had been considered immoral behavior. The document taught that although abortion was a bad choice, it was at times a necessary one.

By this time I had come a long way in my own views on abortion, and found myself in agreement with the teachings of the Catholic Church. This was an issue on which I could not compromise. Suddenly, being Lutheran meant more to me than sitting in a pew. I began to question. Why had Luther split with the Church? Hadn't the Church made significant changes following the Reformation? Why wasn't the Eucharist the center of the Lutheran church service as it was for Catholics? Who was the Virgin Mary and what did Catholics really believe and teach about her? The questions flowed forth and I wanted answers.

The last thing I wanted to do, or wanted anyone thinking, was that I had converted simply to please Mary. It had to be a decision I came to on my own. Mary was a cradle Catholic. I needed the example and support of someone who had chosen Catholicism on his or her own. God provided exactly what I needed, but in a most unusual way.

Conversion

Her Side

During the summer of 1993, as we walked home from church one morning, Tim expressed his desire to learn more about Catholicism. I was both shocked and excited. At the same time I was cautious; I didn't want to say too much. I didn't want him to feel pressured, since I knew he might resent it later on. I didn't want Tim converting because of me. I did offer to be his sponsor, and he accepted. I began praying all the more.

His Side

During 1992 and 1993 several events occurred simultaneously that played a major role in my conversion. In August of 1992, my father showed up at our apartment unexpected and alone. His very presence, unaccompanied by my mother, foretold that something was not as it should be. Calmly, but tearfully, he told me that I was not his son. After enlisting in the Air Force, my father was stationed in Guam shortly after he and my mother were married. He came to me now, bearing papers, to show that he had been discharged from the Air Force and returned home from Guam during the summer of 1967. When he came home, my mother was five months pregnant. I was born in September. Having grown up with divorced parents himself, he did not want that for me. And so, honorably, he stayed with my mother, albeit with a great deal of pain and a lack of forgiveness.

To say that such news was shocking is an understatement. Learning the truth turned my whole world upside down. It threw everything I thought I knew into question. Growing up, I had never once questioned whether my parents were who they said they were. While my younger brother, Jeff, and I looked little alike we simply thought that he took after Dad and I took after Mom. Perhaps even more shocking was to learn that my father had wanted me aborted. Thankfully, my mother did not.

One would not expect good things to result from sin, but God in his wisdom can use evil to bring about good. Learning the truth turned out to be a blessing. It helped to explain some of the misdirected hostility I received from my father as a child. It helped to explain why my younger brother and I were so different. But I was also blessed with undiscovered family.

Not only did I learn about the true identity of my father,

but I also discovered two older half-brothers that I had not known existed. Two months after learning the truth and coming to terms with who I was, I placed a phone call to one of my half-brothers, Rich. We spoke for a long time and agreed to meet at a nearby restaurant. I was nervous about our meeting and didn't know what to expect. As I walked into the restaurant that evening, there was no mistaking who my brother was; we shared an undeniable resemblance. Meeting him was like looking into a mirror and seeing myself thirteen years later. As we sat eating our hamburgers and comparing stories, the waitress asked, "Are you guys brothers?" Here we were meeting for the first time in our lives, and a stranger could see the resemblance. We laughed, thinking, "If you only knew . . ."

In meeting Rich, a unique and inseparable bond was formed. We each felt more complete. Yet our bond was more than genetic. Although we are thirteen years apart, have different mothers, and grew up in different homes, our looks, voices, personalities, and mannerisms are similar. We share the same values. We have a similar sense of humor. We both share a passion for action films and pizza. We also share some of those uncanny separated-at-birth likenesses. Our wives are both named Mary. Rich works for the Archdiocese of Denver; I work for the Diocese of St. Cloud, Minnesota. We are, in fact, more like each other than like the brothers we each grew up with.

Most importantly, in Rich I found someone I could identify with. Rich had grown up Lutheran. However, because of his friendship with a priest, he had converted to Catholicism at age eighteen. I found most compelling not the details of Rich's story, or even his specific reasons for converting. Quite simply, as he shared his story I came to realize that people can and do come to the truth and embrace it, in spite of the obstacles that family or society places in the way. God speaks to each of us differently, and so our conversion stories are uniquely our own, or rather, God's own.

Not long after I met Rich, a couple of other events pointed me toward the Church. The new *Catechism of the Catholic Church* was published and we purchased a copy. I liked having it around because when I had a question I knew I could find an answer. It also impressed upon me the validity of having all that the Church believes in a single source, and gave meaning to the statement "one, holy, catholic, and apostolic Church."

Also at about this time Mary's church, St. Columba's, started Perpetual Eucharistic Adoration. Feeling the need to pray more, I signed up to pray an hour each Sunday evening. When I began, I did not fully understand the meaning of the Blessed Sacrament. It didn't take long for Christ to teach me about his Real Presence. Adoration was the key that unlatched the lock for me. For in adoration, before the Lord, I realized how pivotal the Eucharist is to the Catholic Church. In the sacrament of the Eucharist Christ humbles himself and allows us to take him into our very own imperfect bodies. Could there be anything more? Through adoration, Christ revealed to me how the Eucharist is the source and summit of his Church. Once I realized this, there could be no turning back.

Unfortunately, the Rite of Christian Initiation for Adults (RCIA) program at our local church left something to be desired. Had it been for the RCIA alone, I never would have converted. Thankfully, a friend offered to go with me to a thirteen-week "Fundamentals of Catholicism" class at a nearby parish. An orthodox, faithful, and humble priest capable of handling any question put to him taught the class. It didn't take long for the Holy Spirit to work within me. An audiotape on the conversion of former Protestant minister Scott Hahn clinched it for me. Hahn clearly exposed the errors in the Protestant Reformation's battle cries of *sola fide* and *sola scriptura*. If Hahn was correct, then Luther had been wrong. If Luther was wrong, then the entire foundation upon which Luther had built his church had been in error. If his foundation was unstable, then every Protestant denomination since Luther had been conceived in the divorce caused by that error.

Incredibly, the issues I had long contended with were no longer problems for me; they had melted away. Having heard female Lutheran pastors preach, I had never understood the Church's teaching that priests had to be male. After the "Fundamentals of Catholicism" class the Catholic teaching made great sense to me. For one thing, the priesthood was not a role of power, but one of service. If females were allowed to be priests, men would abdicate the role. I also learned that asking Mary or the saints to pray for me was no different from asking a friend to pray for me. I understood that the stained-glass windows and the statuary within the church were not idolatrous, but merely another way to focus one's attention on the things of heaven. I understood the Church's respect for the sanctity of all human life and her teaching on the selfishness of contraception. I came to know the differences in belief on the Eucharist, and why non-Catholic reception of our Lord's body and blood implies a wholeness that hasn't existed since the Reformation. I felt as if I had been infused with a complete acceptance of the Church and her teachings. I wanted our family to be one spiritually. I was on the road to reconciliation.

Confession was my last major obstacle, more out of fear than any lack of understanding. I found it difficult to overcome my belief that we are "dung heaps covered with snow." My priest-teacher compared the Lutheran concept of forgiveness to typing with an old typewriter. If a sin were like a mistake, you could white it out, but you would always be able to tell that the mistake had been made. In contrast, he compared the Catholic idea of forgiveness to using a computer. Confession, he described, was like hitting the delete key. Once the key was struck, you would never be able to tell the mistake had been made. If this were true, I thought, confession had to be the most powerful and freeing sacrament Christ had given his Church.

On Ash Wednesday I was moved to go to confession. Compiling a laundry list of twenty-seven years' worth of sin was a very humbling experience. The Cathedral of St. Paul seemed an appropriate place to go. There I poured out the sins of my life and was filled with the grace that accompanies the sacrament — not a lightning bolt of grace striking me suddenly, but rather a gradual appreciation of the sacrament and its power. After confession, things moved quickly.

Converting is a covenant one enters into with God. Like marriage or parenthood, it is one of those things you can't really try out beforehand. Once I decided to convert, there was no going back. It was all or nothing, with no room to pick and choose. Either I accepted the Church and her teachings, or I wasn't Catholic. The RCIA and the "Fundamentals of Catholicism" classes were very much like marriage-preparation coursework and Engaged Encounter. There was only so much prayer, reading, discussion, and discerning I could do. My intellect could only take me so far. Now my heart had to follow. Through adoration of the Blessed Sacrament I had acquired an unquenchable hunger for the Eucharist. Truly, I was in love with God, and was being moved to take a childlike leap. I did not have all the answers, I did not know where it would lead, but I had to trust in God. As the Church teaches, some things have always been and will continue to be a mystery. This is what faith is given for.

I felt unable to wait until Easter to convert. My heart had been opened to the Truth. To wait felt like denying God. On March 19, 1995, the feast day of St. Joseph, gathered with my friends and family and Mary as my sponsor, I professed my belief in the holy Catholic Church and all her teachings, was confirmed, and accompanied Mary to the Lord's table for the first time since we had begun dating ten years earlier.

On the occasion of my conversion, Mark, who had forgotten he had ever given me the original St. Joseph prayer card, gave me a new one, with the same prayer on it. I related to him the significance of the original card and how I had lost it. Not more than a week after converting, as I was leafing through my Lutheran confirmation Bible, the original St. Joseph prayer card literally fell into my lap, bringing everything full circle.

I am now able to look back on these remarkable events and clearly see the hand of God in their timing. Had my stepfather not told me the truth, not only would I still be living without knowledge of my father or my brothers, but I probably never would have met my biological father before his death, and I may not have come into the Church.

New Life

HER SIDE

It is a sad statement about my own Catholic education that I grew up so ignorant about my faith. In some ways I was not taught my faith; in other ways I took it for granted, and made no effort to actively learn more about it. I now realize how thankful I am that Tim converted. The questions that Tim raised through his "Fundamentals of Catholicism" class inspired me to learn more. His questions and reading taught me things I had never known about my faith. Tim shared with me what he was learning and he taught me the true differences between Lutheranism and Catholicism. In countless ways I learned why we believe the things that we do and rediscovered the richness in our Church's traditions. I learned about Christ's Real Presence in the Eucharist. I understood the authority of the pope. I understood the reasons behind the Church's teachings on contraception and abortion. All in all I realized just how much I love the Church and also came to understand why she is not just another denomination; she is *the* Church. Tim's conversion was a great blessing to me. I am a more faithful Catholic because of it.

I'm also thankful that the Spirit moved Tim to convert when he did. I feel selfish for saying it, but Tim's conversion did make raising our children easier. It is an incredible blessing to be a family strong in one faith. It helps to make our decisions easier. We feel more united in how we discipline and raise our children, and we share common friends who feel strongly about their faith as well.

HIS SIDE

Although I believed in Christ, my faith did not hold the fullness of Truth so beautifully expressed in Christ and his Church. Therefore, through my conversion, 1 Corinthians 7:14 was fulfilled; an unbelieving husband was sanctified by a believing wife. Even more miraculously, God took my love for Mary, combined it with my love for him, and created new life, not only within me, but within us. Shortly after my conversion, after a struggle with infertility, my wife and I learned we were expecting a child. Our joy was compounded in discovering that we would join in the pregnancy of the Holy Family — our projected due date was Christmas.

In September, Mary and I traveled to Rome and Assisi. How fitting it seemed, as a convert, to be visiting all things Catholic as a new Catholic. The beauty of St. Peter's, the Vatican, Michelangelo's Sistine Chapel ceiling, an Italian Mass — all these filled us with awe, along with the comfort and peace we found in Assisi.

On December 27, 1995, our son, Elias Joseph Drake, was born.

It used to be that both the Lutheran and Catholic Church seriously cautioned against mixed marriages because of the "danger of loss of faith." While I understand the Church's caution and the potential that mixed marriages have for causing pain I marvel at the joy that Mary and I now share. Our own mixed marriage has not only strengthened my faith, but Mary's as well.

Afterword

As I wrote my conversion story, I naïvely envisioned creating something profound, perhaps something that would touch others. Because it is so deeply personal, I discovered it to be the most difficult writing I have ever undertaken. Dr. Karl Stern, Jewish convert to Catholicism, wrote, "How do you begin to write about how you fell in love with God?" To write a conversion story from only the human perspective is to provide an incomplete tale. Clearly, in ways seen and unseen, the Holy Spirit was acting and moving in me, opening my ears, mind, and heart. Likewise, the prayers of my wife, Mary, and others known and unknown, were being raised in unison to heaven. As complete as this story may seem, our perspective pales in comparison to the heavenly events we are unable to relate.

Chapter 13

Burdens as Blessings

by Michele L. Fitzpatrick

At first it seemed like a pretty ordinary Sunday at Orchard Hills Church. Our pastor decided to celebrate communion after the sermon. In an inspired moment between his office and the worship space, on his way to begin the service, he and the coordinator for children's ministries agreed to try something new. The children would be brought in during the service to observe communion. Little did I know that this seemingly innocent decision would abruptly change my life, not to mention the lives of my husband, John, and our three children.

My husband, John, and I began dating when we were sixteen and eighteen years old. Our parents were acquaintances, and our fathers shared a passion for motorcycles. One Labor Day weekend, the day I was due to be born, John and his parents stopped by my parents' house to take a look at my father's new motorcycle. In an inspired moment, the men decided they must take the bike out for a ride. John and his mother shared their Labor Day picnic on our living room floor, while my mother waited for me to arrive.

Since our parents were only acquaintances, John and I didn't get to know each other until I was about eleven and had become friends with his stepsister. When he was sixteen, he would drive me to their house for visits. I loved him almost immediately. When he walked by me, my knees would get weak. He was handsome, sweet, funny, and smart. He hasn't really changed.

We were married before my twentieth birthday. I worked full-time and attended college part-time. John was about to finish his bachelor's degree and was already seeking employment. We considered a garden wedding, but my grandfather, who was also my godfather, declared that he would not attend the wedding if it were not held in a Catholic church. I loved and respected my grandfather, and so we conceded.

I was baptized as an infant, raised Catholic, and attended twelve years of Catholic schools. My angelic sister, fourteen months older, was born developmentally disabled and never matured beyond the mental capacity of a two-year-old. She was both a blessing and a burden. Since she was such a lovable child, it's hard to recall what a trial it must have been for my parents. Now I recognize that her disabilities impaired our ability to be a practicing Catholic family. My father gave up attending Mass in order to stay home to care for my sister. The Catholic teaching on artificial birth control became an obstacle for my parents, trying to cope with a child who needed constant attention and another child born so soon afterward. My mother and I went to Mass every Sunday, but we were not a terribly religious family.

During my teen years I worked part-time on the weekend, and found it easy to avoid going to Mass with my mother. When I was nineteen, my sister passed away suddenly from a complicated seizure. I leaned heavily on my belief in God and in heaven. The same year, two weeks prior to my wedding, my grandfather was diagnosed with lung cancer, and died two months later. Again, my faith was all that saw me through this sorrowful time. Perhaps all I held were the seeds of faith, for I quickly took for granted the way God had carried me through and I continued ahead without him.

John was raised in a very moral but agnostic home. His family did not practice any form of religion or hold to any particular ideas about God. He has a logical, highly scientific mind — the world around him is concrete and rational, and his feet are firmly planted on the ground. Ideas about God were a waste of time as far as he was concerned, and necessary only for those who needed a mental crutch in difficult times.

Although we started our marriage off in the Catholic Church, we spent very little time there for the next several years. Those early days were filled with work, my education, the purchase of our first home — and its subsequent repairs — and many wonderful weekend camping trips. If you had asked me then, I would have explained that I didn't have time to go to church. It wasn't until we were expecting our first child that I began to notice the spiritual rumblings starting within.

My son, Christopher, was born by emergency cesarean section. In the delivery room I cried, and in those drug-fogged moments following his birth, I was struck with awe that he had finally entered the world — through me! I wonder if other mothers gaze deep into the tiny dark eyes of their first child and see God within. The most earnest prayer I ever prayed was the silent joy that swelled my heart in thanksgiving for my son. It wasn't long before my mother began to ask if we were going to baptize him.

We registered at our local parish, and signed up for the baptism class. We started attending Mass regularly, but if getting to Mass before we had children was difficult, it wasn't going to be any easier with a newborn. We went as a family a few times; I went alone a couple of times. John said it was boring, I was tired, and we gave up.

Our second son, Nicholas, was born two years later. Captivated once more by the miracle of life, and determined not to repeat the same hypocrisy, we set about getting involved in the parish. We joined a couples group, which met once a month to discuss relationship issues within the context of the Catholic faith. John was still not thrilled about going to Mass, but with the social element added, he was more inclined. Nick was baptized, and we began attending Mass on a more regular basis. Just when things were starting to get comfortable, John was offered a new job in another community.

Our new parish was small and didn't offer the same types of groups as our previous parish. They were happy to involve me in parish work, but didn't offer adequate support to get my ideas going. I had a difficult time connecting with other mothers in the parish, since they were working mothers and I was home with my children. Friends came more easily outside the church. The following year brought about the birth of our third child, Margaret, whose baptism was followed by another departure from Catholicism.

The obstacles resulting from having to either juggle three children at Mass, or attend by myself felt insurmountable. If I pressed to get everybody ready for church on time, I felt like a villain. John again began voicing that the ritual meant nothing to him. I felt sad going alone, watching the families and knowing that my family was at home, but I didn't have the knowledge to explain why my faith was important to me, or for our children. So I gave up formal religion for several months and began to search for a new solution to my faith crisis.

My friend Alison invited us to attend her Evangelical church. It was known as a "seeker" church, specifically focused to attract new believers. The service was unstructured, and the environment was stark, except for some nice green plants. There were no regular prayers, no crosses, and no creeds. Instead there were thematic discussions filled with Bible references. It was basic, and at the time I thought it would be easier for John to accept. It also offered the social element we felt was missing from our Catholic parish. John wasn't eager about going to any church, but he knew how I desired family unity, and he began attending with us.

It was easy to get involved. I joined the women's Bible study, volunteered to teach Sunday school once a month, to chair the women's Christmas tea, and to assist the youth pastor with the junior high group. Our life revolved around church, encompassing all of our friends and all of our activities. Sometimes we were at church three times a week. While

I enjoyed the sense of community and belonging, there were times when I was uncomfortable with how the church celebrated its rituals.

I was especially apprehensive about how it celebrated communion. I remember questioning my friend Alison about whether the pastor did anything to bless the bread and grape juice. (And using grape juice instead of wine was foreign to me.) She assured me that it was no different than in the Catholic Church. But to me, it was too informal, too infrequent, and often it didn't seem connected to the rest of the service. I buried these concerns because I thought that I was wrong to think there was a difference. Almost two years later, one Sunday, my life abruptly changed.

My oldest son, Christopher, was seven at the time and just beginning second grade. I remember feeling a sense of regret that he would not be making his First Communion, as he would have been if we were still practicing Catholics. My friends consoled me with the thought that children in other Christian churches don't generally receive communion until they are eleven or twelve, when they understand it better. Again, I buried my concerns.

I was surprised when the children were ushered in to observe communion, and then without any further preparation, given permission to receive it. They had been given a short explanation of what would be happening and were told that it tasted a little like peanut butter and jelly.

This particular Sunday, at the prompting of several former Catholics, the congregation was asked to process up to the front of the worship space to receive communion. I watched with shock and profound disappointment when my son sauntered up to receive his bread and grape juice. A confused and disgusted look crossed his face when the pastor told him it was Jesus' body and blood. Each person was to tear off a small piece from a larger loaf of bread, but my son took a massive handful and stuffed it into his mouth, resulting in a wave of giggling from the surrounding congregation. My stomach turned as my eyes welled up with tears. Had Christopher really made his First Communion without my knowing it?

God might as well have struck me over the head with a two-by-four that day. I was appalled that the parents had not been consulted, and that the children had not been adequately prepared for the reception of communion. After the service was over, I questioned several people about whether this was considered acceptable, but received no clear answers. One of the several former Catholics attending this church told me she understood how I felt and she was relieved that her daughter had not gone up. The pastor's response to my grief was that it had been an accident. Again I was offended by the nonchalant manner with which they regarded the body and blood of Jesus. I tried to extract from the pastor the specifics of their beliefs, asking him point-blank, "Is it Jesus, or isn't it?" Perhaps to confuse or maybe to intimidate me, he blurted out, "Well, I'm not going into transubstantiation!" I responded, "What's that?" I realized that this was a significant word, and it became a jumping-off point for rediscovering why I am Catholic today.

The pastor loaned me an impressive stack of Protestant theology books. I learned the meaning of the word "transubstantiation" — a word attributed to St. Thomas Aquinas to describe the physical change of substance that takes place within the bread and wine blessed for communion. St. Thomas taught that the substances of bread and wine changed into the body and blood of Jesus, while all the appearance of bread and wine remained. The Protestant books I read were opposed to the dogma of transubstantiation, but they offered the thread of logic I sought to inspire me to learn more about the Catholic position.

Despite my twelve years of Catholic education, I realized that I understood very little about Catholicism. I thought a sacrifice was giving up chocolate for Easter, and the sacrifice of the Mass meant I had to give up my time on Sunday to attend. I thought the Immaculate Conception was when the

Angel Gabriel appeared to Mary, and I didn't know there was a difference between the Ascension and the Assumption. I hadn't been to confession since eighth grade, and I thought that it was good enough to go to church most of the time. Most importantly, although I had been raised to believe that the Eucharist becomes the body and blood of Christ, I had cynically chosen to believe it was only symbolic in order to justify my departure from the Church. I was suddenly faced with the responsibility to choose what I would teach my own children, forced as it was by observing my son's casual participation in a ritual I viewed as sacred. If I had truly believed that the Eucharist was only symbolic, then I would not have been so deeply offended. I needed to humble myself to seek to understand what God intended so that I could faithfully teach my children, in place of picking and choosing what I wanted to believe.

I lost about ten pounds trying to decide whether to stay within my comfortable circle of friends, or return to the Church I had once abandoned. I felt responsible for the commitments I had made to several ministries. I worried that my children would be angry with me for taking them away from Sunday songs, crafts, and games and instead making them sit through Mass. The pastor reprimanded me, saying that John would never become a Christian if I went back to the Catholic Church. This was the deepest jab, for this was the reason that I had opted to try something else.

Leaving was a painful choice; my church had become my identity. To my benefit, the pastor handled the matter so poorly and hurt me so deeply that John rose to my defense and supported me. Rumors began to spread that I was leaving because of what had happened, and other mothers began calling and complaining about the handling of communion that Sunday. I was told to stop talking or I would cause a schism in the church. I didn't understand this concept. I was informed that I had offended the coordinator for children's ministries, the one who had offered the peanut-butter-and-jelly analogy, and that I needed to apologize to her. When I told the pastor I was leaving, he threatened to call me before the board of elders to have me held accountable. I didn't understand that either. His parting words to me were, "You have vomited all over the place here, and you are leaving us behind to clean it up!" With those words, I turned decisively toward my true home, the Roman Catholic Church.

My return to Catholicism hinged specifically on the dogma of the Real Presence of Jesus Christ in the Eucharist. After the Lord graciously shed some light on the word "transubstantiation" I set about to systematically study each of the teachings of the Church. I was introduced to the *Catechism of the Catholic Church* — a book I hadn't known existed. Digesting book after book, I discovered the meaning of this other mysterious term, "Tradition." I found a new family in St. Ignatius, St. Irenaeus, and St. Justin the Martyr. Within the writings of these Fathers of the Church were the rational answers to the several misconceptions about Catholicism I had adopted during my brief sojourn in Protestantism. Most significantly, I had been led to believe that many of the central beliefs of Catholicism were developed in the Middle Ages. I dismissed this notion when I saw for myself evidence in the nearly two-thousand-year-old writings by the Fathers of the very beliefs I was seeking to better understand.

Returning to our former Catholic parish was humbling. I was happy there was a new priest in place to welcome us, but we had to face many people who remembered our departure. Some of them welcomed us warmly, but some received us with tentative reservation. There were no fanfares for our return, only a long overdue visit to the sacrament of reconciliation, which I made certain I understood completely! I studied the Scriptures, particularly John 20:21-23, whereby Jesus commissions the disciples, gathered in the upper room, with the authority to forgive and retain sins. What was more significant to me was that this sacrament encourages an ongoing formation of one's conscience and continually inspires humility, perhaps the most basic of all Christian virtues. Father was kind and patient in walking me through the rite and when I was finished I felt as if I could fly.

As joyful as my journey home was, it nearly cost me my friendship with Alison. She had been the one person with whom I could endlessly discuss our mutual love of Jesus. Everywhere we went, people would ask us if we were sisters, and we would laugh and say, "Yes!" The more than two-year-long faith journey we shared made us inseparable friends. She was hurt when I chose to return to Catholicism and she wanted no part of my new direction. Each time I would unravel a misunderstanding about the Church, I wanted so badly to explain it to her, but she was unable to hear my defenses because they struck at the foundations of her faith. Faith sharing was such an essential element of our friendship that when I chose this new path I felt like I was leaving a part of myself behind. For the past three years we have managed to maintain our friendship despite our differing theological views, but not without strained dialogues and many tears. Just weeks ago, Alison shared with me her family's intention to begin the RCIA process. It seems the Lord graciously shed some light on a few good books I sent her way. Once again we are joyfully lost in endless discussions!

John supported my decision to return to Catholicism. He withstood my enthusiasm to relearn all things Catholic, and consequently I was able to offer answers to his questions. He overheard me defend the Catholic perspective so many times that now he is able to present the defense himself. He struggles with the traditional concept of God, but acknowledges that religion provides a good moral foundation for raising children, and so he supports and promotes the religious formation of our children. Sometimes I think he is very close to accepting Catholicism as his own, and sometimes I think he follows along out of love for us.

Many of my Catholic friends are married to non-Catholic spouses. The materialism of our society has made God an obsolete concept in their lives. Sometimes these spouses want to know what a church can offer them, not what they can offer to God. Unless the Sunday service provides some form of entertainment, as many churches now do, they have no desire to participate in something they view as an unnecessary repetitive ritual. I know deeply the sad ache that frustrates the Catholic wife who desires to draw her family closer to Christ, yet is hesitant to impose her beliefs upon the husband she loves and respects. The situation is even more difficult when she cannot adequately communicate why these beliefs matter. There were times when I wished I had placed more emphasis on my spouse's religious affiliation prior to making my choice, but in the same breath I know in my heart that, given the choice all over again, it would have been the same.

I once viewed my husband's lack of faith as a burden, and used it as an excuse to ignore my relationship with Jesus Christ. Part of my conversion has been an attitude adjustment. The "burden" was actually the inspiration to deepen my faith by knowing Jesus better. My children have been the leaders in my faith journey, since I began this journey in response to their need for direction. The beginning of my path was fairly steep, and I felt like my husband was a rock I was dragging along behind me. It was unfair of me to expect him to follow me to a place I wasn't certain existed, on a path I didn't understand. Now I know that by compelling me to learn how to explain what I believe, he is not dragging me down. He is driving me forth! Now that my direction is set with certainty, he nearly has to run to keep up with me. I no longer view his lack of faith as my burden; I acknowledge it as my greatest blessing.

I pray for a future Easter Vigil, hoping to watch John receive the sacraments of initiation — baptism, confirmation, and the Eucharist — realizing it is a dream I might never see fulfilled. But if the fruit of my journey brings glory to God, I'm certain he will know that John was an essential part.

Chapter 14

Your Pride, My Prejudice, and 'Festina Lente'

by Lynn Nordhagen

(I wrote this piece for our local diocesan paper when I had been married just over one year. The editor's note in that edition reads: "Author Nordhagen says this article reflects an actual conversation between her husband and herself, and that she was prompted to share her experience when she learned that thirty-five percent of marriages performed in the Catholic Church are mixed marriages. 'I was impressed,' she said, in learning of this, 'that I am not as alone as I feel.' ")

My beloved Protestant husband and I paused. That always emotional topic, religion, was up again. This time the subject was prejudice — his and mine.

"You want me to tell you about Protestants?" I had challenged. I began my litany of Protestant error. "OK. They go to church only when they feel like it. They think the world is a good enough church. When they *do* feel like going to a Sunday service, I can't imagine why, because all they do there is listen to a long-winded, yelling preacher tell them about sin and hell. And sometimes about loving Jesus. Which according to their interpretation means just believing in him. They think they don't even have to be good if they just 'believe' hard enough. And the ones who do think they should be good, mean don't ever drink or smoke. Now that's completely irrelevant."

Here I paused for breath, but didn't stop before I had covered everything from faith versus good works to private interpretation. Then, in a moment of inspired openness, I said, "So why don't you tell me about Catholics?" Actually, I was curious. I have admitted before that sixteen years of Catholic schooling have had a sheltering effect on me. I used to think anti-Catholicism was based on misunderstanding of Church laws and doctrines (like no meat on Friday and papal infallibility). So I've always been sure a rational explanation would dissolve all prejudice and reveal the beauty and wholesomeness of my own tradition.

Now I'm bewildered. It doesn't work. My husband and I are face-to-face with the facts. We have fears, prejudices, disagreements, and a child to raise. We must teach each other.

So he begins, "Catholics, my dear, see nothing wrong with smoking or drinking. For me, just setting foot in a tavern would be a statement of what I am and what I am looking for. I couldn't do that and still say, 'Look to Jesus Christ.' I couldn't buy a six-pack or even sell cigarettes and hope to be a Christian influence."

I think of the bar in the Knights of Columbus Hall. I say nothing. I hear about his youth — in church nine times a week, able to count the number of times he's heard his father say "damn" on the fingers of one hand, expecting and receiving physical healings, serving God and country as a conscientious objector in the army. I know him now as he listens critically to and learns from his pastor, as he thanks God for his baby daughter, as he bears witness to his fellow workers that his marriage grows deeper and better after the honeymoon. So his life teaches me about those "Protestants."

I hope my life teaches him about Catholics. Can he see past our hypocrisy? Catholics drinking, swearing, getting Mass "over with" on Saturday nights. Lord, I pray, let him see your glory in tradition, your guidance in authority, your life in the sacraments. But first, Lord, take the beam out of my own eye.

(More than twenty-five years later, I wrote this story shortly

after returning to the Catholic Church I had left. I have pondered in recent years whether the tensions of living in two churches contributed to my leaving the sacraments, not just once, but twice. May our gracious Lord now grant me perseverance.)

Make Haste Slowly . . . Or . . . 'Father . . .'

My husband is reading from his Bible, following me from room to room, expounding for me in an earnest voice. "That's wonderful," you may be thinking. And indeed it would be wonderful, if he weren't scouring the pages for ammunition to use against my pending conversion to the Catholic Church. " 'And call no man father; you have one Father in heaven.' Why does the Catholic Church ignore that Scripture?" he presses. I finally turn to him in exasperation, "I have explained it a million times, and you just don't want to hear it!" He raises his voice: "I do hear what you say, but it so plainly contradicts Scripture!" "I cannot explain every little detail to your satisfaction! You will have to ask someone else who can answer calmly. I can't do it any more!" I turn my back angrily. "You have to answer to me; I am your spiritual head." He is trying not to yell. My words quaver, "Yes, but Jesus is even more my head, and I have to obey him before I can ever obey you."

Tears wet my pillow. How many times were we going to replay that scene? "Lord, why can't you make us one? Why all this strife over trying to obey you?" Perhaps the answer lies deep in our past, which has indeed been a crazy-quilt of church issues. My growing up Catholic and his growing up Protestant have been cardinal issues at many junctions in our marriage. But for now, only the present and the future matter, as we struggle to understand this threat to our unity. For the threat seems to lie precisely in what we thought was the foundation of our marriage — our obedience to Christ. Now what I am beginning to see as a matter of conscience, my husband sees as a betrayal of our unity. The impasse is agonizing.

Two days later, in the office of a parish priest, I still blink back tears, waiting for a man I insist on calling "Father" to give me some words of wisdom. "Maybe he's afraid of losing you," he suggests gently. "He's not going to lose me — not if this is about obeying Jesus. How could he think that?" Father patiently waits for me to consider. It is so hard for me to get inside my husband's mind. "How could he think that?" I repeat to myself.

I suppose he thinks I am leaving the path that had seemed so straight. It had been a straight way through the years of raising children in a Protestant home, children who now love the Lord and who may be confused by this sudden disagreement. The path took us through years of worshiping side by side in a community of Bible believers. The evangelical church had been a support in times of sickness and crisis, the fabric of life year in and year out, the source of loyal friendships — the doubling of our joys, the dividing of our griefs. Our cherished friendships found their meaning in the common love for the Lord we worshiped.

"Is worship the key?" I wondered. My husband and I won't be worshiping together. Will we even be worshiping the same Jesus? I think he doubts it. Jesus to him, after all, seems to clearly say not to call any man Father. He thinks Jesus belongs more to a pristine early church than to what appears to be a medieval system of indulgences and statues. He believes Jesus has no regard for liturgical vestments and holy water and rosaries, nor for popes, sacrificial Masses, or bowing down to a "wafer of bread." Do we really worship the same Jesus?

Or perhaps it's a matter of style. My husband's imagination is not attracted to incense, processions, or high altars. Or is it about basic authority? His allegiance is to the Bible only. Is it our understanding of the Church? His fellowship with other Christians is limited to the living, breathing believers he can see with his own eyes. I embrace angels and saints in heaven. All my attraction to beauty, hierarchy, and mystery is a mystery to him. He wonders why I can't see that I'm replacing the "simple truth" with superstition and shadows.

As I ponder, Father still waits patiently. (Is this the patience of the ages?) Maybe I can understand my husband's fears. Maybe I can feel the confusion he must feel, and begin to see as he sees: the terrible threat to our straight and narrow way, the path through the craziness of life. But there is no way I can change my course, even if, to us, the road seems to diverge, and we cannot see from here what that will mean to our marriage, or to our children. I see the Lord of my life beckoning me down one way, and apparently my husband cannot see him there at all. I sigh and shake my head. Through my tears, it seems that the man I call Father seems to have understood these things for eons.

Finally I find words. "Father, I have no choice, as perilous as it seems. Sometimes it seems like sacrificing Isaac. Wasn't this Christian marriage of mine promised God's help? Why does it seem that now God is the cause of its trouble? My husband keeps insisting that God wants our unity, and that I must be wrong to disrupt it.

"But I must come home to the Church. My husband will not lose me through this. I trust that obeying Jesus in this way will be good for our marriage in the long run, even if my husband cannot see it. We simply have to walk in darkness, holding his hand. Daylight will come, and our children will all have their own pilgrimages to make. They, too, will have to walk trusting in God."

Father still suggested I take more time to discern prayerfully, to be gentle about my decision and God's timing. Waiting became more and more difficult. I longed to receive our Lord in the Eucharist. I wanted to receive the sacraments, to be fully incorporated into the life of the Mystical Body. But Father's words of wisdom were: *Festina lente!* "Make haste slowly!" The words both captured my eagerness and called for patience. I waited in a kind of puzzled obedience, wondering what possible good would come of the delay. And during my waiting, I studied and prayed and longed my way into an even deeper assurance that the Catholic Church was where I belonged. I saw that the timing would be God's, and that the priest exhorting me to patience was a reflection of my Father in heaven. No wonder I called him "Father." Months later, when I did finally return to the fullness of the Church, it was with a greater peace for myself, and hope for my husband, than if I had rushed into the decision.

To make haste slowly was counsel from a wise Father. Someday, my husband will understand. And although I would certainly like that to happen before we get to heaven, I can wait.

Meanwhile, John Henry Newman's prayer is my own: "Oh, my Lord and Saviour, support me . . . in the strong arms of Thy sacraments, and by the fresh fragrance of Thy consolations. Let the absolving words be said over me, and the holy oil sign and seal me, and Thy own Body be my food, and Thy blood my sprinkling; and let my sweet Mother, Mary, breathe on me, and my Angel whisper peace to me, and my glorious Saints . . . smile upon me; that in them all, and through them all, I may receive the gift of perseverance, and die, as I desire to live, in Thy faith, in Thy Church, in Thy service, and in Thy love. Amen."

Chapter 15

Biblical Submission: An Interview with Kenneth Howell

by Lynn Nordhagen

> But I want you to understand that the head of every man is Christ, the head of a woman is her husband, and the head of Christ is God.
>
> — 1 Corinthians 11:3

Be subject to one another out of reverence for Christ. Wives, be subject to your husbands, as to the Lord. For the husband is the head of the wife as Christ is the head of the church, his body, and is himself its Savior. As the church is subject to Christ, so let wives also be subject in everything to their husbands. Husbands, love your wives, as Christ loved the church and gave himself up for her, that he might sanctify her, having cleansed her by the washing of water with the word, that he might present the church to himself in splendor, without spot or wrinkle or any such thing, that she might be holy and without blemish. Even so husbands should love their wives as their own bodies. He who loves his wife loves himself. For no man ever hates his own flesh, but nourishes and cherishes it, as Christ does the church, because we are members of his body. 'For this reason a man shall leave his father and mother and be joined to his wife, and the two shall become one flesh.' This mystery is a profound one, and I am saying that it refers to Christ and the church; however, let each one of you love his wife as himself, and let the wife see that she respects her husband.

— Ephesians 5:21-33

Wives, be subject to your husbands, as is fitting in the Lord. Husbands, love your wives, and do not be harsh with them.

— Colossians 3:18-19

Likewise you wives, be submissive to your husbands, so that some, though they do not obey the word, may be won without a word by the behavior of their wives, when they see your reverent and chaste behavior. Let not yours be the outward adorning with braiding of hair, decoration of gold, and wearing of robes, but let it be the hidden person of the heart with the imperishable jewel of a gentle and quiet spirit, which in God's sight is very precious. So once the holy women who hoped in God used to adorn themselves and were submissive to their husbands, as Sarah obeyed Abraham, calling him lord. And you are now her children if you do right and let nothing terrify you.

— 1 Peter 3:1-6

In these passages from Scripture, we have important teaching on marriage, which Protestant evangelicals take very seriously. In my experience, many an evangelical wife feels the tension between her own spiritual growth and the authority of her husband. In some circles, the wife may be encouraged to such extreme submission that it can be unhealthy; yet we believe Scripture is speaking to us with all the relevance it had to the Ephesians or Colossians. I've asked Kenneth Howell, a convert to Catholicism from the Presbyterian Church in America, to address this concern and some related questions. Ken has taught Scripture on the seminary level, is a linguistic scholar, and has served as the co-director of the Coming Home Network, an organization dedicated to supporting Protestant clergy who convert to Catholicism. His experience and his understanding of the issues involved in conversion are an extremely valuable resource.

LN: Ken, among Catholic converts from evangelical backgrounds, I often hear that the wives have struggled with the idea that they needed their husband's permission to convert. Evangelical Christians have been taught firmly that the husband is the spiritual head of the family and should make all the important decisions on behalf of the household. Yet biblical submission isn't a concern to many Catholics because they haven't considered it in the same way that evangelical churches have. In your experience, do many people agonize over the biblical passages about submission when it comes to only one spouse feeling led to convert?

KH: Unfortunately, in my opinion, this is not a problem as much as it should be. I know that might sound like an unusual answer, but what I mean is that the biblical patterns of leadership in marriage, and obedience in marriage, are not talked about enough today. That is true both in the Catholic Church and in many Protestant denominations. It's very clear from Genesis 1 and 2 and Ephesians 5, St. Paul's description of marriage, that the husband in a marriage is indeed the spiritual leader of the home. When people don't even consider the question of the structure of authority that God has placed in the family, it shows that they simply don't know what the biblical teaching is. And, unfortunately, they're not hearing it from the leaders of the Church. They may hear it in official documents, but often in the practical, day-to-day things they don't consider it. But this is important because there's also a structure of authority within the Church. God has given authority to the pastors, the priests, the bishops, and particularly to the Holy Father, but people tend not to see that authority-structure, or the importance of obedience to it. St. Benedict said that the beginning of humility is unhesitating obedience. In our culture today, at least in American culture, people almost don't know what the word obedience means any more. That's why I say that it's often not as much a problem as it should be; people should recognize the biblical and Christian call to obedience.

LN: What official documents should people be reading to understand authority both in the Church and in marriage?

KH: On marriage, they could do no better than *Familiaris Consortio,* Pope John Paul II's encyclical on marriage. Another very important document about marriage is *Casti Connubii* by Pope Pius XI. Collections of official documents about marriage are available from Catholic publishers. But even more importantly, the official Church documents are the Scriptures. Sometimes we think of them as being separate from the Church, but they are truly the documents of the Church.

We ought to take seriously the statements that Paul makes in Ephesians 5:21-33, where he gives his absolutely beautiful description of what a marriage should be, because it reflects the marriage between Christ and the Church. A parallel passage is Colossians 3:18–4:1. And another text of Scripture where we find these teachings about marriage emphasized is in Genesis. In fact, it all goes back to Genesis chapters 1 and 2, because at the beginning of human history we find that the marriage relationship is a model of our relationship with God. Not only is it a model in the sense of an analogy, but also marriage becomes an instrument by which the divine life of God can dwell within our souls. Now people who are hurting and suffering from the problems of a bad marriage have a difficult time grasping that. Indeed, all of us have a hard time grasping that, when things are not going well. But nevertheless it is objectively true that in a sacramental marriage — that is, a marriage between two baptized Christians in which there was full consent to the union — there is grace that flows through that marriage. But grace flows in a multifaceted way. It flows through the leadership of the husband, through his loving his wife. It flows through the wife loving and giving honor to her husband, and the submission of both of them to the authority of Christ.

And we must always remember that the Church is the model here. What that means is that the pope or the bishops of the Church do not just make up arbitrary rules for people to follow and say, "Be obedient." The rules, even the nondoctrinal rules of the Church, such as whether one should eat meat on Friday and so forth, are guidelines that are based on solid biblical and historical precedent. In the same way, in the home, the husband and the wife together in guiding the children base their rules on biblical principles. The husband, in guiding the wife and the children, is not to make up arbitrary rules, but his authority is a derivative one. It comes from God and is answerable to God.

So that means two things: first, that we recognize his authority as being from a higher source than himself as an individual. But it also means that the person who is in authority should have a very deep sense of his responsibility to ensure that his leadership is according to biblical, historical, and Christian patterns.

LN: That's not nearly as easy as it sounds! In fact, it seems like a lifelong proposition.

KH: Yes, indeed.

LN: Often, when one spouse wants to convert, but the other doesn't favor that decision, some advisers will say that if there is any conflict at all, a person should wait. They say that peace in the marriage takes first precedence in this decision-making. And I know some people have waited a long, long time. Would you say that that should be the pattern?

KH: I don't think that there's one pattern for a solution. The scenario that often comes up is that a husband, for example, wants to convert to the Catholic Church and his wife either doesn't understand it or has expressed opposition to it. And of course it may be that the wife wants to and the husband doesn't. Those situations have to be dealt with biblically, precisely because of the authority structure that is given in the Scriptures with regard to the home.

In talking about these things, I would say that marital

harmony is a very important ideal to maintain. No one should ever run roughshod over one's spouse's beliefs and feelings about this issue. Here is a situation where people can learn the virtue of patience in waiting for someone to see their point of view. Whether that point of view is right or wrong, part of marriage is being able to understand your spouse's viewpoint.

So I try to counsel people to go very slowly, to try to understand where their spouse is coming from. That may be extremely difficult. But at the same time, we are to understand that ultimately our responsibility is to obey God, and that no one in authority has any inherent right to ask us to disobey God, or to stand in our way when God is asking us to walk in obedience to him. That's true whether it's the pope, one's spouse, an employer, or anyone else. Our ultimate responsibility is to be obedient to God.

Oftentimes in life we are not at that crisis of final decision. More often, we're in the situation where we simply have a spouse who doesn't understand and who needs to have things explained, and we need to listen to find out what the spouse's viewpoint is.

For example, I've often discovered in counseling people that there is a different perception of what the problem is. A wife may say to me, "My husband doesn't understand that I believe in Catholic doctrine, and he doesn't, and that's an irreconcilable difference. We'll never be able to overcome this." Then I ask the husband, "Is that the problem?" And the husband says, "No, that's not the problem. The problem is that she's not willing to listen to my viewpoint." In other words, they see the problem quite differently. Both husband and wife need to seek the humility to be able to listen to one another. At the same time, they must be careful that they do not simply compromise the pursuit of truth. No husband has a right to bind his wife's conscience with respect to biblical truth. Nor does the wife have such a right.

I would say where one spouse wants to proceed with joining the Catholic Church, and the other one is not in favor, the first goal is to come to enough understanding that the spouse who does not want to convert can at least accept the conversion. Short of converting together, the next thing to work toward is acceptance of the conversion without animosity or resentment. If that can be done, then I would say that the person who wants to become Catholic can go ahead and join the Church. What we need to understand about this, and this is certainly true of my own marriage, is that it can be precisely in learning to love and accept each other in spite of our differences that our love can grow even deeper than before.

You see, there's a certain type of Christian culture that thinks that unity can only be when we completely agree on things. Unity does mean agreement in doctrine. But we must also realize that we live in a world that is less than perfect, which means we often have to learn to love people despite the differences between us.

Let's return to your question, "What is the model?" Again, I don't think there is one model, but there is a very important fact to remember. The Catholic Church has always taught — and it reaffirmed in Vatican Council II, in the "Dogmatic Constitution on the Church" (*Lumen Gentium*, 14) — that no one can be saved who, knowing that the Catholic Church is the true Church of Christ, either willingly leaves it or refuses to enter it. When people reach the point where they believe that the Catholic Church is the Church founded by Jesus Christ, and they know of their obligation to join that Church, then they must be obedient to God, no matter what anyone says.

LN: Did that influence you?

KH: Absolutely, it did! That was the point at which I knew I could not remain outside anymore. Because I did believe that this was the Church that was founded by Jesus Christ.

LN: Now what happens when a husband or wife comes to that point, and the spouse is still angrily resentful and not accepting?

KH: The person who wants to join, and is convinced that he or she should join out of conscience and out of obedience to God, must approach his or her spouse as gently and as lovingly and pleadingly as possible, and say, "Do you see that if I don't do this, I will be disobedient to God?" Hopefully, if that spouse is a Christian and understands the importance of this step of faith, that person will at least recognize that his or her spouse wants to be obedient to God above all things.

There's one thing we must remember: obedience to God inevitably brings blessing to our lives. In other words, if we know the good and do not do it, then we are withholding from ourselves, and those in our lives, the blessings that God wants to pour out on us and on them. As painful as obedience can sometimes be, there are hidden blessings. So I would counsel the person to sit down and talk to the spouse and say, "Don't you see that I have no choice? I must be obedient to God." Then all you can do is to leave the result to God, and pray for the person to understand. But even if the person doesn't understand, you can't be disobedient to God.

LN: When I told a priest how terribly opposed my husband was, he said that my baptism is primary over my marriage; it was the first sacrament I received, and his point was just what you said, that our ultimate obedience is to Christ, and that no one can forbid you to obey God.

This brings up another question. What about entering secretly? Is it permitted? Is it wise?

KH: If I'm ever a priest I'll know the answer to that! But with these sensitive pastoral issues we can never give blanket answers. Anyone who wants to enter the Catholic Church should enter with the counsel of a local priest or bishop. There may be some circumstances in which secretly entering might be appropriate, but I would tend to counsel people against it, because it has a psychological effect that is unhealthy. It puts you in a position of having to live a double life. One of the great virtues that we learn as Christians is the virtue of simplicity. Simplicity of heart means to be focused without duplicity. It means we don't try to live a lie. Entering secretly would just invite duplicity. Even though it may be necessary in extreme circumstances, I would tend to counsel against it.

LN: You certainly are in a position to understand these issues, being in contact with so many converts. I think your experience has given you a lot of wisdom.

Now some other practical things that have come up with other people and in my own situation, too.

A couple may go for counseling to a Protestant pastor, and the Protestant pastor naturally says, "Of course, you're not supposed to become Catholic!" How can this be discussed between the couple? Should the one who wants to become Catholic try to get counseling from a Catholic counselor, or is there a way to avoid the situation where each counselor seems to be totally biased?

KH: First, we have to go back to the principle we enunciated a few minutes ago: the person we're going to be answerable to on the Day of Judgment will be Jesus Christ. It's not going to be the pastor of a church or even the priest of a parish. That doesn't mean we can disregard the advice being given, but the pastor of the Protestant church and the priest of the Catholic church each have an obligation to explain the principles by which this conversion process is to proceed. The Protestant minister will have a responsibility to demonstrate to the couple from the Scriptures, or even from his own tradition, the reason why this conversion should not take place. Likewise, the Catholic priest has an obligation to explain from the Scriptures and from the Tradition of the Catholic Church, why this spouse should be allowed to convert. Then the responsibility for the decision does not lie with the priest or the minister; it lies with the individuals in the marriage. The spouses have to take all of the knowledge and advice they have received; they should hopefully pray about it together, and then they have to come to a decision.

LN: Here's a fairly common experience: the pastor says to the one who wants to convert, "Well, the really self-sacrificial thing to do for your family and your spouse would be for you to ignore this call, what you *think* is a call. You've been called to this marriage for a long time, and it's already in place, and you have no right to rock the boat. If you really want to be Christ-like, you'll give up this selfish desire."

KH: That is a very good question. There's some pretty clear biblical guidance in the Gospels: the call of the disciples. We know that St. Peter was married, because Jesus went to his mother-in-law's house to heal someone. But when Jesus said to Peter, "Come and follow me," he did that. Why? Because the authority of Christ is greater than the authority of our spouse. We must follow Christ, even to the point where our Lord said, "If anyone comes to me, and does not hate his own father and mother and wife and children and brothers and sisters, yes, and even his own life, he cannot be my disciple. Whoever does not carry his own cross and come after me cannot be my disciple" (Luke 14:26-27). We must forsake father and mother, brother and sister, wife or husband, to follow him. We must not forsake them on our own will, but only according to the will of Christ.

Now the advice to forget about this sense of call is very different. Let's put it this way: to say that we should deal delicately and move slowly and judiciously is very good advice. But to say we should ignore the call is absolutely different, because if the call to the Catholic Church is the call of Christ, it cannot be disregarded. We can never ignore the call of Christ. Even if no one understands, we need to follow Christ and what he says.

LN: Of course the psychological challenge is that everybody may be understanding the call of Christ but you — you who want to become a Catholic. And it should be clear from the Scripture, says the Protestant.

KH: We should rejoice that in the evangelical Protestant churches today there is a firm belief in the truth of Scripture. For well over a hundred years, there has been a very deep-seated division between what is called liberal Protestantism and evangelical Protestantism. The good side of liberal Protestantism is that it tends to promote tolerance, but the bad side is that it promotes tolerance at the cost of truth. In evangelicalism, the adherents believe in truth, but there's a great culture of intolerance. But a Catholic can rejoice that evangelical Christians do believe in the truth of the Scriptures. They believe in the basic truths of history in the Christian church, so we should be very pleased that we have a very similar foundation. But that also places the burden on the evangelical Christian to demonstrate why joining the Catholic Church is wrong. Likewise a Catholic has a responsibility to show, from the common base of the Scriptures, why it is the right thing.

LN: So it needs to be reasoned out from Scripture between them, without intolerance.

KH: We need to understand that the virtue of tolerance is not a matter of saying, "It doesn't make any difference what you believe." It's recognizing the difference and still accepting and loving the person anyway. You may have deep-level disagreement, but you still love and accept the person.

LN: I think we are back to the question of authority. For instance, if the husband wants to convert, the pastor has a much different approach than if a wife wants to become Catholic. Suppose I am a Mormon wife and I come to an evangelical pastor and say, "I want to convert to your church." The pastor may very well support the wife's insubordination in such a situation. But if the wife wants to leave evangelicalism, then suddenly the evangelical husband's authority is much more important. Do you see what I mean?

KH: You're saying that the advice given by evangelical pastors is that it's okay for a woman to convert to the evangelical church, even against her husband's wishes, but it's not okay if she wants to convert from evangelicalism to Catholicism?

LN: It seems to come down to the question "Does the husband's authority depend upon his belief structure?" If he is a Christian, does he have authority he would not otherwise have?

KH: No, the husband's authority is not dependent on his belief structure. The reason is that the marriage relationship and the husband's headship are grounded in creation. It doesn't matter whether the husband is a Buddhist or a Hindu or a Catholic or an Evangelical. This is seen in 1 Peter 3. Peter counsels women whose husbands are not believers. He says in that context that wives should be submissive to their husbands so that if any of the husbands do not believe the Word, they may be won over without words by the behavior of their wives, when they see the purity and reverence of their lives. Now we must understand that Peter was addressing a particular situation. Nevertheless, his advice holds true not only for wives, but for anyone who is under the authority of someone else. We are to show reverence and the respect that is due to that person because of the position the person is in. The position has been given to that person by God, whether it is a husband, a president, a schoolteacher, or any other authority. So if a wife wants to convert to Catholicism out of evangelicalism, she must do everything she can to be respectful and submissive to her husband. But there are two things to remember here. A human being, being imperfect and flawed and sinful, will sometimes exercise authority in improper ways. What is an improper way? When someone asks us to do something that is contrary to the will of God. That is why Peter and John could stand up against the Sanhedrin, whose authority they were under, and say to them, "We must obey God rather than men." In a similar way, the Christian wife must do everything that she can to be lovingly respectful and obedient to her husband, no matter what he believes. But when he exercises his authority in an improper way, against the will of God, she has the right and even the responsibility not to follow his dictates.

Let me give you an example that I think everyone would agree with. Suppose there is a husband who is physically and verbally abusive of his wife. Now she has a responsibility in general to be loving and obedient toward him. But she does not have a duty to accept physical abuse from him, because he has misused his authority to the detriment of his wife rather than to love her. So she does not have a responsibility to remain physically in his presence when he is doing this, nor even to live with him if it's a constant problem.

So with respect for her husband's authority, the wife must still discern, with the help of the Scriptures and Christian counsel, whether or not God is calling her to the Catholic Church. In that case, she must obey God.

LN: Another thing for careful discernment is the timing of what God is calling us to do.

KH: I'm so glad you brought up the question of timing. The call to the Catholic Church is not something that can be questioned. Every Christian is called to the unity of the faith. We are called to be part of the Church that Jesus Christ founded, because that is what the Scriptures teach in Ephesians 4, where Paul says there is one Lord, one faith, one baptism, one God and Father of all. He goes on to talk about the ministries of the Church, given for the purpose (4:12-13), until we all attain to the unity of the faith and the perfect knowledge of the Son of God. In other words, the unity of the faith is through coming into the Church. Now that call is unequivocal. But what is a question of discernment is *when* that is to be done. There we must take into account many different factors: the relationship with the spouse, the relationship with the children, the employment situation that one is in, one's state in life, etc. There are many factors that influence the timing. This means that entering the Church could proceed slowly or proceed quickly. Often it means it will proceed more slowly than one wishes. But one learns the virtue of patience in that suffering as well.

LN: There may be intense suffering for people who really believe in the Eucharist, yet have to wait.

KH: And the longing for the true body and blood of our Lord Jesus Christ is a true sign that a person is being called to the Catholic Church.

LN: There is a certain teaching in some evangelical circles that the wife's responsibility is simply to obey her husband and let God deal directly with her husband in cases of conflict. It is said that the husband's authority is an umbrella of protection for the wife, even to the extent that if you just obey your husband, short of sinning, of course, that takes your responsibility away.

KH: There's no question that any Christian heart can rejoice in an emphasis upon proper authority, but obedience to proper authority does not take away our responsibility to do and to live the truth. If we know the good to do and we don't do it, it's sin to us. If someone is asking us to do something wrong, and that person is unaware that it's wrong, we still have the responsibility to follow Christ and do what's right.

LN: Well, I can easily imagine most Protestant pastors saying, "It's certainly not sinful not to join the Catholic Church!"

KH: That's a point of theological difference that is extremely important. To most of twentieth-century Protestantism it doesn't matter which church you belong to. A Catholic can never believe that. It does matter which church you belong to.

LN: Now a practical question: How can you encourage a spouse to study? It's one thing to talk together, but often that is not enough. For instance, in my case, there's such a resistance on his part to read anything, partly because he thinks I should be able to summarize it for him, partly because he thinks I'm trying to indoctrinate him. I don't know what to do with that.

KH: The spouse who is Catholic and wants to share that with a non-Catholic spouse should first of all begin with prayer and penance. To pray for the salvation of your spouse is an act of love and obedience to God and love for your spouse. And we must remember that conversion of the heart is something that only God can do. So we should not try to convert our spouse; we should pray for that spouse's salvation. Now if the spouse is open to discussion or exploration, the second suggestion is to find out the way in which that person receives information. Not everybody is attuned in the same way. Some people are willing to read; others are willing to listen. We have to work very hard on explaining the Catholic faith to that person in terms that person will understand. Maybe he or she would prefer videos, or maybe it's a matter of watching EWTN or listening to tapes.

But perhaps the only thing that will be effective in having a person understand the Catholic faith is the way that we live. I will give you an example. In my own marriage, I think the most effective way that my wife understands the Catholic Church is when she sees it being lived out in my life, especially through confession. Of course I never tell my wife the things that I confess, but I demonstrate that I have a continuing need for both the forgiveness of Christ and the desire to be more obedient to him. Then she is more open to understanding the importance of what the Catholic Church teaches, especially with regard to confession, forgiveness, and repentance, and penance and growth in virtues. The other day my priest anointed me with the sacrament of the sick, not because I was physically sick but because I've been sick in my soul. I've struggled with a particular sin, which I don't have the willpower to overcome.

He perceived rightly that something has affected my psyche and my soul and has kept me bound to these particular sins. So he administered the sacrament of anointing of the sick. We believe that Christ was coming to heal that particular part of my soul. Now my wife did not understand this at first, but after I explained it to her, at least she could see that I had a desire to be more truly loving and obedient to Christ, which is why I received that sacrament.

The Catholic spouse needs to say, "How does my spouse receive positive information about the Catholic Church?" And once we understand, that's the avenue we have to use.

LN: Some non-Catholic spouses are not only flabbergasted that we would tell our sins to a priest, but they're also jealous, in a way, that we would be confiding in someone else. Not that they want to know our sins, but they don't understand how we could tell these intimate details to someone else.

KH: Well, there's a profession of substitute priests. It's called barbers and hairdressers. People tell all kinds of things when they're sitting in that chair that they wouldn't tell to their most intimate friends. But we are privileged to have the sacrament of penance and we can be confident, precisely because there is a sacramental seal over the confessional, that the priest will never reveal his knowledge of that life. And I also think (this is my own personal belief) that God gives the gift of forgetfulness to our priests. They don't even remember what they've heard.

LN: Maybe part of it is that they have heard it all so many times; part of it is also the special grace of forgetfulness.

KH: Part of the charism of receiving ordination is the ability to love even the most recalcitrant sinner. I've seen this with our priests again and again. I've gone back to confess this sin over and over, and they don't lack love for me, even though I don't seem to get any better.

LN: Here's another practical question: How can I assure my spouse that in spite of my rejecting his authority (in favor of Christ's ultimate authority) and all his objections, I still love him?

KH: Wonderful, wonderful question. This is a question that every married couple has to have, not only with regard to religious differences, but in all of life. People receive and understand love in different ways. In general (there are all kinds of exceptions to this), the makeup of a woman is such that a man must show her love by tender understanding, physical affection, and a heart that is really listening to what she says. Some women understand love by gifts, and some understand love by the commitment of time, so to a husband

I would say, commit time to your wife, commit yourself by showing her tender affection, by giving her a listening ear. Those are the things she will understand.

To a woman I would say that very often a man understands love by respect. If she can show respect to her husband in any genuine way, whether it's respect for his accomplishments in his work, or if it's respect for his intelligence, or if it's respect for his love of the children, or if it's respect with regard to his understanding of human nature, whatever way it is, she needs to try to show him that respect. But of course, each couple must pray and work to find the way that particular person understands and receives love, and seek to show it in that way.

In my experience as a Protestant pastor, and even now as a Catholic lay adviser, I find the most difficult situation is when a Christian wife has very little reason to respect her husband, really very little objective reason. I have talked to many wives whose husbands are (excuse the technical word) slouches, who are insensitive brutes, and they can almost legitimately ask, "Why did I marry this guy?" Sometimes it works the other way around, but more often I've seen it in this way. That is a very difficult position for a Christian woman to be in. Then all I think we can counsel is: "Pray that God will reveal to you the ways in which this person's soul has been damaged. What kind of damage keeps this person from doing things that would ordinarily be occasions for respect?"

I'll give you an example. There are people, both men and women, but often I meet men who seem to have an inability to understand another person's viewpoint. There's something wrong with a person's soul that makes such a person so self-centered that he can't get out of himself to understand another person's viewpoint. But the Christian who seeks to understand why that person is not able to do things or say things or be the kind of person who would command respect — the person who seeks to understand that kind of person grows in the virtues of patience of love and hope by doing that.

LN: Those words are food for thought!

One question I don't want to forget: what about the issue of confusing the kids, which is a big objection. A spouse will say, "You can't do this to our family; if you are Catholic and I am Protestant, the kids will think it's even okay to be Buddhist."

KH: This is a great problem. That's where the husband and wife must seek the common areas of their Christian faith. If one is Catholic and one is not, that doesn't mean that they can't pray together, that they can't emphasize Jesus Christ. They should emphasize the common faith that they have, and they should attempt to pray together as a couple, as a family. By doing that, they see Christ as the way to salvation. The children see that it does make a difference what you believe. And the parents should try to steer the children to healthy Christian activity.

LN: The truth does matter, and it matters what you believe. But here husband and wife are going back and forth with each other saying, "My belief is true, yours is not true." That's where the kids look on and say, "Who can know the truth anyway?"

KH: We must always emphasize that the truth and our understanding of the truth are not the same. The truth that Christ teaches in the Scriptures and in the history of the Church is not exactly the same as what we're saying in this moment. That's putting it negatively, but to put it positively, we can say, "We always understand the truth imperfectly, and our goal is always to continue searching out the truth that Christ taught us." Catholics and Protestants have different understandings of what that truth is, but the truth is there, to be understood and to be found. The reason that's so important in our context today is that young people in our postmodern era hear all around them that you can make up your own truth. We must firmly remind young people that there's no such thing as making up your own truth. Truth is what it is, apart from whether we believe it or not. Just because we don't believe it, doesn't mean that two plus two does not equal four. It's true regardless. In the same way, Christ's truth revealed in the Scripture is there objectively whether we understand it or not. Our goal is always to keep searching for truth. One healthy thing about differences is that the more we examine them the closer we get to understanding what truth is.

LN: Some have expressed the feeling that our sufferings in "mixed marriages" somehow reflect the suffering of Jesus in his broken body, his divided Church. Is it a participation in the suffering of Christ to be in a marriage where we are struggling over truth and worship and unity?

KH: To be in a marriage — to be in any marriage — is to experience the suffering of Christ. It doesn't matter whether you're both Catholic or both Protestant or whatever, because in any human relationship you're going to have times of great hurt and misunderstanding, and those times are the times in which we share in the sufferings of Christ. For example, you can have a marriage and still have loneliness. You can have a marriage and have misunderstanding; you sin against each other. But the virtues of our faith — the ability to forgive, the ability to be united to another human being (a spouse in this case) — are things we seek more and more, although we always experience unity imperfectly. Consequently, it's very important to understand that when we experience these things, we have to positively embrace these problems and difficulties as part of the suffering of Jesus in our life. We are to understand that the marriage we're in is God's means of giving us holiness, both in the joys and in the sufferings.

Besides, our disunity is not so much a suffering of the broken, divided Church, as it is the imperfect union of Christians with the Church. Indeed, the Catholic Church teaches that the Church is not divided. The Church believes, and every Catholic should believe, that the Church is always one. When we confess that we believe in the "one, holy, catholic, and apostolic Church," we are confessing that the Church by its very nature cannot be divided. But individual Christians can be imperfectly joined to the Church. So the pain that we feel is that there are genuine Christians of good will who are not yet joined sacramentally to the Church. And that pain is something we should feel. Every Christian should have the desire of Jesus when he prayed, "Father, that they might be one even as we are one" (John 17:11). So when we see Christians who do not experience the fullness of unity in the truth, we should feel the pain of Christ's heart in that way.

Chapter 16

The Courage to Love

by Gregory K. Popcak,
MSW, LCSW

Eric and Maureen, an attractive couple in their early forties, sat scowling at each other in my office. Maureen, raised Presbyterian, had recently begun the RCIA program in a local Roman Catholic parish and her husband, a nonpracticing Methodist, was — shall we say — unhappy about this recent development. Though Eric himself did not attend his church regularly, his family was very active (his brother is a minister) and he considered himself "a good Christian."

"I wish I could share my faith with my husband," said Maureen, "but he gets angry every time I bring it up."

"I don't appreciate her shoving that Catholic stuff down my throat," said Eric. "First it was weekly Mass, then it was this RC-whatever-you-call-it. Now she won't even have sex with me because Catholics think sex is a sin unless you have a baby every time you do it, and I'm not about to touch her without some kind of birth control. Frankly, I don't see why I shouldn't be resentful."

It is sad when issues of faith, which by rights should draw a couple closer together, end up being clubs with which mates bludgeon each other. Nevertheless, it is a regular occurrence, and it is a problem that has been with us since the earliest days of Christianity.

To help couples faced with the tension resulting from a unilateral conversion, I'd like to look at the issue from several sides. First, what should the ultimate goal of the couple be? Second, what are some common concerns and/or questions for such couples? And finally, what other faith and marital factors complicate the already stressful circumstances surrounding a unilateral conversion?

The Ultimate Goal

"I want my whole family to go to church together," says Martin, a recent convert to Catholicism who is married to Jennifer, a woman who is, to Martin's chagrin, happy to remain Protestant.

Sharing a unified vision of the faith and attending church services together is often the ideal expressed by those who have a conversion experience. Having found what one considers to be a great treasure, it is only natural to want to share that treasure with loved ones. And yet, such a sharing is not always immediately possible. In fact, at first, it is not always advisable to pursue such a goal. Normally, there needs to be a transition phase; a stage in which the couple at least agrees to be tolerant — though not necessarily enthusiastically supportive — of each other's involvement in different churches.

While this goal is more modest and, in many ways, less satisfying than total unity of faith, it is an important stage during which many issues are worked out. For example: How can we still find ways to fulfill Christ's command to be loving toward each other even though we disagree on such important issues? How can we expand our capacity for generosity and learn to appreciate the good to be found in both faith traditions? How can we protect the peace of our home even while asking very direct questions about our respective faiths? How will we pass on a unified vision of the faith to our children, even though we have such clear differences? Does your rejection of our previously shared spirituality mean that you will reject me next? And so on.

Making basic tolerance the first relationship goal in the presence of a unilateral conversion affords both the husband

and wife the time needed to adjust to the changes they are experiencing. Likewise, it stops the non-Catholic spouse from feeling pressured to do something he or she is simply not ready (and may never be ready) to consider doing. By making basic tolerance the first goal, the converted spouse sends the message that "I have found something that gives me great joy, but I am willing to wait until you are ready to share it with you. Moreover, I am willing to continue to support you in your faith journey even while you are still trying to figure out how to support me in mine. No matter what churches we worship at, we both still love Jesus, and I still love you." This can be a powerfully loving message to send. And while basic tolerance does not always lead to a shared vision of faith, a shared vision does not often occur without passing through this stage first.

Common Concerns

There are several concerns that couples raise as they are experiencing the tension that results from a unilateral conversion. While space does not allow us to address all of these concerns, the following represent some of the biggest: How much should I try to convert my spouse or argue about questions of faith? Should I wait for my mate's permission before I convert? Should I follow my passion and enter the Church immediately, or does prudence require me to wait and test the waters? And finally, How do I introduce my spouse to the Church's teachings on NFP (natural family planning) and sexuality? Let's take these one at a time.

Should I Try to Convert My Spouse?

In a word, no. The harder you work to convert your mate the more defensive your mate will become and the more likely your relationship will be poisoned by resentment. While it is perfectly acceptable to offer to explain or share things that you find fascinating, interesting, or comforting about Church teaching or practice, it is quite another thing to try to "make" your mate find those things similarly fascinating, interesting, or comforting. Your job is not to argue your mate into the Church. But if you are not to be a Crusader, then what are you to be? Well, you are to become Christ. In order to have any credibility to possibly lead your mate into the Church, your mate must first be able to see that your Church involvement is making you into someone worth following. Your first and most important job as a married convert to the Catholic faith is to learn how to use the grace of the sacraments to become the spouse your partner always needed you to be, but you previously lacked the courage, strength, or will to become.

If your Catholicism is not at work in the way you relate to your spouse and children, then it is not a true conversion, but merely an intellectual exercise or social outlet. In order to help you understand — in practical terms — what it would mean for you to bring the faith home, I recommend making a list of all the things that your mate has ever asked you to do or be. Some examples might include: be more attentive to the kids, be a better listener, be more disciplined, be more romantic, be a better communicator, or any other request that does not expressly violate the principles of your faith but you have simply avoided doing because it forced you out of your "comfort zone." And then as you receive the sacraments, meditate on what it would take to fulfill those requests. For example, if you go through the RCIA, when you are preparing for baptism or confirmation, ask yourself what new relating skills you would need to learn or what changes you would need to make in order to live out the virtues of faith, hope, love, temperance, prudence, peace, patience, understanding, wisdom, self-control, and all the other gifts and fruits of the Holy Spirit at home with your spouse and children. When you receive the Eucharist (or if you are not yet a full member of the Church — when you pray while others receive), meditate on how fully Christ gives himself to you and then ask God for the grace to give yourself as fully to your mate and children. In general, ask yourself how Christ would do everything in your marriage from scheduling date nights, to making love to your mate, to doing yard work, cleaning the house or taking out the trash, and then rely on the strength of the sacraments to help you project this Christ-like image to your spouse. And when you fail to be the loving servant to your family Christ and his Church calls you to be, use the grace of the sacrament of reconciliation to help you get back on track.

As the early Father of the Church Tertullian said, "Look at those Christians, see how they love!" Your conversion must make you a better lover and servant to your mate first and foremost. When you allow the grace of the sacraments to help you become the spouse Christ would be to your mate, your husband or wife may eventually ask, "What's gotten into you?" This is your cue. Simply say, "Every time I go to Mass or celebrate the sacraments, God reminds me how much he loves you, and that makes me want to love you that much more. I'm just sorry it took me so long to see it." Then drop the subject. As St. Francis once said to his disciples, "Go forth and preach the Gospel. Use words if you must." By choosing to focus your energies on becoming the spouse God wants you to be instead of focusing on arguing your mate into the faith, you present an attractive witness that will either lead your mate into the Church through your grace-filled example, or at least gain the respect of your mate and lessen tension in your home, should your mate choose to remain with his or her own denomination.

Do I Need My Mate's Permission to Convert?

This is a big question and many people, wives especially, wonder if they are not betraying the biblical injunction to be submissive to their husbands if they proceed with their conversion despite his disapproval. But let's look at that Scripture.

The passage from Ephesians begins with "Defer to one another out of reverence for Christ" (Ephesians 5:21). Then and only then does St. Paul exhort wives to be submissive to their husbands. This is important to remember because, according to Scripture, deference to one's mate assumes that one's spouse is first discerning and revering the will of Christ for their lives.

Unfortunately, sometimes husbands and wives forget to seek God's will and instead seek to impose their own will on their mates. When this happens, husbands and wives use their God-given authority in a wrong way, a way that seeks to discourage each other from the pursuit of the paths, ministries, and missions God has placed on their hearts. To submit to this wrongful use of spousal authority is not Christian submission — it is idolatry. It is denying God's holy will for your life to follow your mate's will for your life. If you do this, you might as well erect a statue to Baal in the living room while you are at it.

St. Paul tells us, "In life and death we belong to God" (Romans 14:8). And Jesus tells us, "If anyone comes to me and does not hate his father, and mother, and wife . . . and his own life also, he cannot be my disciple" (Luke 14:26). As Christians, we are obliged to follow wherever Christ leads, even if this means following without our mates alongside us. Of course, as Christians, we must at all times attempt to grow in a way that is respectful to our marriages. Even so, our first duty must be to God and the mission he has given us in our lives.

C. S. Lewis addresses this point in *The Four Loves*: "So, in the last resort, we must turn down or disqualify our nearest and dearest when they come between us and our obedience to God. Heaven knows, it will seem to them sufficiently like hatred. We must not act on the pity we feel; we must be blind to tears and deaf to pleadings."

Of course, husbands or wives must be very cautious when the path they believe God wants them to take may inflict some serious growing pains on their marriage. Before causing such pain, they should pray, discern, agonize, and seek guidance from their pastors and counselors, and listen to the good advice they are given. And they should also be sensitive to the reasonably expressed concerns of their mates (see below). But if all their efforts continue to point in a particular direction — specifically the direction that leads one to closer communion with God and a greater capacity for contributing more to the marriage — one must take that route. Even if it means defying your mate.

Should I follow my passion and convert immediately, or does prudence require me to wait — and if so, for what? • This is a judgment call best made by each individual Christian after a whole lot of prayer, discernment, and consultation with respected pastors or other brothers and sisters in Christ. In another chapter in this book, Kenneth Howell gives some very good advice about timing. Beyond this, I would add the following.

In my books *For Better . . . Forever! A Catholic Guide to Lifelong Marriage* (Our Sunday Visitor Publishing) and *The Exceptional Seven Percent: Nine Secrets of the World's Happiest Couples* (Carol Publishing Group) I describe a problem-solving rule I call "Never negotiate the 'what,' only negotiate the 'how' and the 'when.' " In other words, if your mate wants or needs something, it is not your place to deny permission for your mate to have it (this is a parental role, not a spousal one). However, you do have a right to insist that your concerns be addressed before you lend your support to your mate's cause. While the convert's mate does not have the right to forbid his or her spouse from entering the Church (or doing anything for that matter) he or she does have the right to say, "If you are really serious about this, then before I can support you, I need you to give me a specific amount of time to adjust [*or* to help me tell my parents / to find another way to provide for our family first / to figure out how to handle this with our children / etc.]." In this way, the husband and wife can work together to find mutually respectful ways to meet their individual needs. I would suggest that the intended convert, faced with any reasonable requests from his or her mate, should postpone any final actions until those concerns have been adequately addressed. It would seem that, in most cases, Christian prudence and basic respect for one's mate would require at least this much. An intended convert, after diligent prayer and seeking the wise counsel of others, may choose to do things differently, but he or she should realize that unless profound respect is shown for one's mate's concerns (even while they pursue their own conversion process) the future of the marriage could be placed at risk, and the chances that there will ever be tolerance of the different faiths, much less a unified faith vision, are negatively and significantly affected.

How do I introduce my spouse to the Church's teachings on NFP and sexuality? • The best way to answer the question of how to introduce your mate to the Church's teaching on sexuality and NFP is to do it slowly, and emphasize the benefits to the marriage that NFP yields.

Too often, spouses who are converting announce to their mates, "If you want to make love with me, we are going to do it the Church's way (that is, the NFP way) from now on, because the Church says it's a sin not to do so." While this is technically correct, it has the effect of running over one's mate with a steamroller, makes NFP look like so much "popery," and overshadows the myriad benefits to a marriage that NFP can bring. Let's examine some of these benefits.

First of all, there is only a five-percent divorce rate among couples practicing NFP (and only a one-percent divorce rate among couples who teach it). While there are no studies I am aware of that definitively explain this phenomenon, it is a fact with which to be reckoned. My own take on the statistic is that practicing NFP requires the couple to develop and live out a shared vision for their lives, like no contracepting couple can. Also, it empowers couples to constantly seek God's will for their life, economics, marriage, and family size by requiring the couple to prayerfully discern the direction of their lives every month. Besides this, NFP prevents couples from "sexing" their way through problems and instead actually spend a significant amount of time each month loving, serving, and communicating with each other in nonsexual ways. The unique level of loving, serving, and communicating that goes on in marriages where NFP is practiced leads to much more satisfying sex when the couple does make love. Interestingly, the studies of the premier marriage researcher Dr. John Gottman support this conclusion when he asserts that couples with the most rewarding sex lives do not concentrate on the sexual aspects of their relationship as much as they concentrate on nonsexual ways they can love and serve each other on a daily basis. NFP requires such service from couples, who are then empowered by the grace of marriage to reap the benefits in the bedroom.

Finally, it might be helpful to let the non-Catholic spouse know that NFP is not a specifically "Catholic" thing. Many Bible-believing Protestants come to see that Scripture deals quite harshly with those who practice a contraceptive mentality. Kimberly Hahn (wife of Catholic apologist Scott Hahn) came to the Catholic Church through her study of Scriptures in a Protestant Bible college where she realized that contraception was universally condemned in Scripture and that the Church was the only Christian institution that had the fortitude to hold this position consistently for two thousand years. In light of such facts, it is not surprising that a significant percentage of the membership of the Couple to Couple League (an organization promoting NFP) is Protestant.

Regardless, before springing NFP on your mate, you will want to get some basic training in its effective practice. Contact the Couple to Couple League or your diocesan family life office for the telephone number of an NFP teaching couple near you. Invite your mate to attend an NFP class with you, not because you want to bully him or her into submitting to "what the pope tells couples to do in their bedrooms" (as if your spouse could be bullied in such a way). But rather, so that your mate can see first hand what he or she is being asked to accept, and he or she can gather the information needed to make an informed decision rather than merely an emotional one.

Other Factors Affecting the Marriage

While unilateral conversion is often the straw that breaks the camel's back, other issues that predate the conversion can figure into the conflict as well. I'd like to take a brief look at four — one personal factor and three marital ones. They are: the kind of faith the nonconverted spouse exhibits, the lack of generosity in the marriage in general, the spouses' general lack of credibility with each other, and a deficiency in good problem-solving skills.

The Nonconverted Spouse's Faith Stage

Essentially, believers of all denominations fall into three basic categories. In ascending order of mental health, the first group is comprised of individuals who have a kind of "us versus them" mentality about religion. Folks in this group may have a somewhat paranoid worldview and see those who do not specifically identify themselves with their preferred group as dangerous. Individuals in this category tend to use their religious involvement as a way to prop up their inferior self-esteem. Such people believe themselves to be among "the elect." They tend to think of themselves as superior to the rest of the world that is made up of people who, at best, don't get it, and, at worst, are actively plotting against the success of the preferred group.

The second category is comprised of individuals who have a meaningful connection to their faith but attend a particular church because of the emotional connection they have to it ("It makes me feel good to go") and/or because of the social connection they have to the particular church ("All my friends/family attend that church; I like to worship with them"). This category also includes those individuals who attend their particular church out of inertia. (For example: "I've just always gone here." Or "I inherited this church from my folks.") However, these individuals tend to be at the beginning cusp of this stage.

Finally, the third group is comprised of those whom I would call "Truth Seekers." These individuals, though they are solidly ensconced in a particular faith tradition, are eager to question, explore, and study every aspect of their own faith tradition as well as others. (*Note well:* People in this category should be differentiated from those individuals who are merely "open-minded" and whose claims to believe in everything actually prevent them from believing in anything.) As I say, though they usually have a strong devotion to a particular faith group, people in the "Truth-Seeking" category tend to be most concerned with seeking God's will wherever that search may lead them, even if pursuing that truth requires great personal sacrifices at times.

If a convert to the Roman Catholic faith is married to a person in the first category (the "us versus them" believers), then any attempt at conversion will be perceived as a vicious, personal attack by the nonconverted spouse. Regardless of the sanity and generosity the convert may have shown to his or her mate in the past, the convert will henceforth be counted among "the enemy." The convert's attempts to reason with a mate adopting such a posture will most likely be unproductive. This is because such a hostile response merely reflects the paranoid workings of the spouse's own mind rather than the actual circumstances. (For example: "Just because Catholics don't really worship statues and have sex with nuns doesn't mean that they shouldn't be treated as if they do.") In such cases, unilateral conversion can be devastating to the marriage insofar as the convert — in the worst-case scenario — can be branded as a tool of the devil sent to tempt the "faithful spouse" from the true way. If such couples survive a unilateral conversion, the resolution may not come before an extended separation and/or a great deal of counseling to address the other nonreligious issues that are being symbolically played out in the "religious crisis" the couple is suffering through.

If a convert is married to someone in the second category (faith defined primarily by emotional ties and social relationships), most of the conflict is going to center around such questions as "What am I going to tell my family/friends?" "How could you leave behind the security of what we've always known to pursue this crazy idea of yours?" and "If you reject our old 'tribe' does that mean you will also eventually reject me?" If the convert is careful to respectfully respond to such concerns, and work with his or her mate to show that he or she is not going to run irresponsibly into the arms of his or her "new lover" (that is, the Catholic Church), this couple will most likely be able to arrive at the toleration stage we examined earlier with only a moderate amount of difficulty. Even so, total unity of faith may be years away — if it ever comes — as the nonconverted spouse continually examines the emotional and social costs and benefits of leaving one's own denomination and following one's mate. Spouses in this category are most responsive to the idea of converting when they see that church involvement is causing the convert to become a better, more responsive, attentive, and loving husband or wife. When the convert directs his or her spiritual energies into the marriage, it shows his or her spouse that the losses incurred by leaving behind the "old crowd" will be more than made up for by the intimacy of the marriage.

Alternatively, these marriages suffer greatly when the convert spends all of his or her time working at the church at the expense of family relationships, engages the spouse in pointed, theological arguments, and hangs out with his or her Catholic friends to the exclusion of the spouse because "I get most of my support away from home." Such actions on the part of the convert will cause his or her mate to view the Church as a rival — a mistress to be avoided and even fought against at all costs.

If the convert's spouse is in the third category (the "Truth Seekers"), conflicts will be mostly theological in nature as the couple has a series of tense but civil-enough arguments surrounding the finer points of each other's faith. In spite of the tension that does exist, these couples are best equipped to handle unilateral conversion because both the husband and wife respect each other's intelligence, responsibility, and conviction. They may not always agree with each other, but there is enough respect in the marriage as a whole to extend some credit when it is necessary to do so.

While each marriage is different and no one intervention will work for every couple, by helping the convert know the type of personality he or she is married to, the convert can take the appropriate general steps to preserve the marriage even while pursuing his or her own spiritual convictions.

Now that we've seen one of the personal factors that complicates unilateral conversion, let's examine three marital factors that negatively impact couples facing unilateral conversion: a lack of generosity, a lack of credibility, and a lack of good problem-solving skills.

A Lack of Generosity

Some spouses are loathe to join in their mate's interests (religious or otherwise) if they themselves do not share those interests. When one spouse says, "Would you like to come shopping with me [*or* go to that concert / watch the big game / hear about my work / go camping / go to the theater / etc.]?" the other spouse responds with some version of "Ugh. You know that's not my kind of thing. Why don't you do that with one of your buddies [girlfriends]?" Such sentiments represent a marital problem I refer to as a lack of generosity. That is, a general unwillingness to stretch one's own comfort zone for the sake of one's mate and marriage.

The amount of generosity present in a marriage before a conversion is a good indication of the amount of satisfaction (or lack thereof) the couple can expect from their postconversion relationship. If there is a great deal of generosity in the marriage before the conversion, then it is highly likely that the couple will be able to reach at least the toleration stage we examined earlier, because both the husband and wife are used to stretching their own comfort levels for the sake of a mate. However, if a spirit of generosity is lacking in the preconversion relationship, estrangement will increase exponentially following conversion as the converted mate becomes more and more interested in the Church and the nonconverted spouse retreats into his or her own pursuits.

In marriages where generosity is lacking, converts should direct their energies toward taking the time to learn about, participate in, and become conversant in their mate's interests first (especially nonreligious interests — which are "safer"), before they can credibly expect such generosity to be reciprocated on a more religious front. This is a kind of back-door intervention that builds credibility (see below) and encourages the mate — by example rather than lectures — to reach beyond his or her immediate comfort levels and try to understand where the converted spouse is coming from. Developing such generosity is important in all marriages, but it is vital for marriages facing unilateral conversion.

A Lack of Credibility

Henry's wife, Sheila, was received into the Catholic Church six months prior to my meeting them. Their marriage was cracking under the pressure and they came to me in a last-ditch effort to save it. Said Henry, "She keeps pushing me to come to church with her. Honestly, though, I can't stand to be around her anymore. She has become such a bitch since she converted. She's always picking on this thing that I do and that thing that I say. Who the hell does she think she is?"

Who indeed? Sadly, when a person converts or reverts to the Church, his or her passion for the faith can sometimes be expressed rather judgmentally. All of a sudden, everything that irritated one about one's mate takes on a new spiritual significance. As one revert said — only half-jokingly — about her unchurched husband, "I always thought he was an idiot. Now he's a damned idiot to boot."

Clearly, this is a case of seeing the speck in one's neighbor's eye and missing the beam in one's own. As I said, if the convert (or revert) hopes to lead his or her mate into a unity of faith, then he or she must be someone worth following. This is done, not by lecturing or becoming hypercritical of a spouse, but by using the grace of the sacraments to become the mate Christ would be if he was married to the convert's spouse. This is a tall order, but it is nothing less than Christ and the Church require of a married Christian. And it is absolutely necessary to the survival of a marriage facing unilateral conversion.

A Lack of Good Problem-Solving Skills

The final nonreligious factor that negatively affects marriages in which one mate converts and the other does not is poor arguing skills. Effective marital problem-solving is an art form that precious few couples learn to do well. Granted, most couples can stumble through life using a basic, albeit limited, repertoire of problem-solving skills. But when a couple experiences a serious stressor, like unilateral conversion, they are going to need a master class in problem-solving. A wise counselor seeing such a couple would do well to avoid the religious issues at first, and instead teach the couple the skills they need to argue effectively and respectfully. Such skills will enable the couple to then come to their own solutions regarding the "religion question." (For tips on effective arguing in a Christian context, see my books, *For Better . . . Forever!* and *The Exceptional Seven Percent: Nine Secrets of the World's Happiest Couples.*)

The problem with many pastoral counselors (and pastors who counsel) is that they try to tackle the religious issue head-on, which can't be done without appearing to take sides. This results in one mate or the other becoming alienated by the process and withdrawing from the counseling. The only way to deal with this issue respectfully is to lead the couple step by step through the skills they must learn to solve their own problems in the unique ways God is calling them to do so.

Again, converts in marriages where arguments in general are circular and ineffective should first do whatever is necessary to learn effective problem-solving skills so that religious discussions (and indeed, all discussions) could be as productive as possible. I would invite couples struggling with any aspect of unilateral conversion to contact me at the Pastoral Solutions Institute (740-266-6461) for specific guidance on how to protect the intimate core of the marriage even as they pass through this very challenging time.

Conclusion

In short, unilateral conversion is a difficult reality, but an eminently survivable one, assuming married couples learn to respond well to the challenges such conversions present. In fact, if couples use the opportunity to grow in maturity and generosity, increase their credibility by becoming more thoughtful mates, and learn more effective problem-solving skills, such couples might find themselves in the enviable position of having a better postconversion marriage than a preconversion one even when the religious differences persist.

Of course, the real key to the whole process is prayer. Regardless of the churches they attend, couples must continue to worship God in the "domestic church" that is their family. Couples must work together to constantly discern God's will for their lives, and seek the Lord's grace to be loving to each other, especially when being loving is hard and makes little sense.

Of course, the fact remains that even when couples experience religious differences, they remain each other's best hope, second only to the saving work of Jesus Christ, for arriving properly attired at the heavenly banquet. It is my sincere hope that every couple reading this would remain deeply committed to their marriage, experience the peace and wisdom of the Holy Spirit, and work to see that God's love reigns in their hearts and homes. Regardless of the degree of unity between your and your mate's form of religious expression, it is my wish and prayer that you and your house will continue to serve the Lord.

Chapter 17

A Marriage Saved in Heaven: Elisabeth Leseur's Life of Love

by Robin Maas, Ph.D.

The name Elisabeth Leseur is unknown to most American Catholics; but the English translation of her remarkable journal, long out of print, is once again available. The recent release of a beautiful new paperback edition by Sophia Institute Press provides occasion for rejoicing, for this French housewife's spiritual odyssey is sure to give hope to the countless Catholic wives in this country whose suffering mirrors her own. For several years I have assigned Elisabeth Leseur's journal to my students at the John Paul II Institute for Studies on Marriage and Family. Without exception, they are stunned by what they read and are deeply moved.

Many American women will find Elisabeth Leseur's writings psychologically inaccessible, for they witness to a vision of marriage and an experience of silent, sacrificial love for which our contemporary culture offers no explanation or support. At a time in history when women feel they have a right to personal fulfillment in both the major spheres of their lives — domestic and professional — this particular life may register with many as an enigma and a rebuke, for it reminds us that our personal ambitions are narrow and impoverished, lacking the luster and verve of the heroic.

Married in 1889 in Paris, Felix and Elisabeth Leseur were both from relatively prosperous and cultivated backgrounds.

They and their impressive circle of friends were part of an intellectual elite who indulged themselves in a constant round of receptions and soirees, evenings at the theater, and frequent travel abroad. The young husband was a medical doctor, and like so many ardent suitors, Felix had promised his fiancée that even though he was no longer a believer — having lost his faith in medical school — he would always respect her Catholic piety and never interfere in her practice of the faith. Elisabeth was attractive, good-natured, and intellectually curious. A lover of all the arts, when she was not busy entertaining or being entertained, she pursued her own intellectual advancement through self-directed study projects, mastering Latin, English, and Russian.

Indeed, this was a couple that seemed to "have it all." To look at the handsome newlyweds one would never guess that the relationship would soon be permeated by the deepest and most hidden psychological anguish imaginable; and even more astonishing was the survival of their affection for one another in the midst of a massive failure of communication of the sort that would topple most middle-class marriages today.

The Cross of Spiritual Isolation

At the time of her marriage, Elisabeth Arrighi Leseur could be fairly characterized as a sincere but somewhat conventional Christian. There was no particular reason, given her background, for Felix to expect the kind of spiritual seriousness that emerged in her early thirties, just as there was no reason for Elisabeth to expect the dramatic change of attitude that developed in her husband not long after their marriage. From a staunchly Catholic family, the Jesuit-educated Felix was able to discard his religious formation surprisingly quickly under the pressures created by his own professional and social ambitions. Originally willing to tolerate what he himself had left behind, Dr. Leseur soon came under the influence of anticlerical friends and adopted their attitude of militant resistance to Catholicism. His innate capacity for zeal came to full bloom in his conversion to atheism and the subsequent efforts he made to evangelize his wife.

Felix began to undertake a study of polemical anti-Catholic literature in earnest and in his enthusiasm thrust much of it upon his wife. Soon, it began to take effect. Elisabeth came to have serious doubts and started to look favorably on the arguments of liberal Protestantism, positions that Felix gladly endorsed, since he saw these as only a short step away from radical agnosticism. One work in particular, Renan's *History of the Origins of Christianity*, he expected to produce the much desired coup de grace that would demolish the last remnants of his wife's religious convictions. To his surprise and dismay, the effort backfired:

> . . . Thanks to divine Providence, the very work that I thought would accomplish my hateful object brought about its ruin. Elisabeth . . . was not deceived by the glamour of the form, but was struck by the poverty of the substance. . . . She felt herself approach the abyss, and sprang backwards, and from then on she devoted herself to her own religious instruction.[1]

Elisabeth's reeducation in the faith, which she herself planned and implemented, consisted of an extensive reading program devoted to the New Testament and the writings of the saints. Her husband's eager efforts to sway her had taught her the arguments; her own program of study gave her the background to reply confidently. Thus the net effect of Felix's attack on Elisabeth's Catholicism was to ground her much more firmly in her faith than she had ever been before.

Furious at this unexpected turn of events, Felix redoubled his efforts to get his wife to see the light, but there was an unmistakable change in Elisabeth that even her frustrated husband could not ignore. He saw her faith become a new thing, unassailable, unshakable, and radiant, opening henceforth to her the way to the sanctification in which she was so marvelously to progress. Her ascension to God had begun. And this faith "that could move mountains" had been set by God upon the firmest rock of all — that is, upon suffering.[2]

In Elisabeth's case, the primary source of her suffering was her marriage, but as we shall see, it had nothing to do with having married "the wrong person" or in the death of marital love. The radical tension between husband and wife over the issue of religion was to be a constant, implacable reality in their marriage, and a source of unremitting pain for Elisabeth. The following entry captures accurately the poignant nature of the isolation she endured: "I thirst for sympathy, to bare my soul to the souls that are dear to me, to speak of God and immortality and the interior life. . . ."[3]

Elisabeth confided to her journal the acute pain she suffered when not only husband but friends as well attacked or made light of what she treasured in her heart:

> Bitter suffering of an evening spent in hearing my faith and spiritual things mocked at, attacked and criticized. God helped me to maintain interior charity and exterior calm; to deny or betray nothing, and yet not to irritate by too rigid assertions. But how much effort and inner distress this involves, and how necessary is divine grace to assist my weakness![4]

That a young wife should be deeply wounded — and angered — by such a betrayal is to be expected. What is remarkable here is Elisabeth's capacity to make use of her suffering for the benefit of those who inflicted it on her. Where human nature seeks just reparation for pain inflicted, Elisabeth is unwilling to indulge that very natural demand; nor will she simply suffer. Instead, she "spends" that pain to benefit those who caused it. Immediately following her description of her distress, she adds this plea and a resolution:

My God, wilt Thou give me one day . . . soon . . . the im-
mense joy of full spiritual communion with my dear husband, of the same faith, and, for him as for me, of a life
turned toward Thee? I will redouble my prayers for this intention; more than ever will I supplicate, suffer, and offer
to God communions and sacrifices to obtain this greatly
desired grace.[5]

An Apostolate to Souls

Felix recalls that when asked to inscribe a motto in the
daybook of her beloved younger sister, Elisabeth had written
the following: "Every soul that uplifts itself uplifts the world."
He continues, "In that profound thought she defined herself."[6]
This message to someone she loved presaged what was to
become the leitmotif of her own life and the meaning of her
personal mission as she understood it.

While still a young woman, Elisabeth had come to the
conclusion that the popular conviction, that for activity to be
valuable it must have a widespread and measurable social
impact, was mistaken. Aware of the profound and transfor-
mative action worked by grace in the depths of each soul, she
claims to "believe much more in individual effort, and in the
good that may be done by addressing oneself not to the
masses but to individual souls. The effect one can exert is
thereby much deeper and more durable. . . ."[7] In one of her
earliest journal entries she voices an aspiration that will mark
the special character of her apostolate: "I want to love with a
special love those whose birth or religion or ideas separate
them from me; it is those whom I must try to understand and
who need me to give them a little of what God has placed
within me."[8]

One thing God certainly gave Elisabeth Leseur in abun-
dance was a profound empathy to the sensitivity — and fra-
gility of individual souls. Thus she accepted as her special task
to learn, first, to understand those who, so different from herself, took delight in abusing what she loved; and second, to

love these same souls. Moreover, she must love them "for themselves alone and for God, without counting on a single recompense or sweetness, simply because they are souls and because Christ, the adored Master, in looking upon them . . . uttered . . . 'I will have pity upon the multitude.' "[9]

Her prayers for a productive apostolate were certainly answered, for in the end, a great multitude were blessed through their encounters with her. The passing of time and the addition of trials in this woman's life were consistently accompanied by resolutions such as the following:

> To go more and more to souls, approaching them with respect and delicacy, touching them with love. To try always to understand everything and everyone. Not to argue; to work instead through contact and example; to dissipate prejudice, to reveal God and make him felt without speaking of him; to strengthen one's intelligence, to enlarge one's soul. . . ; to love without tiring, in spite of disappointment and indifference. . . . Never to show the wounds that are caused by certain hostilities, declarations, or misunderstandings; to offer them for those who cause this suffering.[10]

This craving to give what she herself almost never received becomes the means through which Elisabeth's personal purgation proceeds. Toward the end of her life, this desire burns through her entire being like an invisible flame:

> To learn from the Heart of Jesus the secret of love for souls and deep knowledge of them: how to touch their hurts without making them smart and to dress their wounds without reopening them; . . . to disclose Truth in its entirety and yet make it known according to the degree of light that each soul can bear. The knowledge required for the apostolate can be had only from Jesus Christ, in the Eucharist and in prayer.[11]

The Highest Form of Action

Although for Elisabeth no physical or additional emotional suffering could compete with the pain that Felix's spiritual alienation caused her, along with her lifelong sorrow in not being able to have children, she met with and was forced to endure suffering in almost every area of her life. Unbeknownst to most of her friends — but not to her physician husband — she fought a constant battle with a variety of physical afflictions.

Eventually Elisabeth's physical suffering made it increasingly difficult for her to leave the house, let alone maintain the active involvement with socially worthy charitable causes she had previously enjoyed and continued to support financially. Living with these severe constraints, she came to see that her suffering, rightly used, could be a source of formidable power.

Trying to explain this to a friend whose very active husband was facing the prospect of blindness, she wrote: "I know by experience that in hours of trial certain graces are obtained for others, which all our efforts had not hitherto obtained. I have thus come to the conclusion that suffering is the highest form of action, the highest expression of the wonderful communion of saints, and that in suffering one is sure not to make mistakes (as in action, sometimes) — sure, too, to be useful to others and to the great causes that one longs to serve."[12]

Again, we see an attitude that strikes at the heart of contemporary assumptions about how a work of value can be accomplished in the world, especially by a woman. The demand for the freedom to be actively involved in worthy projects (if not actually in charge of them) has become a predominant theme for modern women; yet here is someone who claims to have found the secret of personal effectiveness in a form of action that far transcends the only type of involvement that most of us can imagine. Indeed, a life consisting of constant physical pain, emotional suffering, and undiminished social obligations would not appear to offer much scope for a late-twentieth-century woman who is zealous to accomplish some great work for the world. Yet as Elisabeth's body steadily weakened, her convictions about how souls are captured for God were just as steadily confirmed and clarified:

> When we feel impotent against hostility and indifference, when it is impossible to speak of God or the spiritual life, when many hearts brush against ours without penetrating it, then we must enter peacefully into ourselves in the sweet company that our souls never lack; and to others we must give only prayers and the quiet example of our lives and the secret immolation which makes the most fruitful apostolate.[13]

As we have seen, Elisabeth's generosity of spirit and sensitivity of soul created in her a space large enough for each person who entered her life and a willingness to love and respect them all by meeting them where they were.

But in many cases, this level was far below the higher reaches toward which she was herself drawn. Thus, when she would much prefer to be praying or studying in solitude, she would instead willingly converse with husband or friends about a host of things of only secondary importance, at the same time refraining from mentioning those subjects that spoke to her own deepest interests and needs, since she knew this would provoke alienation or ridicule.

While the modern preoccupation with "personal authenticity" would quickly condemn such a strategy, it is important to recognize that there is no effort here to pretend that what she detests has great intrinsic worth and that somehow she must either learn to appreciate its value or resign herself to inevitable suffering. What interests her is the soul itself, and so the hidden effort she makes to accommodate herself to the needs and interests of each person she encounters is not a form of passive acquiescence. For her this was a gesture of love, an intentional and active apostolate, a reaching out to souls in desperate need of what she loved and wanted to offer openly but could not because of the dread it inspired in unconverted hearts. It was the simple power of her own God-possessed presence she learned to rely on in these encounters, and, in the end, it was to have an enormous impact on many souls, including the one whose resistance hurt her the most.

The soul whose well-being obsessed her was, of course, Felix's own, and she never stopped praying for his conversion. She came to recognize that any deliberate efforts to bring about his conversion would be doomed to failure. The change she so ardently longed for in Felix would be God's work entirely; in the meantime, she must love and not give in to temptations to self-justification that might only serve to make that work more difficult.

The Conquest of Love

The power of Elisabeth Leseur's freely embraced apostolate of suffering, born of her love for a soul in grave danger of being lost, was finally manifested in the life of Felix Leseur. The first signs that it was having its desired effect came in a cessation of hostilities as Felix found he could no longer ignore the growing and unmistakable evidence of sanctity in his wife. Several years before her death he found his attitude toward her persistence in the faith softening:

> When I saw how ill she was, and how she endured with equanimity of temper a complaint that generally provokes much hypochondria, impatience, and ill humor, I was struck to see how her soul had so great a command of itself and of her body; and knowing that she drew this tremendous strength from her convictions, I ceased to attack them.[14]

Then, in 1911, while Elisabeth was recuperating from a difficult operation, Felix accompanied his wife on a pilgrimage to Lourdes. Expecting to see only "hucksters in the Temple," he was taken completely by surprise when, unobserved, he witnessed Elisabeth praying at the Grotto, apparently levitating.

> I had before my eyes the spectacle of something that evaded me, that I did not understand, but which I recognized clearly as being "the supernatural," and I could not withdraw my eyes from so moving a sight. I returned from Lourdes troubled by what I had seen and felt in that land of miracles. Oh, I was certainly still a rationalist, on the surface at any rate — deeper down, Elisabeth acted upon me without my perceiving it; and this action grew stronger during her last illness. I could never weary of admiring her moral force in the midst of a real martyrdom.[15]

At the time of Elisabeth's death (from cancer), Felix made another dumbfounding discovery in the vast scope of her spiritual outreach, evidenced in a huge correspondence with people from all walks of life and of whose existence he had had no inkling. Amazed, he watched what seemed like a never-ending stream of visitors come to visit Elisabeth during her last days, and an even greater number of entirely unknown mourners file past her body prior to the funeral. He reports that following the outpouring of grief at the funeral he heard that the attending clergy asked in astonishment, ". . . Who was this woman? We have never seen such a funeral before."[16]

It was not until after her death, when Felix discovered, read, and reread her journal and a document she entitled her "Spiritual Testament," that he realized what was working in him was the direct result of Elisabeth's own self-conscious offering of her life to God for his conversion. This realization was one of those momentous revelations that overturns what has been in an individual's life to make way for the new:

... A revolution took place in my whole moral being. I understood the celestial beauty of her soul and that she had accepted all her suffering and offered it — and even offered her very self in sacrifice — chiefly for my conversion. ... Her sacrifice was absolute, and she was convinced that God would accept it and would take her early to himself. She was equally persuaded that he would ensure my conversion.[17]

By the spring of 1915, Felix's conversion was complete, and he soon decided to publish his wife's journal. He had found in this document the meaning of her life and, finally, he felt the full extent of her love for him.

A New Vocation of Love

The story of Felix Leseur does not end with his conversion. The power of the love with which he was loved continued to work in his life in the most surprising of ways. The very same zeal that had been focused on Elisabeth in an effort to get her to apostatize came to the surface once again in Felix's life, but in a vastly altered and purified form.

Two years before her death, Elisabeth and Felix had what would prove to be a fateful conversation in which they speculated about what each would do when the other died. Elisabeth's response was: "I know you. I am absolutely certain that when you return to God, you will not stop on the way because you never do things by halves. ... You will some day be Père Leseur."[18]

Indeed, Felix had thrown himself back into the faith of his childhood with fervor, reading the Gospels and the books in his wife's library, going to daily Mass, and even becoming a Dominican tertiary.

Elisabeth was right. Felix conceived a desire to become a Dominican priest. His Dominican director said no, dismissing his request as evidence of the inordinate zeal of the new convert. But with the same persistence with which he once attacked his wife's faith, Felix persisted in his quest for the priesthood. In the fall of 1919, at the age of fifty-seven, he became a novice in the Order of Preachers. At the age of sixty-two he was ordained.

After twenty-five years of marriage, his priesthood would cover a span of twenty-seven years. Much of his time as a cleric was spent speaking publicly throughout Europe about his wife and her apostolate. Eventually he was given the task of petitioning Rome to begin the process of her beatification. Père Leseur died in 1950 after several years of hospitalization. When an inventory of his room was made, "they found only his breviary and his rosary."[19]

Felix Leseur discovered that under his very roof a life had been lived, the meaning of which had entirely escaped him. He had witnessed much suffering without guessing that it was he who had benefited most directly from it and would continue to be the chief beneficiary of that life's redemptive value. The life of Elisabeth Leseur was a life of love, a vivid testimony to the possibility of loving totally despite the absence of every opportunity for personal fulfillment and meaningful "activity" as the world understands these things. This was a life that completely changed another life — perhaps many lives — because it was willing to open itself fully to the possibility that in her and through her own pain and loss, God could do the loving.

Endnotes

1. Felix Leseur, "In Memoriam," in Elisabeth Leseur, *My Spirit Rejoices: The Diary of a Christian Soul in an Age of Unbelief* (Manchester, N.H.: Sophia Institute Press, 1996), p. 13.

2. Ibid., p. 15.

3. Ibid., p. 62.

4. Ibid., p. 148.

5. Ibid., pp. 148-149.

6. Ibid., pp. 26-27.

7. Ibid., p. 49.

8. Ibid., p. 45.

9. Ibid., p. 76.

10. Ibid., pp. 79-80.

11. Ibid., pp. 125-126.

12. Ibid., p. 22.

13. Ibid., p. 146.

14. Ibid., p. 30.

15. Ibid., p. 31.

16. Ibid., p. 27.

17. Ibid., pp. 32-33.

18. Quoted in June Verbillion, "The Silent Apostolate of Elisabeth Leseur," *Cross and Crown* (March 1959), p. 42.

19. Ibid., p. 43.

Recommended Reading

The Catechism of the Catholic Church, Second Edition (English translation for the United States of America, copyright © 1994, 1997 United States Catholic Conference, Inc. — Libreria Editrice Vaticana; available from Our Sunday Visitor Publishing, 1-800-348-2440; www.osv.com).

(If you are unable to find the following, please contact Pauline Books & Media, 1-800-876-4463; www.pauline.org.)

Casti Connubii (On Christian Marriage), Pope Pius XI.

Ut Unum Sint (On Commitment to Ecumenism), Pope John Paul II.

Matrimonia Mixta (On Mixed Marriages and Statement on the Implementation of the Apostolic Letter on Mixed Marriages), Pope Paul VI — NCCB.

Letter to Families, Pope John Paul II.

Familiaris Consortio (The Role of the Christian Family in the Modern World), Pope John Paul II.

Matrimonii Sacramentum (Instruction on Mixed Marriages), The Congregation for the Doctrine of the Faith.

Ecumenical Directory (Directory for the Application of the Principles and Norms of Ecumenism), The Pontifical Council for Promoting Christian Unity. (*Note:* Section IV, C, is in regard to mixed marriages. Paragraph 151 is excellent concerning the obligation of the Catholic spouse in the religious education of his children.)

More Good Reading

Grodi, Marcus C., ed. *Journeys Home.* Santa Barbara, Calif.: Queenship Publishing, 1997.

Henesy, Michael and Rosemary Gallagher. *How to Survive Being Married to a Catholic.* Liguori, Mo.: Liguori Publications, 1986.

Johnson, Kevin Orlin. *Why Do Catholics Do That?* New York: Ballantine Books, 1994.

Leseur, Elisabeth. *My Spirit Rejoices: The Diary of a Christian Soul in an Age of Unbelief.* Manchester, N.H.: Sophia Institute Press, 1996.

_____. *Light in the Darkness.* Manchester, N.H.: Sophia Institute Press, 1998.

Madrid, Patrick, ed. *Surprised by Truth.* San Diego, Calif.: Basilica Press, 1994.

_____. *Surprised by Truth 2.* Manchester, N.H.: Sophia Press, 2000.

Nordhagen, Lynn. "Once, Twice, Three Times a Catholic," in *Envoy Magazine*, edition published in March-April 1998 (www.envoymagazine.com/samplearticles/mar_apr98/mar_apr98story1.html).

Travnikar, Rock, O.F.M. *The Blessing Cup: 40 Simple Rites for Family Prayer-Celebrations,* rev. ed. Cincinnati, Ohio: St. Anthony Messenger Press, 1994.

About the Author

In this, her first book, Lynn Nordhagen draws on her experiences as well as those of others who have converted or reverted to the Catholic faith. She has gathered these essays to offer comfort, understanding, and hope to married people who are converting to the Catholic Church in the face of a spouse's opposition. This opposition may take the form of indifference, grief, anger, threats, or other behavior that may bring pain to both parties. Furthermore, she offers these stories to the spouses who are not becoming Catholic, praying that they may gain insight and hope, recognizing that this can be, for them also, a time of discovery and growth in the Christian life.

Those who have shared their experiences in this book are very human and struggling Christians who offer their stories to fill a need they themselves had felt deeply — to know they are not alone, and to be understood in a situation that is becoming increasingly common.

Lynn was born and raised in Spokane, Washington, and graduated from Gonzaga University. She and her Protestant husband, Marvin, have four grown children, all of whom love the Lord.

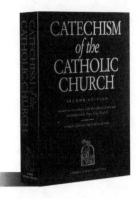

Our Sunday Visitor. . .
Your Source for Discovering
the Riches of the Catholic Faith

Our Sunday Visitor has an extensive line of materials for young children, teens, and adults. Our books, Bibles, booklets, CD-ROMs, audios, and videos are available in bookstores worldwide.

To receive a FREE full-line catalog or for more information, call **Our Sunday Visitor** at **1-800-348-2440**. Or write, **Our Sunday Visitor** / 200 Noll Plaza / Huntington, IN 46750.

- -

Please send me: ___A catalog
Please send me materials on:
___Apologetics and catechetics ___Reference works
___Prayer books ___Heritage and the saints
___The family ___The parish
Name_____
Address_____Apt._____
City_____State_____Zip_____
Telephone ( ) _____

A13BBABP

- -

Please send a friend: ___A catalog
Please send a friend materials on:
___Apologetics and catechetics ___Reference works
___Prayer books ___Heritage and the saints
___The family ___The parish
Name_____
Address_____Apt._____
City_____State_____Zip_____
Telephone ( ) _____

A13BBABP

- -

Our Sunday Visitor
200 Noll Plaza
Huntington, IN 46750
Toll free: 1-800-348-2440
E-mail: osvbooks@osv.com
Website: www.osv.com